FAMILY

"Dr. Cahill's work is a welcome addition to the ongoing discussion on family and 'family values' taking place today. Of critical import is her openness to the cultural values of other racial/ethnic groups, most significantly African Americans, to whom she devotes an entire chapter. It is a rare and welcome example of the dialogue that needs to take place within not just the Roman Catholic Church but all of Christianity. . . . I hope this work will serve to encourage further dialogue across lines of race, ethnicity, class, gender, and sexual orientation."
—Diana L. Hayes
Georgetown University

FAMILY
A Christian Social Perspective

Lisa Sowle Cahill

Fortress Press
Minneapolis

FAMILY
A Christian Social Perspective

Cover art: "Family Plan" by Diana Ong
Cover design: Marti Naughton
Interior design: Beth Wright

Scripture translations from the Revised Standard Version of the Bible, copyright © 1946, 1952, and 1971 by the Division of Christian Education of the National Council of Churches of Christ in the United States of America, are used by permission.

Library of Congress Cataloging-in-Publication Data

Cahill, Lisa Sowle.
  Family : a Christian social perspective / Lisa Sowle Cahill.
      p.   cm.
  Includes bibliographical references and index.
  ISBN 0-8006-3252-4
    1. Family—Religious aspects—Christianity. 2. Sociology, Christian—United States. 3. Family—Religious aspects—Catholic Church. 4. Sociology, Christian (Catholic)—United States. 5. Catholic Church—Doctrines. I. Title.

BT 707.7 .C35 2000
261.8'3585—dc21
                                                                          00-056182

Manufactured in the U.S.A.
07   06   05   04   03   2   3   4   5   6   7   8   9   10   11

To my children,
Charlotte, James, Will, Don, Ae

Contents

What is the Christian family? This is the question that motivates this project. It is a question with a context. During the 1990s, North American social theorists and cultural critics seemed to divide into two schools of thought about families. Both agree that family forms are changing, but they diagnose the causes and results of this phenomenon very differently. On one side are those who pinpoint rising divorce and illegitimacy rates as symptoms of unfettered individualism, narcissism, moral laxity, and hedonism. These vices lie at the root of widespread family disintegration. They are devastating civil society while depleting the "social capital" (important social institutions that promote inclusive social participation and support) that depends on healthy family life and is so necessary to a viable society. Crime and poverty follow in the wake of such trends. Key to their reversal is a renewed ethic of family life built around responsibility, fidelity, and self-sacrifice.

On the other side stand those who view newly pluralistic family forms as a liberation from the patriarchal nuclear family, which is in reality not traditional but a product of the industrial revolution, capitalism, and the public-private split. The nuclear, middle-class family is structured according to hierarchically ordered gender roles and owes its economic security to a racially segregated underclass perpetually excluded from economic prosperity. Diversity in families is a welcome change, and it should not be judged socially or morally inferior.

These opposing camps were vociferous and influential during the 1992 and 1996 U.S. election campaigns and continue to be vocal in this century. They have fought for different approaches to family, health care, and welfare policies, and they both try to manipulate cultural symbols to form public consciousness in support of their own agenda.

To oversimplify, religious responses to those two views of the family have tended to break down into evangelical-conservative and mainline-feminist categories, with black churches occupying a complex middle position that will be investigated in this book's first and fifth chapters. The evangelical-conservative and mainline-feminist reactions, however, seem to focus on two different North American experiences of family and to put the problems, successes, and future of one rather than the other at the center of debate and political action. Evangelical Protestants and conservative "pro-life" Roman Catholics focus on the middle-class family, disrupted by new rates of sex and childbearing outside of marriage and by infidelity and divorce in marriage, all of which destabilize the economic base of the nuclear family. That base consists of a male breadwinner providing indirect access to material and social goods for his wife and children. Liberal Protestants and Catholics, on the other hand, especially feminist theologians and churches that are rapidly institutionalizing nontraditional roles for women, focus on families that are outside of or excluded from the social structures that protect the model of family built on the male wage earner and female domestic support. They are looking for new patterns of access via different family forms, or they have found access within the standard middle-class forms constraining or oppressive. Hence they seek to institutionalize "nontraditional" patterns of family life. A counterpoint to both of these contrasting religious responses, one that will be explored at some length in chapter 5, is found in African American interpretations of family life. Writers from this perspective often acclaim the strengths of black kinship patterns outside the nuclear model and call for socioeconomic reform, even while they seek to enhance marital and parental stability to improve the social position of blacks in our society.

The evangelical-conservative Christian response answers what it defines as the problems of families today by championing strong family relations and bonds, urging sacrifice and altruism within the family. Yet, this approach often fails to provide a socioeconomic critique of internal family relations (especially male-female relations), and of the social positioning of families (especially why economic factors make it impossible for some families to thrive on the nuclear model). The mainline-feminist model typically undertakes a more radical critique of gender, race, class, and sexual orientation as they appear in family forms and social functions, but it, in turn, has difficulty regaining its normative balance around some vision of what is a healthy family or a Christian family. It tears down oppressive forms without building up better ideals of kin-derived, spousal, and parental relationships or of how families serve the common good of society and are served by it. While advocates of the first approach claim that "the Christian family" denotes the monogamous, reproductive pair who sacrifice for the welfare of their children, advocates of the second maintain that the "Christian" values of compassion, love, and inclusion not only prohibit the condemnation of other types of family but demand the acceptance of all families who have been the victims of social injustice. African American authors tend to agree with the latter position while still supporting and encouraging the formation of two-parent families within an extended kin network.

The family is here understood as basically an organized network of socioeconomic and reproductive interdependence and support grounded in biological kinship and marriage. Kinship denotes affiliation through reproductive lines. Marriage, in turn, is a consensual and contractual manner of uniting kin groups, especially for the purpose of reproduction, and for perpetuation of the kinship structures through which social and economic relations are managed. While modern societies invest affective, interpersonal relationships within the family with primary significance, this has not universally been the case. Moreover, the extended consanguineous family is more ancient and more universal in social importance than the modern so-called nuclear family, consisting of spouses and children and considered to have been formed through marriage. The fact that *family* is defined primarily in terms of kinship in virtually all cultures signifies the importance of *the body* and of essential material needs in defining the family and its functions. The fact that marriage, however, is also a way of creating and defining family cross-culturally represents the importance of affiliation through *free choice* in defining family ties. Both are important elements in understanding and defining family.

Although family as created by kinship and marriage is the most basic family form or definition of family, it is not the only or exclusively legitimate form. It is basic in that it prevails across cultures as an important social institution and provides the fundamental working concept of family for most individuals and societies. There are other types of human alliance, however, for mutual economic and domestic support, as for reproduction and child rearing, that are analogous to the basic kin- and marriage-based family. These need not entail biological kinship or male-female marriage. For instance, forms of adoption are familiar in most societies, though in many cultures adoption of children within the kin group is preferred over adoption of non-kin. The outer boundaries of family are thus perhaps impossible to define, since analogous forms arise according to particular circumstances and needs. In any event, it would be imprudent to attempt to set definitive limits on what counts as family if, as I do, one wants to advance an inclusive and supportive approach to family life, one that can hold up ideals such as male-female coparenting and sexual fidelity without thereby berating and excluding single-parent families, divorced families, gay and lesbian families, blended families, or adoptive families. Such family structures are often very worthy and successful adaptations to particular circumstances and, given appropriate support, can fulfill family functions as well as more traditional families. As I hope to show, the ideals of Christian family life should focus more on function (fostering gospel-informed commitments and behavior) than on regularity of form.

My thesis is that strong family, spousal, and parental relationships are important, but that these very ideals are undermined by condemnatory and punitive attitudes and policies toward nonconforming families.

Attitudes and policies advanced under the aegis of "Christian values" often do in fact support the economic advantages of the middle-class nuclear family at the expense of those who are excluded and rejected. In my view, the Christian family is not the nuclear family focused inward on the welfare of its own members but the socially transformative family that seeks to make the Christian moral ideal of love of neighbor part of the common good. Family responsibility and fidelity need to be combined with altruistic social action that makes it possible for all families to participate in the common good of society and for women and men to be equal participants in family and in social life, including economic life. Increasingly, Christian theories of family life place it in this larger social context.[1]

Unfortunately, however, so-called Christian ideologies of family life are at least as likely to sanctify injustices of gender, class, and race as they have been to challenge and reform them. The term *Christian family* is ambivalent. Often the family is preserved at the expense of any real Christianity, while "family values" rhetoric becomes a means of reinforcing social inequalities. On the other hand, if the socially radical meaning of Christianity is taken seriously, Christian families can become vehicles of social justice, even as they strengthen and build upon their bonds of kinship, affection, and faithfulness. Examples will be given from the New Testament, the early church, the Reformation, and contemporary culture. Positive ideals of Christian family will also be sought in an interpretation of the Roman Catholic model of family as "domestic church" and in the writings of African American theologians of family life.

My experiences as a white, upper-middle-class academic living in New England during the last quarter of the twentieth century and into the twenty-first century obviously influence the questions I think important and the answers I give them. There are other relevant factors: my Roman Catholic roots and Jesuit university education, as well as my long and happy association with the Catholic and Jesuit traditions during my career in higher education; my graduate school education at the University of Chicago Divinity School, at a time when students were privileged to enjoy courses with the likes of James Gustafson, David Tracy, Langdon Gilkey, Martin Marty, Norman Perrin, Paul Ricoeur, Nathan Scott, Mircea Eliade, Schubert Ogden, Brian Gerrish, Bernard McGinn, and other notables who taught and advised me; my now twenty-eight-year marriage, which has produced one daughter and four sons, three of whom are adopted from Thailand; my increasing interest, fostered by the bonds our family has formed with Thailand and our friends there working in family services, in the status of women worldwide; friendships with gay and lesbian people who have also adopted "hard to place" children from other countries; my sister Maryann, who, having ended a marriage almost as long as mine, has recently entered the nursing profession while continuing to shepherd her six children, three of them adopted, and who has been a foster mother to many more over the years.

I have been reflecting on and writing about the ethics of sex and gender for most of my years as a theologian. Married women who were also ethicists (especially Roman Catholic ones) were enough of a rarity in the 1970s that my original interest in bioethics was soon almost overwhelmed by invitations to speak, write, and teach about issues related to sex, marriage, family, and women's roles. I learned from my teacher and mentor, James Gustafson, that one cannot be a good theological ethicist without a strong commitment to the fundamental theological and philosophical matters underlying topical debates about practical dilemmas. It is necessary to bring Scripture and tradition, as well as human experience, the social sciences, and contemporary philosophy, to bear on all the concrete aspects of Christian ethics. In considering the situations of families today,[2] it is important to refer to biblical and theological teachings about marriage and the household, to studies of divorce rates or child welfare, and to philosophical theories of freedom and justice. It is also essential to probe the more basic question of how all these sources can or should work together as authorities for Christian ethics.

Gustafson has always insisted that all theological convictions are culturally located and perspectival. Without necessarily being a relativist, one must recognize the influences of what is now more trendily called one's "social location" in the formation of one's theological and ethical positions. The importance of social location has become more and more clear to me over the years, although I remain just as firmly dedicated as ever to the (typically Roman Catholic) view that there are in fact moral values that are in some sense objective because they are rooted in common human needs and purposes. Figuring out just what these are, and just how pliable they are in the face of different forms of social instantiation, is a difficult project, but it is at the heart of normative ethics, whether religious or secular.

In earlier writings, the social dimension of family relations that most occupied my interest was patriarchy. While always aware that race and class bear on sexual and gender ethics, I tended to think of this subject matter from the perspective of the struggle for women's and men's equality in the middle classes of North America, where women's access to paid employment, the juggling of professional and family responsibilities, and the definition of stable but more flexible norms of sexual behavior after the "sexual revolution" were central issues.[3]

As a result of my family's adoption experience, and as more and more feminist theologians from the "Third World" and from Latina and African American traditions on this continent become highly visible in the mainstream discourse of the North American theological academy, I began to see how to place my original concerns in a more intercultural framework. As a result, I became increasingly aware of the deeply entrenched and violent nature of patriarchy in the cultures of the world. Specifically in relation to the family, women worldwide are often defined in terms of childbearing roles but are subjugated to male interests in the fulfillment of these roles, having little or no independent access to economic and social resources. This also results in the depreciation of female children and in an immense degree of suffering for those women among "the poorest of the poor" whom the greed and violence of rich nations and corporations have devastated. Concern about "our" (North American, privileged) responsibility for this suffering led to a more urgent concern with the possibility of establishing some cross-cultural standards of moral discourse and accountability, so as to resist the more relativist aspects of the postmodern intellectual culture that stamps the coinage of much North American and European academia.[4]

In 1992, I was invited to become a member of the Religion, Culture, and Family Project, a cooperative research and writing group that was directed by Don Browning of the University of Chicago Divinity School and funded by a grant from the Lilly Endowment. This group met annually for five years, published eleven monographs and edited volumes,[5] and sponsored several conferences and symposia on the family in North American culture, some of which continue still. Participation in this project has added further dimensions to my research interests and capacities, reflected in the present work.

While my own "official" contribution to the Religion, Family, and Culture Project is the volume *Sex, Gender, and Christian Ethics*, I have gone on during the past four years to think more about the social situation of families in my own culture, particularly in relation to current debates about welfare reform. Much indebted to the mix of ideas and politics that came about as a result of the project, this book is the result of my continued attempt to understand what is "the Christian family" as critically informed by Christian tradition and as ethically responsive to today's social realities.

Chapter 1

Families, Christian Ethics, and Civil Society

Families in North America are in crisis. Such is the founding thesis of the Religion, Family, and Culture Project, according to its brochure. I endorse that thesis, if properly qualified. The crisis in American families looks different for women compared to men, for people of color compared to whites, and for the chronically undereducated and unemployed compared to the middle class. Divorce and births to poor, teenaged mothers are in fact bad signs for families. But the family crisis has other social and economic roots that are just as truly matters of Christian moral concern as are narcissistic individualism and unwillingness to make and keep commitments.

In 1991, the Religion, Culture, and Family Project took as its point of departure the fact that the American family is in decline, with terrible consequences for children and hence for social stability and prosperity in the next generation. While recognizing that working mothers and the freedom to end abusive marriages are here to stay—and not bad developments—leaders of the project fault an individualist ethos of self-fulfillment for family breakdown.[1] As one authority frequently cited by members of the project has written, an American ethos of "expressive individualism" is the cause of much of America's family woes.[2] In this ethos, fostered as the baby-boom generation reached its professional phase in the 1980s, individual fulfillment takes precedence over the well-being of the family as a whole. During this period, sexual experimentation and divorce rates rose, while birth rates declined.

A special concern is fatherlessness, attributed—here drawing heavily on sociobiology—to the "male problematic."[3] Evolutionarily tilted toward sexual promiscuity, so the argument goes, men, unlike women, need powerful cultural norms to ensure their parental investment. A cultural ethos of narcissism points men in the wrong direction: away from mates and children. This ethos must be shifted toward greater concern for the common good, and, near to home, a greater sense of responsibility for family ties.

Religious traditions and ideals—faithful marriage, self-sacrifice, care for children, male-female family cooperation—can engage the imagination, inspire conversion and dedication, and unite us in a new project of family well-being. The new pro-family atmosphere of church and society

1

must be structured by equality and justice in gender, economic, and racial relations. Social institutions that support families, including poor and minority families, are the right and responsibility of all members of society. As Don Browning and co-authors state it,

> the new postindustrial ideal should be the egalitarian family in which husband and wife participate relatively equally in paid work as well as in childcare and other domestic responsibilities. This family will need new preparations, new skills, new religious and communal supports, and a new theory of authority.... [The] *new family ideal* ... [is] *the committed, intact, equal-regard, public-private family.*[4]

I support wholeheartedly the project agenda of addressing the state of family life in relation *both* to a culture of individualism *and* to socioeconomic factors, of examining both positive and negative aspects of changing gender and workplace expectations, of bringing the contributions of religious institutions and faith traditions to bear on the strengths and problems of families, of devoting explicit attention to the experience of the African American churches in America, and of building bridges between liberals and conservatives. Attention to the complexity of these dimensions became stronger as the project progressed, fostered by Browning's efforts to ensure a relative degree of pluralism among the positions represented.[5]

Nonetheless, I suspect that among many critics of today's families there remains a tacit assumption that the modern nuclear family is normative and that its decline is more or less traceable to a single cause: lack of moral commitment, self-sacrifice, and perseverance among an increasingly narcissistic childbearing population.

I agree that an individualist market mentality pervades the social attitudes of much of the middle and most of the upper classes. This includes their attitudes toward sexual exchange and family relations. In particular, too many young adults make and keep commitments only on the basis of clear short-term advantage, while prosperous middle-aged men "trade up" by acquiring trophy wives. This has devastating effects, both psychological and financial, for women and children.[6] Furthermore, in segments of society under economic duress, economic factors can militate heavily against the ability of persons to make and sustain commitments to sexual partners and children, as has been ably demonstrated by William Julius Wilson.[7] The values, motives, and shaping social circumstances of the higher classes cannot be projected facilely onto the poor. Instead, according to Wilson, it is the ruthless market individualism of the well-off that creates the socioeconomic climate inimical to family formation in the "underclass."

Moreover, the proposed solutions to the supposed rise of home-wrecking self-indulgence are often unfair to women, since it usually turns out that women are expected to make asymmetrical sacrifices of educational and professional development to care for young children and that women are urged to accept male authority in the home to entice mates away from the infidelity that causes so much fatherlessness. The solution to "expressive individualism" proposed by Barbara Dafoe Whitehead is a "new familism," in which both parents sacrifice for children, but the woman makes more concessions, rearranging her professional life to defer advancement in favor of domestic responsibilities.[8] Equality of the sexes in the family, the need for flexible alternatives in reconciling family responsibilities with other social roles for both sexes, and even the importance of equalizing access to employment and its benefits are much more in evidence in the "critical familism" of Browning and his co-authors, who hope that a sixty-hour *family* work week (sixty hours combined work outside the home by both adults) will become the norm for employed couples in America.[9]

At around the same time that the Religion, Culture, and Family Project was developing under Browning's guidance, the United States Catholic bishops were pursuing a program of family evangelization focused through the metaphor of family as domestic church. The purpose of this program was not so much to bring families "into line" according to ecclesiastical norms but to reach out to families that had not experienced themselves as part of the church and to encourage the growth of spirituality in the family setting. Those the bishops hoped to address included single-parent families, blended families after divorce, and African American and Hispanic families.[10]

In 1993, as president of the Catholic Theological Society of America (CTSA), I received a letter from Cardinal Joseph Bernardin, the late archbishop of Chicago who was then head of the United States Catholic Bishops' Committee on Marriage and Family. He requested that the CTSA encourage more theological study of the concept of family as domestic church. This request eventually resulted in the formation of a CTSA research seminar—chaired first by Susan Secker of Seattle University, then by Christine Firer Hinze of Marquette University—that produced several papers and the projected publication of a book (to be edited by William P. Roberts of the University of Dayton). While not a direct participant in this seminar, I continued to pursue similar research. I also learned through the Religion, Culture, and Family Project discussions with colleagues that the domestic church metaphor has a long if not very highly developed history in Christian thinking. Consequently, I have chosen in this book to examine varied uses of the metaphor—in the New Testament, in the work of John Chrysostom and Martin Luther, and in Puritan and Catholic social teaching.

The Family as Church

The idea that the family itself is a domestic church and the idea that the churches should address the family crisis in the United States today are connected in important ways. Yet these connections are ambivalent. From the beginning of its concern with families of believers in the New Testament, Christianity has recognized that the family is an important institution of what is today termed "civil society." Every individual's self-understanding, character, and integration into social roles are achieved through participation in the institutions of civil society, not just by one-to-one or small-scale interpersonal relationships, much less by the lone individual's experience, introspection, or choice.

Identification of the Christian family with the church is one way of transforming an important formative institution of civil society—family—to represent better and to educate for Christian values and practices. But an underrated fact is that the transformative process will necessarily go both ways. Herein lies a sometimes unrecognized danger for Christian faith and behavior. Just as the Christian family can change cultural norms, so can family membership change Christian ideals. (Stanley Hauerwas is among those who have recognized this, though he paints greater conflict between the natural and the Christian family than I in the end think necessary.[11]) Thus, comparisons of the family to a domestic church, little church, or church of the household can work either to convert families and their members to the standard of God's reign or to undermine the radical reorientation of values that the eschatological reign of God demands. Usually both dynamics occur at the same time. The proposal of a "new familism," or even a "critical familism,"[12] is not unproblematic for Christian ethics.

As I will argue in chapter 2, the symbol "kingdom of God," or "reign of God," in the teaching of Jesus invokes an inclusive community united in love of neighbor and enemy. Christian community as "kingdom present" is resistant to worldly hierarchies of gender, race, and class, especially when such hierarchies exclude the poor from the basic necessities of life. As I will argue further in chapters 2 and 3, however, Christian ideologies of the family have not always served this ideal or have served it with mixed success. After all, the kingdom is simultaneously present and not yet present. In many cases, the image of "the Christian family" is used to reinforce, not overturn, patriarchal hierarchies within the family. Beyond the individual family, an image of the kind of normative Christian family that is truly "church" can be used to reinforce socioeconomic hierarchies of privileged ("Christian") families over others and to browbeat those who do not conform to the leadership's ideal. And very often the family ideal of

Christian leadership comes virtually to be equated with the family form that best serves the interests of the cultural elites, because these elites exist in a symbiotic relationship with ecclesiastical leadership.

This ironic development occurs in our own culture, for instance, when "welfare mothers" (who are disproportionately African American and Hispanic[13]) are blamed by self-professed Christians for sexual and maternal irresponsibility and required to take up low-paid employment without adequate childcare. Meanwhile, the white churches and higher classes praise the fidelity of middle-class parents whose ability to maintain their marriages and nuclear families is in effect underwritten by others denied equal access to education and employment and thus to life in communities with civil institutions (like churches, neighborhoods, and schools) supporting "intact" family life.

William Julius Wilson pinpoints some of the social causes of family "disintegration" when he observes, "as the disappearance of work has become a characteristic feature of the inner-city ghetto, so too has the disappearance of the traditional married-couple family." Moreover, "in the African American community, rates of marriage are positively correlated with levels of education."[14] In other words, failure to marry and provide a two-parent home for children is, for the disadvantaged, due less to individualism or lack of conviction about the desirability of such a home in principle than it is to realistic hopelessness about the prospect of achieving it, given poor education and joblessness. Yet part of the "dominant American belief system" that has recently ended guaranteed federal support for poor families with children is that "it is the moral fabric of individuals, not the social and economic structure of society, that is taken to be the root of the problem."[15] Attributing family "failure" primarily to personal moral weakness allows the more advantaged to avoid the uncomfortable conclusion that they themselves are in some way responsible for the factors that lead to family "breakdown" among the urban poor and the even more distasteful conclusion that restoration of the family and of other institutions of civil society will require a redistribution of social assets.

The brilliant American social ethicist Reinhold Niebuhr captured the dynamic at work in much of the American family debate (and in much historical usage of the metaphor "domestic church" or "church of the home") when he coined the term *collective egotism* to explain the social aspect of sin. All persons have sinful tendencies to assert their own advantage over the rightful place of others. These tendencies are constrained by social norms limiting the acts of individuals. By identifying with the higher purposes of a group, an individual is able to make claims to supremacy that he or she would never dare to advance on his or her own. The egotism of the individual is sublimated to self-sacrifice for the group, but by claiming the identity of the group as one's own identity, the individual also secures a share in the prerogatives attained on the group's behalf:

> The social group asks for the individual's unconditioned loyalty, asserting that its necessities are the ultimate law of the individual's existence. But on the other hand it is a pretension which the individual makes for himself, not as an individual but as a member of his group. Collective egotism does indeed offer the individual an opportunity to lose himself in a larger whole; but it also offers him possibilities of self-aggrandizement beside which mere individual pretensions are implausible and incredible.[16]

The point here, of course, is not that all desire for or praise of family ties is sinful, only that family belonging is potentially idolatrous, a socially acceptable form of arrogance and greed. Advocacy for the family can reduce to advocacy for one's own kin group and the conditions perceived essential to its support. But not only that. It can also become advocacy for one's own social class, to the security of which one's own privileges, as well as those of one's friends and relations, are attached. Protection and reinforcement of the family, sacrifice for the family, and argument about the superiority of the Christian family can lend a moral veneer to what in reality amounts to the self-interest of the middling and prosperous classes, and especially of their adult male members. The pro-family agenda becomes socially exclusive when the prerogatives of family well-being—especially the luxuries of families in the upper social echelons—motivate rationalizations against class-spanning love of neighbor, care for the poor, and table fellowship with the stranger, those moral duties that distinctively mark the Christian life.

As I will show in chapter 4, use of the domestic church metaphor in recent Catholic teaching has been directed specifically at the responsibility of Christian families to serve the common good by enhancing the participation of the least well-off, enabling all to share in the responsibilities, rights, and benefits of society. Yet even modern Catholic analysis of the family is insufficiently critical of patriarchy and needs to pursue a deeper analysis of the ways in which global capitalism produces unjust social relations at the local level, thus undermining families. Therefore, while I accept the metaphor of family as domestic church as a valuable instrument of evangelization and catechesis, I do so recognizing that it requires a dangerous, if unavoidable, liaison between the transformative social impulses of Christian faith and the ordinary infrastructures of human society. The latter tend to protect and channel social goods within groups of shared identity and to favor those at the top of the chain of command.

Many critics of the state of American families cite astronomical divorce rates, rising numbers of teenage pregnancies, and the paternal absenteeism caused by both as key contributing factors to the plight of America's children. But a 1994 Carnegie Corporation report also cites persistent poverty, child abuse, high numbers of children in foster care, inadequate health care, dangerously inferior childcare, and lack of subsidized parental work leave as part of the bleak picture of children's welfare.[17] Clearly, not all of these factors can be resolved through the moral rearmament of unfortunate parents. Children are a social responsibility. The well-being of children and families will require affirmative action on the part of those with the resources. This means sacrifice. It also means the cooperative transformation of many of the mediating institutions of society that channel material and social goods to some families and away from others.

The Family and Civil Society

The family is an institution of civil society, and it is interdependent with virtually every other. Though many commentators have argued that the troubles of families are caused largely by the decline of civil society, family vulnerability is due at least as much to the kinds of civil institutions our society fosters. Of particular importance are the larger purposes or interests that mediating institutions serve. Civil society is not disengaged from the economy or system of government, for example, but functions both to disseminate and to resist or reorder the values and norms inherent in broader, more inclusive patterns of social organization. Mary Ann Glendon cautions that "to revitalize the fragile structures of civil society, however, would involve nothing less ambitious than reshaping the large economic and political structures that impose constraints on and offer possibilities to families and their surrounding institutions."[18]

The institutions of civil society are not simply local entities, in which neighborly interactions are insulated from the megasystems of market and state, nor are they necessarily benign.[19] The problem is to frame the question of civil society within criteria of justice that relate the more comprehensive realms of human association to the more local forms, such as family, neighborhood, church or synagogue, school, commercial or shopping district, workplace, local politics, and voluntary organizations (for example, fraternal or charitable ones). The values dominant in the larger spheres can only take hold and have practical effect insofar as they are refracted through local institutions and realized in outcomes or actions at the local level. But local individuals and groups also have the opportunity to influence the big systems of government, economics, politics, and institutional religion. After all, these large-scale organizations acquire agency in and through constellations of component small-scale groups and their individual members.

The current debate about civil society (including the family) was enormously invigorated by the catchy title (and striking analysis) of Robert Putnam's 1995 article "Bowling Alone."[20] Yet the debate is rooted at least a decade before in Eastern Europe, when Vaclav Havel and others called for popular activism against the socialist state. Many carry the discussion back to Alexis de Tocqueville's observation that, though Americans "are forever forming associations," their independence and individualism tend to undermine their efforts and make it necessary for government to intervene.[21] Putnam makes the claim that association memberships have fallen by about a quarter among Americans over the last quarter century. He argues that this decline correlates with a loss of social trust and political engagement, spelling diminishment of the social capital necessary to sustain the institutions of a democratic society.[22]

When the family is placed among these institutions, the conclusion may be drawn that the family itself has been infected by this loss of trust and committed investment and that the weakening of the family contributes to the decline of social capital that characterizes American social life in general. Therefore, according to David Blankenhorn, "the centerpiece goal of a civil society strategy should be to strengthen marriage as a social institution" and thus to "increase the proportion of children who grow up in two-parent homes, assuming that such homes are the best family form to offer security to children."[23]

Less often is it noted by the theorists of civil society that the weakening of civic institutions that support families is in a significant way responsible for the difficulty that family members have in sustaining long-term relationships. This interplay of institutional strengths and weaknesses is increasingly apparent to contributors to the American family debate. Blankenhorn adds that a second piece of the strategy should be to enhance supportive communities that enable "stable families, linked by communal institutions based on shared values, [to] maintain a common life."[24] Those assessing the health and importance of civil society have moved from an initial strong focus on the local context, in contrast to large-scale market forces and state bureaucracies, to an apparent consensus that both local and national or federal efforts are important to the vitality of civil institutions. William Sullivan is hopeful that the fast-changing shape of the world economy and geopolitics may offer a window of opportunity to undertake the vast sociopolitical adjustments necessary to create the kinds of civic infrastructure that justice and human flourishing require.[25]

A point needing more attention all around is that neither the family nor other institutions of civil society forging a "common life" for some necessarily serve the inclusive common good; to the extent that surrounding institutions are not inclusive across class lines, many families stand to lose. This last reality comes more clearly into focus in Christian social ethics when the roles of institutions and groups in society are illumined by a concept of social and structural sin ("collective egotism") and by an ideal of Christian living that is both social and inclusive across class boundaries ("reign of God"). As chapter 4 will illustrate, using the example of welfare reform, Christian ethics maintains a place for government intervention in civil society precisely because, as Reinhold Niebuhr argued, sin as pride and self-assertion always intrudes on harmonious social relations, and groups that attain power are loathe to give it up. Some coercive element is always necessary to right the balance.

In *Whose Keeper?* sociologist-philosopher Alan Wolfe had already arrived in 1989 at the concern of Putnam and others that American civil society is on the wane. Wolfe nuances his analysis in important ways. Borrowing from Jürgen Habermas's "colonization of the life world," Wolfe contrasts civil society to the market and the state. But he neither portrays these larger systems of modernity as thoroughly debased nor disconnects them entirely from his ideal of civil association. What he does argue is that, while Americans have always taken care to limit government and political authority, they have been incautious about the incursions of the market into ties that they assumed would always be characterized by "trust, friendship, . . . intimacy and community."[26] The market and the state support the modern values of individual choice and equality respectively; what is wrong is not their emergence but their undue influence in the wrong places. "We need civil society—families, communities, friendship networks, solidaristic workplace ties, voluntarism, spontaneous groups and movements—not to reject, but to complete the project of modernity."[27] This means recreating civil society in new ways, so that institutions like the family are not so thoroughly interpenetrated by market values that the preponderance of family decisions is made on considerations of rational self-interest. Self-interested calculation of immediate harms and benefits will always work in favor of the adult agents who exercise most control over their own fate—over the "marketability" of their assets on the marriage and reproduction markets. The moral code of the market need not be abolished, according to Wolfe, but it must be resisted in the spheres of intimacy and trust that civil society is designed to serve.

A vulnerability in Wolfe's analysis is his assertion that one asset of the modern mentality is our recognition that we are free to invent our own moral codes, rather than simply to accept them from traditional authorities. A similar problem will arise in any theories of, or advocacy for the renewal of, civil society that are radically tradition based or in which the ultimate appeal is simply to a community's past or its current moral sensibilities. On the one hand, Wolfe exhorts fellow citizens to build up the infrastructure of civil society so that through intimate relationships we may learn compassion for and obligation to future generations, distant strangers, and diverse cultures.[28] Historically, "Americans found in the family, in community spirit, in the voluntary group, and in principles of altruistic charity a self-image that stood in sharp contrast to the materialism of their economic life"; it is this altruism, nurtured in intimacy, that must be recovered.[29] In a more recent work, Wolfe offers hope that middle-class Americans are not in fact so divided by hostilities and competition as "culture wars" theorists would have us believe.[30] But, beyond tolerance for others' differences, it still has to be shown that Americans are willing to balance a sense of entitlement to government-provided benefits for oneself with a sense of duty to the common good, or of obligation to sacrifice for fellow citizens who are less well-off.[31]

At the end of the day, Wolfe does not finally show why civil society should prefer to teach altruism or why we will select altruism rather than self-interest as our moral code. And if altruism is not now or in the future in fact being selected as the moral code of most Americans, there is little ground on which to argue for it that could not simply be chalked up to unrealistic nostalgia for an imagined past.

Some normative judgment about human well-being and flourishing is required. As a Niebuhrian analysis indicates, the "capital" of intimacy, trust, and cooperation can be either spent on exclusionary tactics that protect group assets by drawing clear boundaries for "civility" or invested in opening social borders to former outsiders, expanding networks of care and assistance so that social goods are shared among more, not fewer, participants. But for a shift toward the latter to happen, it must be agreed that compassion is finally a more noble and rewarding disposition than greed. A choice for compassion and open networks of cooperation also requires that limited resources be more widely and hence more sparsely distributed and that associations of the most local and homogeneous variety be interlinked with concentric, collaborative, and ever more heterogeneous affiliative circles. This, in turn, demands the expansion of altruism beyond the projects of immediate mutual reward. It requires sacrifice. A judgment in favor of inclusive altruism can, of course, by supplied by a religious tradition like Christianity. I maintain that it can also be arrived at inductively, consensually, and experientially by public and dialectical reflections on the nature and conditions of a humane society.[32] Such an agreement requires patience, perseverance, and hard work; it is not easy to achieve.

The mere fact of civil society is, sadly, as likely to illustrate the predominance of group self-interest over care for the common good as the reverse. The family, along with the neighborhood and the voluntary association, has been as implicated in this dynamic as any other civil institution. Families may be where individuals learn empathy and sacrifice, but families do not always expand the circumference of their virtues past the mutually rewarding love of family members or past the mutual support of other families similarly structured and socioeconomically, racially, or ethnically situated. Putnam's article already acknowledges that a decline in "intolerance" and "overt discrimination" may in fact be due to "the erosion of traditional social capital." Traditional social bonds are often strengthened by exclusionary group identity and tactics. A cautionary note regarding nostalgia for the civil institutions of the past is sounded in Wolfe's 1989 book and is struck again and more loudly in recent writing by Wolfe and others, in response to critics.[33] Caveats in place, it remains necessary that the would-be rebuilders of civil society be hardheaded about its inevitable double dynamic.

More research on the actual state of civil society has shown that the proclivity of Americans to "join" may not be disappearing anyway. According to a 1990–1991 survey, 82 percent of Americans belong to at least one voluntary organization, and the backbone of civil society in the United States is the churches and religiously affiliated groups.[34] Religious membership has been correlated with voting, political activity, volunteering, and charity.[35] Many church groups, in turn, are among the most active in sponsoring forms of volunteerism that lend their strengths to community development, helping to lift many out of inequality.[36]

Worrisome, however, is the conclusion drawn by Theda Skocpol that in recent years the more educated segment of the American population has pulled out of national organizations and broad-based community groups, which traditionally united people across class lines, even if by only one gender (in separate male and female associations). Today people in the upper middle class—professionals, managers, and businesspeople— are preferring professional and specialized organizations that are more gender-inclusive but less socioeconomically diverse. "America's largest cross-class organizations have withered. The best-educated people are still participating in more groups overall, but not in the same groups as their less well-educated fellow citizens."[37] In other words, civil society still serves special interests, although the purview of those interests can be defined in varying ways.

Examples abound of civil society at its not-so-benign. These range from the Michigan militia to my local PTA in a well-fixed suburb. No dearth of community activism there. Nonemployed, highly educated mothers with lots of leisure time banded together to advocate for resources to be redistributed to "talented" children from those with "special needs" (serving a disproportionate number of minority children who had been bused out from downtown or who were enrolled in the school's magnet English as a Second Language program) and to build a new school playground with private funds after the city ruled renovations an unfair drain on a budget shared with the schools of less-wealthy neighborhoods.

I also recall spending summers in a small town in Michigan, where the nuns who taught my dad still carried on in a close-knit Irish-Catholic community, where the people are simple, open, friendly, working-class, and always ready to "do" for their neighbors. Families were large, and everyone chipped in to make sure chores got done. At a family reunion in 1998, however, my women cousins from a family of seven children still resented having to polish their brothers' football shoes. My maternal grandfather, a farmer outside the same city, supported a wife and four children but kept a mistress in town. Families were strong, but the double standard reigned. And in her seventies, my own mother had still not been able to come to terms with and move beyond the abuse she had suffered as a child. In those days, that was family business.

On a far more serious note, in the times when my parents were growing up in Michigan, and even when I spent idyllic summers playing with cousins there in the 1950s, lynchings were widespread in the South. In the insulated world of my childhood, I was unaware of this violence. The institutions of civil society furnished my protections just as, by binding our attention, fellowship, and loyalty so close to home, such institutions enabled the violence that transpired in equally intimate associations elsewhere. More could be said, no doubt, of the politics and economics that created these two symbiotic worlds within the same nation.

One memorable example of effective yet nefarious civil association can be found in Studs Terkel's *American Dreams: Lost and Found*.[38] Terkel tells the story of C. P. Ellis, who was born in 1925 and raised in Durham, North Carolina. For his family, life was a constant struggle between low-paid work and unemployment. C. P. was close to his father, a problem drinker who could not afford to clothe his children decently and who "never seemed happy" but who took C. P. fishing and to ball games. When his father died of brown lung, C. P. was left—at seventeen and with an eighth-grade education—to support his mother and sister.

The pattern continued for C. P. He married young and had four children, one of whom was blind and "retarded." Barely scraping by while pumping gas and working a bread route, C. P. saved enough money to buy a service station and worked seven days a week, only to lose his business after a heart attack. After that, C. P., who claimed to have always felt a sense of inferiority, really "began to get bitter" and tried to find somebody "to blame." "They say to abide by the law, go to church, do right and live for the Lord, and everything'll work out. But it didn't work out. It just kept gettin' worse and worse."[39]

About that time, C. P. found support, a sense of belonging, and an outlet for his bitterness in the Ku Klux Klan. "The natural person for me to hate would be black people, because my father before me was a member of the Klan." Klan members hung around C. P.'s service station; they bought Cokes, had a few drinks in their cars, then stood around talking; they had meetings every Monday night. C. P. recalls making his oath of loyalty in a dark meeting room, filled with the applause of four hundred robed men. He knelt before an illuminated cross and made his vows. "Here's a guy who's worked all his life and struggled all his life to be something, and here's the moment to be something. I will never forget it."[40] C. P. rose through the Klan membership and ranks, eventually to become Durham chapter president ("exalted cyclops"). At one time, C. P. was state organizer of the National Rights Party. He organized a Klan youth group for kids who "were havin' racial problems." The first rally, playing "Dixie," drew a hundred young people who were "just thrilled to death." C. P. taught them the principles of the Klan.

As C. P. recalls, this was also the time when the Civil Rights Movement was beginning. More prosperous members of the Klan, city councilmen, and county commissioners who secretly opposed desegregation would phone up C. P., call him "friend," and urge him to attend city meetings to oppose "niggers in our schools." Passing C. P. in town, however, these same notables would cross to the other side of the street. C. P. gradually realized that he was being used. "As long as they kept low-income whites and low-income blacks fightin', they're gonna maintain control. . . . We got the greatest system of government in the world. But those who have it simply don't want those who don't have it to have any part of it."[41]

C. P. finally had a change of heart on race, brought about by his election to the school committee. He co-chaired the committee with a black woman whom he initially loathed. The feeling was mutual. Over time, however, both realized that working together was better than dividing their energies. A particularly forceful moment for C. P. came when the two commiserated over ridicule that their respective daughter and son had suffered in school because each parent had been "selling out" their race. Later, C. P. was elected to the school board, got deeply involved in union organizing across racial lines, was elected union business manager, and hung on his wall a plaque for service from the Durham Human Relations Council.

The interview concludes with a postscript, in which C. P. receives a phone call in his office. He reports that the caller was "a black guy who's director of Operation Breakthrough in Durham. I had called his office. I'm interested in employin' some young black person who's interested in learnin' the labor movement. I want somebody who's never had an opportunity, just like myself."[42]

The union, Operation Breakthrough, the local school board, and the school committee are all part of civil society. Strong local bonds and loyalties, based on intimate knowledge and trust, make possible personal and social relationships that reverberate from one telephone conversation throughout the national ethos of race and class. Of course, the same is true of Klan membership passed from father to son. The Klan is civil society; only it feeds on class insecurity and racial animosity. It makes one group strong by making another weak. It is strengthened through adult male dedication to youth formation, male-bonding rituals in parking lots and assembly halls, and confidential phone calls in which those from society's lower echelons are made to feel "important" by those to whom they are useful at the top.

A rendition of uncivil society at the opposite end of the economic spectrum comes from a 1998 *New York Times* story about Mark Forrest Gilbertson, social and marital "gatekeeper" of the scions of New York's blueblood families:

> Anyone between 20 and 45 with an active social life in the Anglo-Saxon bastion of the Upper East Side has probably been introduced to Mr. Gilbertson or members of his Director's Council of the Museum of the City of New York—whether through boarding schools, summers in Southampton or the post-debutante party circuit.[43]

Talk about enmeshment of civic institutions. Talk about market values. And "the family" is certainly strong here. One descendant of an old New York family slipped Mr. Gilbertson her nephew's name and address, knowing that when "Mark put him on the list . . . his social life would be taken care of." Gushed a twenty-something "party planner," "Mark didn't like the guy I was dating. . . . He kept telling me, when I'm ready, he will introduce me to someone from a nice background with the same values." After a recent move to New York, one California native with a Harvard MBA also accomplished list inclusion. "Mark makes New York feel like it's your own personal country club," said the fortunate new arrival, owner of a leveraged-buyout company. Perhaps he will meet a suitable mate *cum* social investment at one of Mr. Gilbertson's exclusive cocktail parties, hosted every other month at his town house.

Both of these examples make it seem too optimistic, if not naïve, to describe civil society as the realm that recognizes "obligations to other people simply as people," the realm constituted by "the bonds that tie people together because they want to be tied together without regard for their immediate self-interest or for some external authority having the power to enforce those ties."[44] The fact is that *all* social groups and spheres, no matter how intimate and trust-laden, are prone to perversion by self-interest and the drive to dominate others. Sometimes the overarching "authorities" for whose sake personal relations are being conscripted are not immediately in evidence, just as when C. P. Ellis failed to perceive the socioeconomic game plan in which the cultivated fellow-feeling of the service station parking lot was one small piece. Sometimes the authorities of civil society are bluntly on the surface, as in the crass matchmaking of some well-to-do urbanites (whether denizens of modern New York or ancient Rome).

No doubt many of the social circles in which we live and have our being are ambivalent regarding the authorities to whom allegiance is owed. After all, even while affiliating with groups that we perceive to serve our own best interests, we also achieve admirable levels of other-concern and dedication to common causes. Sometimes real compassion, altruism, and self-sacrifice without hope of gain are even achieved among and between groups, not just between inspired individuals. Compassionate action of a group beyond its own sphere of "belonging" is virtually always mixed in motivation and never extends far or lasts long. That is why Reinhold Niebuhr said that mutuality and justice (not love) are the highest possibilities of groups,[45] and why Jesus illustrated the morality that follows on faith in shocking yet engaging parables. In these stories, for example, wrongdoing children are not stigmatized but forgiven and feasted, and neighborly giving is directed to those whom the donor's culture regards as least deserving.

The New York-based Institute for American Values, whose council includes several notable politicians and educators as well as Judith Martin (a.k.a. "Miss Manners"), holds symposia on social and family issues in New York's Carlyle Hotel, and some of these have been sponsored jointly with the Religion, Culture, and Family Project. I respect and commend the genuine and well-placed public concerns of these sponsors. There is a clear need for those with funds and clout to mobilize at the top in order to get their resources into play at subsidiary levels. Yet I wonder whether meeting to discuss religion and family at upscale spots in Manhattan doesn't threaten collusion with the forces that keep "undesirable" families down and "successful" ones up in a manner inconsistent with core Christian traditions about faith, family, and community. I do not mean to be invidious.

I have participated in more than one of these symposia in the recent past and will likely do so in future. Thus I have all the more reason to urge that trenchant self-criticism and a sense of perspective are in order, especially when we undertake to judge others while assuming that our own feet tread the right path—something for me to ponder as I disembark the jet and taxi into midtown.

Conclusions: Three Convictions

Addressing the plight of the family in light of the state civil society, the following chapters are shaped from three convictions that can be briefly stated.

The first concerns human nature. Human beings are intrinsically social; they affiliate in all kinds of groups and communities, from the most intimate to the most expansive that available means of communication and material exchange will allow. If there is a distinctive mark of the postmodern age, it is not that civil society is disappearing but that humanity has at its disposal incredible means of mass communication and fantastic technologies that have expanded the interconnective web of human affairs all around the globe. Hence all the institutions of civil society are inextricably connected not only to the systems of the nation but also to global markets, governments, and proliferating global and multilateral institutions, from the International Committee of the Red Cross to terrorist organizations.[46] Humans have a natural capacity for intimacy, empathy, compassion, and altruism that can be learned and fostered in close associations like the family and gradually extended, with the help of cultural symbol systems and the communications media, to larger and larger communities. The moral task of families and of civil society in general is to enhance these capacities and to discourage their opposites.

Second, however, is the reality of human wickedness, or, in religious terms, sin. Sin resides in individual hearts, but it is most effective when it permeates social groups, allowing individuals to conceal even from themselves the deepest motives for and violent consequences of their actions. And, in turn, groups like families, schools, neighborhoods, and civic associations shape the individual for good or for ill, that is, for open-hearted compassion or for xenophobic self-defense and domination.[47] Collective egotism does not make the formation of morally responsible communities—large or small—impossible. But it does constitute a dark side of all human associations that family theorists do well to keep in mind, so as to counteract it more effectively. Sin as selfish irresponsibility for others does not affect men more than women, though it may affect typical patterns of male and female behavior differently. Confidence in the relational and altruistic potentials of our distinctively human nature, however, will preclude any capitulation to female or male sexual or reproductive fecklessness. Christian ethics can provide symbols and ideals to capture and convert the imagination, showing us that in embracing the duty of compassionate co-responsibility for and with others, we will discover our truest reward and fulfillment.

Finally, Christianity—its symbols, traditions, practices, and teachings—always takes on earthly existence in and through "earthen vessels."[48] Though we live to become "body of Christ," the ambiguity of our sanctification has been a theme of Christian ethics from the New Testament to the present. This means that neither the interpretation nor the incarnation of Christian moral ideals is a simple matter. Christian traditions about family are two-sided, from the exhortations of Jesus and Paul, through centuries of theological endeavor, and into our own era. Cultural norms of gender, class, and race, entwined in time and place with the family as an institution of civil society, threaten to undermine the "good news" that Christian family members are called to witness. The vocation of Christian families is to embody discipleship in all the concrete ways and in all the particular relationships that make up their daily existence, with all its complicated ties to others near and far. In so doing, the Christian family will begin to transform civil society and all the other co-arising institutions through and in which Christians exist with others on this planet.

Chapter 2

Family Bonds and Christian Community: New Testament Sources

Today's phrase *family values* connotes a solidarity in family identity that the first Christians found highly suspect, if not condemnable. Families in the ancient world commanded intense loyalty and in return secured one's status and advantages in society. Christians, on the other hand, commit themselves to a new community of believers in Christ, one in which loyalty to the family hierarchy is superseded by solidarity with other believers in a mix of family and class standings. The new family of Christ subverts customary ways of allocating power and resources within the larger society. Although status distinctions are never entirely abolished, Christians form a new metaphorical family, less tied to biological kinship and more class-inclusive than the cultural norm.

In the ancient world, while pagan philosophers and rulers dictate that family relationships be subject to the internal authority of the *paterfamilias* (the male head of the family) and the external authority of the civil government and its laws, Jesus' teachings imply far-reaching changes in family order and control. Although similar shifts are already tentatively appearing in first-century Greco-Roman culture, Christian communities are dangerous to the cultures in which they take root.

But dominant cultural values, especially those centered on the family, can be subversive of Christian commitment as well. This fact accounts, at least in part, for early Christianity's ambivalence toward the family and marriage. Jesus, for instance, warns his disciples away from the value placed on family relationships. At the same time, many of the first small communities of Christians form in and around households of converts.

Moderating the tension between the Christian vision and family life enables these new communities to survive in a sometimes-hostile environment. It simultaneously furnishes them an opportunity to change the institution of family from within. But this very mission can signal a diminution of the Christian protest against culturally normative lines of power and control in marriage, family, and gender relations. This chapter will place early Christian families against their cultural background in order to understand the symbiotic, if critical, relation between Christian values and the family values of the time. It will then investigate what transformative effect resocialization into the new family of Christ could have on social relationships.

Reinterpretation of New Testament perspectives on the family for our own time will require a dialectical approach. The New Testament provides us with a prototype of the socially transformative family, engaged with cultural realities and committed to a positive and constructive renegotiation of natural human relations and bonds. But Christian commitment today requires that we adopt a critical hermeneutic of family relations represented in the New Testament, asking whether a more radical mission of the Christian family is possible and necessary.[1]

Family and Society in the First-Century Mediterranean World

The advanced agrarian society of the first-century Mediterranean is under Roman political control, but Hellenism is the pervasive cultural influence. In Palestine the cultural and religious heritage of the Israelites also is formative.[2] As in traditional Middle Eastern societies today, the central social institution is the family. Christians share common aspects of Greco-Roman family life due to their cross-cultural situation, in which the law of the Roman empire applies to all Roman citizens, including those from Jewish and Hellenistic backgrounds in Palestine and in the Greek-speaking cities around the Mediterranean.[3] Families are complex, extending both vertically to ancestors and descendents and horizontally to relatives, as well as to such unrelated persons as slaves, freedpersons with legal bonds to the family, and servants.[4] Individual identity is defined primarily in relation to the family and its social place; it consists of the duties, responsibilities, and prerogatives one holds within one's family and by virtue of one's family role in the social network.

The family of this period is decidedly not the nuclear family of today. Parents and children never function as a social unit in isolation. The Latin *familia* can refer to all those related through the male line; it can also denote all those under the authority of the *paterfamilias* in a household, the membership of which is not limited to kin. The household (*domus*) includes a married couple and their children but also incorporates slaves, clients, unmarried relatives, freedmen or freedwomen, and other tenants of the property. The *paterfamilias*'s authority over his slaves and children is by law almost absolute, though harmony and moderation are the ideal and, in practice, the actions of heads of households are moderated by affection and prudence. In Roman Palestine, as in ancient Israel, married sons live with their parents, and multiple wives are permitted by religious law.[5]

While all societies have systems of social prestige, the link between prestige, social access, and inherited family status is especially strong in the small "face-to-face" communities of the ancient Mediterranean, whether the agrarian economy of the village (as in Galilee), migrating tribal groups (which also existed in Palestine), or pre-industrial cities (like those of the Hellenistic culture in which Paul founded churches). These societies are organized by the social categories of honor and shame. Honor references a patronage system in which those with higher status channel social and material goods to those of lower status who have petitioned for or earned their favor. Honor is not a personal, inner sense of satisfaction or integrity but the place one occupies in the eyes of others and of the community as a whole.[6] One may have *ascribed* honor because of who one is, for example, being born a male into a high-status political family. One may have *acquired* honor on the basis of one's influence, expertise, or past record.[7] One does not possess, gain, or lose honor by oneself but with and for one's entire family. One's family may hold and convey honor by lineage and birth, or it may acquire it by deeds. The honor of one's family determines those with whom one can do business, what social functions one may attend, whom one may marry, where one may live, and even what religious roles are open to an individual.[8]

Honor within families is also strictly ordered by hierarchies, in which the father holds the position of head, sons follow in order of birth, and women are subject to adult men. Male honor depends to a very large extent on protecting, defending, and enforcing the modesty and chastity of women.[9] Indeed, perhaps the most distinctive aspect of Mediterranean honor and shame societies is the importance given to masculinity, sexuality, and the maintenance of distinct male and female domains, including the seclusion of women from non-kin males. A shameless woman damages the honor of all the males in her paternal kin group, as well as the honor of her husband.

By the time Christianity arrives during Roman rule, the position of women is already somewhat ambiguous in what traditionally has been and still largely remains a highly patriarchal culture. In imperial times, married women usually remain under the authority of their fathers, rather than passing to the authority of their husbands at marriage. Consequently, women can in their own right inherit property from their fathers, but fathers can also command both the marriages and the divorces of their daughters. Hence fathers still exercise an immense control over women and property, through the disposition of which they manipulate alliances in the most advantageous way for their own kin groups. And although women are not legally under the authority of the *paterfamilias*, tradition and custom dictate subordination of the wife to the husband, as well as of daughter to father.[10] Thus, a married woman would still be subject to her father as *paterfamilias*. Nonetheless, sometimes women represent the power of male kin to inferiors or outsiders, and women are active independently in business, public patronage, and public religion, albeit not in politics and not frequently in the arts.[11] Further, it is sometimes possible for women to gain freedom from male guardianship. Augustan legislation permits freeborn women who bear three children, or freedwomen who have four, to gain their freedom. Domestic culture motivates and reflects these legal changes. The segregation of women within the house and at occasions like meals is less pronounced in Western than in Eastern culture. In the first century, Verius Maximus writes that some Roman women are now reclining next to their husbands at banquets.[12]

Women also play both devotional and patronal roles in religious cults under the Roman Empire, enhancing their status and influence. The cult of the Egyptian goddess Isis is popular with women of all social classes throughout Italy and the western provinces, and female devotees are depicted with their ritual implements in art (for example, on funerary altars).[13] Women hold many offices in the cult, including priestess, though not high priest. Ross Shepard Kraemer calls the cult of Isis "more favorable to women than any other religion of the time,"[14] even though it reaffirms women's traditional roles and probably serves as propaganda for them. Where it makes a difference is in making Isis's role as faithful wife more important than her role as mother and in giving equal importance to wife and husband. As such, it reflects cultural trends emergent during the Hellenistic period that recognize the significance of the individual and of the nuclear family. The Isis cult legitimizes the economic and personal autonomy of women that is increasing in the culture, and it downplays even if it does not eliminate the idea that women's primary fulfillment and even salvation are through childbearing.[15]

Inscriptions also record religious roles for Jewish women, including offices in synagogues, although not priesthood. For example, Caelia Paterna is deemed "mother of the synagogue of the people of Brescia." Both Jewish and Gentile women gain "in prestige and social standing in their communities through this honorific service and through their active patronage of buildings and institutions."[16] The first-century Jewish philosopher Philo of Alexandria describes a Jewish monastic community, the Therapeutae, composed of both women and men devoted to living an ascetic and contemplative life. Philo praises among them certain "aged virgins" dedicated to wisdom in whom "the Father has sown spiritual rays."[17]

It is also important to realize that, although women's primary roles may be domestic, the home in the Greco-Roman setting is not a private domain in today's sense. This has implications both for the practical access of women to public influence and later for the function of the house churches as highly social entities. Though men's and women's spaces are differentiated in the house, with women occupying the stereotypical domestic sphere, there is no division comparable to the modern one between public and private space or between work and family life. Excavations at sites like Pompeii, Herculaneum, Ostia, and Ephesus attest to fluid access between domestic and commercial areas. In addition, there are semipublic parts of the spacious houses of important personages (the vestibules, the atria, and the peristyles) to which even the most humble passerby has access by legal right. "The house [is] one of the most important places both for conducting business and for the production of salable goods. The house [is] not the place to escape from work but the place where much of the work [is] done; it [is] not the place to be free of a public role but the place to enhance that role by hospitality."[18] Thus the family and its domicile exist at the intersection of the public and private. Family is a key institution for defining one's social status, and the household anchors the framework of relations that patterns society as a whole.

Even so, some Greek and Roman thinkers foreshadow the later Christian sentiments that there are higher values than family life, that family loyalties should be generalized to outsiders, and that internal family relations should be mutual and reciprocal. Therefore, conversion to philosophy for Greeks and Romans brings the same consequences of social ostracism and persecution risked by the early Christians. As Epictetus describes it, a commitment to the life of a Cynic philosopher requires "radical detachment" from family, household, property, and social convention. In phrasing remarkably evocative of 1 Cor. 7:32-34 ("I should like you to be free of anxieties. An unmarried man is anxious about the things of the world, how he may please his wife, and he is divided"), he urges that the Cynic ought to "be free from distraction," while the married man "must show certain services to his father-in-law, to the rest of his wife's relatives, to his wife herself; finally, he is driven from his profession, to act as a nurse in his own family and to provide for them." This includes having to "get a kettle to heat water for the baby, for washing it in a bath-tub; wool for his wife when she has had a child, oil, a cot, a cup," and so on.[19] Renouncing the claims of a particular family, the Cynic makes "all mankind his children," his "sons, daughters, and brothers"; "in that spirit he approaches them all and cares for them all."[20]

While the Stoic philosopher Musonius Rufus is generally positive toward marriage and raising children for the common good of the family, the city, and the human race, he too warns that to be a philosopher means to follow the will of God, not the commands of one's father, and to be ready to live without property or possessions.[21] He advances the exceptional opinion that the relation between husband and wife should be mutual.[22]

In summary, the family in Greco-Roman culture of the first century is a highly important social institution organized to favor the prerogatives of male elders and the elite classes and to favor access to material and social goods for their inferior dependents. It would not be too much to claim that one's identity is first familial and only secondarily individual. Belonging to a family and holding a prescribed place within a family and a household are a central part of individual identity and a precondition for most people to enjoy the goods and benefits one's local community can provide. Even in the ancient world, some are critics of the system and try to live free from the quest for human respect and rewards. Their views, however, are strikingly unorthodox and place them outside the pervasive networks by means of which worth and power are typically allocated.

Controlling the family—its land, property, marriages, procreation of children, and internal ordering—is a key way for the tribe, village, city, or state to control individuals, groups, and social classes. Families mediate the interests of surrounding religious and political hierarchies reflected, for instance, in norms regarding marriage, procreation, and the transmission of property. Although civil laws and philosophical norms are aimed at regulating the upper classes primarily, the patron-client and honor-shame systems create patterns of social interaction in which poor families are seriously disadvantaged and relatively powerless to change their lot.

The Jewish Context

Jesus and those who first follow him are Jewish, with a long tradition respecting family and lineage as the foundation on which Israel's covenant with God is established and as the conduit through which faith and traditions pour down on new generations. Although both the kinship system and terminology for it are somewhat fluid over Israel's long history, kinship in ancient Israel consists of three basic levels: tribe, clan, and family.[23] The tribe (the twelve tribes of Israel) is the primary unit of social and territorial organization but has the least impact on ordinary life. The clan, the next level, is of somewhat indeterminate size, including a number of related families, for which the clan functions as a sort of protective association. Clans marry endogamously, in order to preserve Israel's system of land tenure, wherein territories are assigned by clan. All the families in a clan have responsibility for the land of members. They are, for example, responsible for redeeming the land of a kinsman who has fallen into debt and restoring it to its original owner or his heirs in the jubilee year.

The third level of kinship structure, the "father's house," is the strongest source of identity and inclusion for the Israelite. It is an extended family, comprising all the descendents of a living ancestor, except for married daughters, who become part of their husbands' families. In such a family, fifty to one hundred persons might live together in a cluster of houses, sharing common courtyards and cooking facilities. Since the ancient Israelite family is patrilineal and patrilocal, the birth of sons is critical to preserve the father's house and its patrimony, especially the ancestral portion of land, which enables the family to be self-sufficient. Although eldest sons are favored in inheritance, all sons inherit; daughters receive dowries that are, in effect, their share in the family inheritance.

In essence, the family is from ancient times the basic unit of Israel's social structure, with both military and judicial functions; it is the basic economic unit, in which inhere rights and responsibilities in relation to the land; and it is central in preserving the covenant relationship with Yahweh, communicating the faith, history, laws, and rituals of the nation from father to son.[24] The identity of the individual is, once again, corporate before it is personal, and the basic corporate form of belonging is the patriarchal family existing within God's covenant people. During the Davidic monarchy, Deuteronomic legislation reduces the power of the father of the family and the authority of the clan, with the aim of strengthening centralized national authority. The effect of these reforms on local solidarity is much greater in Judah, with its focus on Jerusalem, the temple, and the priesthood, than in Galilee.[25] Nonetheless, for all Israelites, unity remains key to family belonging; individuals are always placed and understand themselves in a social and relational context, above all, in the family. "Central to family values was the emphasis placed on solidarity, grounded in the interdependence of members that was necessary for survival and continuity."[26]

As Halvor Moxnes points out, many characteristics of the honor and shame society are recognizable in the "good wife" of the Pastoral epistles, who is subdued in public and submissive at home. "In like manner also, that women adorn themselves in modest apparel, with shamefacedness (*aidos*) and sobriety (*sofrosyne*), not with braided hair, or gold, or pearls or costly array" (1 Tim. 2:9).[27] Nonetheless, there is evidence that the status of women may be more varied or flexible in Israel than has typically been assumed. For example, the historian Josephus mentions nine divorces among the Herodian rulers, five of them initiated by women. The purpose of these divorces was enhancement of individual or family status through the formation of new, more advantageous political alliances. Josephus sees the divorcing women as departing shamefully from Israelite tradition, but the fact is that they are able to act so by being part of the urban elites by whom their behavior is accepted. It is difficult to know, however, to what extent these women act on their own initiative or are pressured or coerced to do so to advance family interests.[28] Not enough is known about the actual lives of Jewish women in the first century to pronounce definitively on the extent of their subordination when Jesus is engaging in his mission or when the first generations of Christians are interpreting and implementing traditions about Jesus. Not only may women have fulfilled roles not reflected in the "authoritative" texts, but these texts may have been written in some cases precisely as "prescriptive" forms of resistance to more varied or independent activities of women.

Carol Myers suggests that all members of the early Israelite agrarian family contribute to the household economy, leading to a high level of interdependence between the sexes and among generations. Although early Israelite society is admittedly androcentric, in that both descent and residence are defined with respect to males, thus privileging males regarding property, Myers objects that this does not necessarily amount to *patriarchy*, in the sense of sexism.[29] In any event, the gendered division of work is not highly developed and structured in peasant Galilee, with its cooperatively arranged living spaces, its common village facilities for threshing and for pressing olives and grapes, its domestic production of crafts and textiles, and its demand for full participation of all available family members in the intensive work of harvest time.[30] Some cooperative activities involve women only, including pregnancy and birthing customs and rituals and the funeral rites of lamentation.[31] Sarah Tanzer offers that evidence from texts beyond the usual rabbinic authorities, as well as from nonliterary sources, suggests that women may be "leaders of various sorts in synagogues, as benefactors and donors, as converts to Judaism and in relation to feminine aspects of the divine, and as highly educated individuals, leading celibate and contemplative lives side by side with men."[32]

In the Galilean towns and villages where Jesus carries out his ministry, the family remains the basic social form, as in other traditional agrarian societies. The Jewish peasant families of Jesus' followers survives in the Roman empire only under duress, eking out subsistence, producing most of their own food, and constantly subject to stress and crises. Richard Horsley outlines "several sorts of disruptions that could have a major effect on the economic and social viability of peasant families, from suddenly disruptive military expeditions through their territory to the steady escalation of economic pressure in the form of new demands from additional layers of rulers"—the Jewish client kings appointed by Roman authority.

Desperate peasants borrow money from state officials and some high-priest families, who can gradually acquire control over land and labor. Heavy taxation on the land and its products often leads to debt and the eventual loss of land that is supposed to be held in trust by a family or lineage. That, in turn, means a serious and spiraling threat to the means of survival for an extended network of kin. Peasants who are losing ownership of their land could become, in effect, the tenants of their creditors, having to concede to prior claims on the fruits of their work and being at the mercy of those who control their indebtedness. But even peasants who still reside freely on their ancestral property are obliged to pay burdensome taxes and tithes to greater and lesser officials representing the Jerusalem temple and priests, Rome, and the line of local Jewish kings subservient to Rome. In such times, "overt social conflict erupted in Galilee, whether escalating banditry, peasant strikes, or widespread peasant revolt."[33]

Richard Horsley's thesis that Jesus' command to "love your enemies" refers to increased generosity and sharing among peasant families[34] attests both to the marginal economic existence of these families and to the drive to protect family interest in competition with outsiders, surely heightened in proportion to scarcity of access to resources. Thus, like Greco-Roman families, Jewish families, struggling under the laws of the empire, provide individuals' primary source of corporate identity and well-being. Conversely, they can function as collective reservoirs of competitiveness, aggression, envy, and greed or spite (depending on whether a family actually succeeds in gaining some of the property, goods, or power available only to the fortunate few). Rivalry within the family leads not infrequently to animosity and occasionally even to fratricide. Dishonor to the family can lead to blood revenge. The internal organization of all these Mediterranean family types tends to favor men and conscript women's sexuality and fecundity for the family's own reproduction and the retention of its patrimony.

A remarkable example of the use—even violent use—of women, marriage, children, and enslaved peoples to secure social position and cement relations among dominant males is provided in the biography of Josephus, as recounted by Stephen Barton. This example spans Roman and Jewish cultures of the first century. Josephus takes pride in the nobility of his own lineage—tracing to both priestly and royal ancestors—as well as in his record in fathering three sons. Having been married three times,

> [he] says that his first marriage was an honor bestowed on him by Vespasian: "it was by his command that I married one of the women taken captive at Caesarea, a virgin and a native of that place." So, as with his treatment of his lineage, marital ties are related to an all-embracing concern with prestige. The woman remains anonymous

while the patron is named repeatedly. She is important primarily for her gift status in the patron-client relationship between Vespasian and Josephus, as well as for her reputation as a [virgin] and native Jewess, factors important to Josephus' reputation as a Pharisee. This marriage was short—apparently his wife left him—and no offspring are mentioned. Josephus' second wife, whom he married in Alexandria, bore him three children, of whom only Hyrcanus survived. Josephus then divorced her, "being displeased at her behaviour," and subsequently married a Jewess "of distinguished parents . . ." by whom he had two more sons.[35]

The family in the ancient world—as in many ways today—is the nexus of relationships of social inequalities maintained by structures of precedence and subjugation. This example says it all: a captive woman given as property by a high-status patron to a client, valuing of women primarily for their ability to produce sons, selection of wives on the basis of breeding and political advantage, and easy ability of dominant men to command or demand both marriage and divorce.

In the families of Josephus's world, each generation is socialized to obedience to the *paterfamilias* and to the social web, which exerts its own pressures on him via its criteria of prestige. Even if kin relations do not "naturally" have this valence, the frequency or even universality with which they tend to function this way in all cultures will lead to a high Christian suspicion of the family.

At the same time, the Israelite faith tradition enjoins practices that resist the boundaries of family loyalty by urging care for the "widow and orphan," as well as for other poor and needy persons who do not belong to one's own family or clan. John Rogerson refers to several "structures of grace" in the Hebrew Bible, that is, social arrangements grounded in divine mercy that are designed to mitigate hardship and misfortune by transcending family bonds (for example, Exod. 22:22-27, which expresses God's compassion for the "neighbor" who cries out and commends lending money to the poor among God's people).[36] In fact, in the pre-exilic edition of Deuteronomy dating from the seventh century, there is a remarkable shift from what had traditionally been duties of the family to care for its members to duties of each Israelite (man) to his neighbor. The "jubilee year" is proclaimed (Deut. 15:7-11; cf. Lev. 25). According to Deuteronomy's brother-ethic, "any needy Israelite, regardless of family or genealogy, has a claim upon his more prosperous neighbour, a claim grounded in the fact that the people as a whole is called by God to be a holy people." Deuteronomy also extends the rights of women somewhat by giving male and female slaves the same right of release and protecting women against false allegations about their chastity.[37]

Leo Perdue likewise suggests that the family ethic extends beyond the structures of literal kinship to shape "a network of understanding and care that moved beyond the immediate compound family to include clans, tribes, and the totality of the 'children of Israel.'" The term *neighbor* could include not only kinsmen but any fellow Israelite or even a resident foreigner, "who was to be loved as oneself and thus provided with the support necessary for survival."[38]

Stephen Barton gives further examples of the brother-ethic found in Deuteronomy from the writings of two Jewish authors who were rough contemporaries of Jesus: Philo of Alexandria (c. 50 B.C.E.–20 C.E.) and Josephus, who lived in Palestine (c. 37–93 C.E.). Philo argues that kinship and marital ties must never cause one to go after false prophets and idols, for "the honour of God" is "the indissoluble bond of affection which makes us one."[39] Josephus depicts the subordination of family ties by the Essenes, a separatist male community, at least some of whom did not marry or have children, as evidence of their virtue and piety. Regarding women as faithless and a distraction, Essenes prefer to "adopt other men's children" and "regard them as their own kin."[40] Both Philo and Josephus praise biblical figures who set aside family loyalty in favor of obedience to God and his will: Abraham was willing to kill Isaac, Saul to kill Jonathan, and after becoming leader of the Israelites, Moses exhibited no favoritism to members of his own family.

The Jewish family has a long and strong history of collective identity, pride, and cohesiveness, commanding individual fidelity, protecting its honor, and being devoted to the mutual well-being primarily of other member families in one's own clan. As in Roman and Greek culture, the family is religiously sacred, handing on religious identity (including membership in the priestly caste) with family belonging, and sanctifying norms of family behavior by grounding them in the divine will. A complementary ethic of care for all the needy, however, expands the family's moral outlook and advances an inclusive sense of community.

Jesus and Families

Jesus' preaching of the reign of God as present and available to those who are commonly regarded as "dishonorable"—sinners, prostitutes, tax collectors (probably associated with imperial oppression), slaves, gentiles, women, and those deemed ritually unclean by disease—is shocking, though not without precedent in his parent tradition. The Beatitudes (Matt. 5:3-11; Luke 6:20-26) constantly reverse the usual expectations about honor and shame. Jesus tells his followers to give freely without expectation of return (Matt. 5:38-48). And since such practices represent the overthrow of cultural norms—like self-identification with one's family, loyalty to the family above all else, strict hierarchy within the family, and antagonism, competition, or reciprocal favoritism among families—Jesus' sayings about family ties are clearly iconoclastic.

In a few notorious instances, Jesus seems to indicate that family bonds are incompatible with discipleship. The adolescent Jesus is depicted by Luke as acting in complete disregard for parental feelings, when he stays behind on his family's return from Jerusalem to pursue theological conversation with religious elders (Luke 2:41-51).[41] Mark portrays Jesus' uncomprehending relatives as believing him to have gone mad and striving to take him home, an effort on behalf of his safety and family honor that is quickly rebuffed by its intended beneficiary. Indeed, Jesus repudiates his family's responsibility for him and his kin ties to them: "Whoever does the will of God is my brother, sister, and mother" (Mark 3:28-30). In a formulation that both dissociates the honor of women from biological maternity and distances Jesus from his familial origins, Luke shows us a Jesus who deflects praise of his own mother from her role in giving birth and nursing him: "Rather, blessed are those who hear the word of God and keep it" (Luke 11:27-28).

Even more strongly, Jesus dichotomizes discipleship and family by seeming to demand that family relations be completely repudiated and abandoned. In response to Peter's avowal that "We have given up everything and followed you," Jesus responds that anyone "who has given up house or brothers or sisters or mother or father or children or lands for my sake and for the sake of the gospel" will be repaid in abundance in "the age to come" (Mark 10:28-30; Matt. 19:27-29; Luke 18:28-30, where "wife" is also included). To follow Jesus will divide one's household (Mark 14:12; Matt. 10:21, 34-36; Luke 12:51-53). Indeed, "If anyone comes to me without hating his father and mother, wife and children, brothers and sisters, and even his own life, he cannot be my disciple" (Luke 14:25-26).

These pronouncements are baffling to those of us who see care for parents and children and loyalty to our spouses as important moral duties. Their meaning comes into focus in the context of the first-century patriarchal family, where familial forms of faithfulness serve as demarcators of social approbation and status and as structures through which material and social well-being is assured for some and denied to others. Loyalty to one's own group and dedication to the status of that group over all others and at the expense of whoever stands in its way are incompatible with a life of mercy, service, and compassion for the neighbor in need or for the social outcasts and the poor existing on the margins of society. Family loyalty certainly conflicts with mercy on competitors for prestige or goods with whom one has established longstanding enmity.

Jesus uses familiar behavior patterns as a foil for his message about the reversal of standard social relationships. In the parable of the Prodigal Son (Luke 15:11-24), Jesus says that the reign of God is like a father who behaves quite unusually, forgiving the son who has shamed the family and welcoming him back even to the extent of sidelining his obedient elder brother. "He also has to fend off an ambitious mother, 'Mrs. Zebedee,' who tries to broker patronage for the eschatological social advancement of her two sons (Matt. 20:28-31)."[42]

Yet Jesus is sympathetic to others who suffer or plead with him on behalf of family members, especially parents distraught over the illness or death of their children: the Synagogue official whose daughter is at the point of death (Matt. 9:18-26; Mark 5:21-43; Luke 8:40-56); the military official with a sick son (John 4:46-53); the Syrophoenician woman with a sick daughter (Matt. 15:21-28; Mark 7:24-30); and the father whose son is possessed by a demon (Matt. 17:14-20; Mark 9:14-28; Luke 9:37-42). These stories reveal parents in apparent states of concern for children for their own sakes, not only in view of future advantages children offer to parents.

Children in Jesus' social world are not generally regarded as having value in their own right; hence the common practice of exposing infants, which the early Christians reject. Jesus' saying that one must become "like a child" to enter the reign of heaven has impact precisely because of children's negligible status. Childlikeness can symbolize the transformation of priorities and radical countercultural lifestyle required of disciples. Disciples are not to seek status in worldly terms or seek to control others to enhance their own position. Like children, they must accept weakness and social scorn, be obedient and willing to be trained, and comply with the demands placed on them by the community formed around the gospel. Instead of seeking recognition for their own greatness, those who would enter the reign of God must become like children, "the last of all and the servant of all" (Mark 9:33-37; Matt. 18:2-5; Luke 9:47-48).

Moreover, anyone who receives a child in Jesus' name receives Jesus himself: the standard criteria of honor and social worth are turned upside down, and Jesus identifies himself with the insignificance of a child. The infancy narratives in Matthew and Luke connect Jesus to his Davidic ancestry and divine parentage, while tensively symbolizing royal glory transfigured in a humble birth. When children are brought to Jesus, he welcomes and blesses them readily, foiling his disciples' efforts to send them away (Mark 10:13-16; Matt. 19:13-15; Luke18:15-17).[43]

The New Family of Believers
The early Christian missionary movement has radical social implications in part because it converts individuals independently of their obligations

to the patriarchal household. The house churches do not coincide perfectly with the household, because entire households are not always converted together. This creates conflict with the expectation that subordinate members of a family will follow the religion of the *paterfamilias*. It is also offensive to the political order, since the patriarchal household is the paradigm and basic unit of the organization of the state.[44]

In contrast to the socially respectable family types of their day, Jesus' disciples are socialized into a new family of those even now living under God's reign. Most obvious in the Pauline letters with their pervasive kin symbolism of "brothers and sisters in Christ," this re-creation of family loyalty can also be discerned in the Gospels. The association of disciples with childhood is one example. Another is the redefinition of the true family of Jesus as the faithful disciples, not Jesus' biological kin. The opposition is strongest in Mark, though it is also suggested in Matthew and Luke. Mark's Jesus, "looking around at those seated in the circle" of his listeners, says in reply to the news that his "mother and brothers" are outside the room where he is teaching, "Here are my mother and my brothers. [For] whoever does the will of God is my brother and sister and mother" (Mark 3:34-35; see Luke 8:19-21; Matt. 12:46-50). The disruptive effect on the natal unit is multiplied by Jesus' characteristic references to God as father. Beyond establishing a personal relation between the believer and God, this metaphor shifts loyalty from the *paterfamilias* to God alone. The fatherhood of God does not necessarily have to be understood in "patriarchal" terms. Indeed, it can challenge human fathers to forego prerogatives that derive from their power over their dependents, if God's fatherhood is imbued with the divine qualities of mercy, forgiveness, and perfection that Jesus urges the disciples to imitate. If God alone is "father" for the disciples (Matt. 23:9), then the authority and power of the human patriarchal father are vastly diminished or even rejected in the Christian community.[45]

In *Discipleship and Family Ties in Mark and Matthew,* Stephen Barton reinforces the case that, for the disciples,

> household ties and kinship-related identity are strongly relativized. They are relativized, first, by belief in the breaking in of the kingdom of God with the coming of Jesus the Son of God, who establishes the nucleus of a new covenant community open to the Gentiles. This new covenant community is understood as the eschatological family of Jesus constituted, not on the basis of inheritance and blood ties, but on the basis of active obedience to the will of God. They are relativized also by the call to follow Jesus in a life of faith and radical detachment enabling participation in the all-important preaching of the gospel to all nations. Third, they are relativized by the story of Jesus himself, rejected not only by the leaders of his own people, but

also by the people of his own hometown, and by the members of his
own family.[46]

Yet Barton is at pains to argue that the Gospel writers do not delegitimize
natural family ties as such and are in no way anti-family. Rather, he sees
the issue as the radical transcendence of kinship by the new identity that
comes from faith in the God Jesus reveals and in whose name he calls for a
new way of life. Hereditary family identity and responsibilities must be
subordinated to the voluntary solidarity of disciples, who constitute "a
new, eschatological family." The imagery of a new family of the children of
God also provides a theological rationale and compelling religious symbolism to account for and respond to the marginalization or rejection by
their own families that many Christians experienced.[47]

Divorce Sayings

A strong counterpoint to the critique of family bonds manifest in some of
Jesus' sayings is his well-attested refusal to tolerate divorce. The repeated
New Testament prohibitions of divorce[48] almost undoubtedly go back to
Jesus himself. They are puzzling insofar as they seem at odds with other
sayings that are highly suspicious of, if not downright hostile to, family
commitments. Carolyn Osiek expresses a common modern reaction: the
divorce prohibition is problematic because it can be interpreted legalisti-
cally and because it causes pain to couples caught in untenable unions. Yet
these sayings "are so ubiquitous and varied and so distinct from their context that their basic content must be taken with utmost seriousness as historical."[49] From the standpoint of social ethics and justice, though, the key
point is that Jesus' sayings against divorce were precisely "distinct from
their context." If divorce was a mechanism for ensuring the primacy of
male interests in patriarchal marriage, then Jesus upheld the right of
women to protection. Prohibiting divorce had the practical effect of limiting arbitrary male control over women and of protecting women from the
social consequences of the fact that they were valued primarily as sexual
prizes, son producers, economic bargaining chips, and tokens of family
political status.

In other words, the anti-divorce stance of early Christianity had exactly
the same religious grounding (the eschatological reign of a compassionate
and redeeming God) and the same subversive social meaning (inclusive
and compassionate social relations) as the sayings of Jesus about abandoning family ties or as the preference of Paul for permanent virginity. All
are forms of resistance to the controlling social hierarchies reflected in and
magnified through the relation of sexes and generations in the patriarchal
family. Although it is probably true that Jesus did not repudiate family

simply as family, it is not enough to say that he only wanted his followers to put family claims in perspective. Jesus as remembered by the early Christian movement presents family life with a deep and momentous challenge. In Barton's statement that there is "no evidence" that Mark was hostile to the family because "Jesus' prohibition of divorce presupposes the continuing validity—indeed the radical renewal—of household relations,"[50] the stress absolutely should be placed on the prospect of "radical renewal," taken in the sense of radical transformation.

Perhaps because of his interest in defending the validity for Christians of natural kin ties and marriage, Stephen Barton, unlike Elisabeth Schüssler Fiorenza and other feminist interpreters, does not develop the potentially radical sociopolitical value of Christian community seen as "family." Although it is neither the only such influence in the first century nor completely successful in realizing its own ideals, the early Christian ethos is highly critical of ordinary family life and in many ways develops over against it. As in many other cultural environments historically, the Greco-Roman family is key to the enforcement and perpetuation of hierarchies of power, permitting those at the top to exploit those at the bottom and to manipulate the middle ranks as intermediaries. The kin-based family with a specifically Christian identity has an opportunity to reorder customary family life, expressing the intrinsic social and ethical dimensions of Christian faith and community formation.

House Churches

The first Christian communities are catalysts for the incipient reconfiguration of important institutions of first-century civil society: first family, then the interdependent sectors of economy, gender, and religion. Even so, the relation of family status, individual status, and patronage continues to be an issue for Christian families. Wealth is never equalized absolutely, and at least some Christians function as patrons in hosting house churches and sacred meals. Carolyn Osiek and David Balch frame a pertinent question: Was the symbolism of baptismal equality in Christ "only an ideology that did not disturb the ethic of the owners, or did becoming Christian make an actual social difference?"[51]

Given the strong contrast between the traditional ways of structuring and regulating social functions through the family and the Christian ideal of forming compassionate, inclusive communities that bound believers of different social statuses together as new families, it might seem reasonable to conclude that Christian families are thoroughly countercultural. In the words of Elisabeth Schüssler Fiorenza, "the Jesus movement in Palestine severely intrudes into the peace of the patriarchal household."[52] Certainly the entire basis of Christian religious identity is faith and a personal commitment to act as a disciple; whereas in both Greco-Roman and Jewish culture of the first century, one belongs to a religious community by virtue of family identity and the traditions of one's kin group and its elders. For women especially, the link between marital and maternal status and religious standing is broken. Women are hearers of Jesus' words and believers in their own right. Neither marriage nor childbearing are mandatory; the new option of religiously dedicated virginity allows both women and men a new way to gain status and holiness outside family duties.

The picture becomes more complex, however, when we consider that, while many individuals become followers of Jesus over familial objections, others convert as members of households. The early Christian movement at least partly owes its growth to the availability of households for cultic activities like the eucharist.[53] In this it follows Jewish precedent. In the Jewish world, the family is the primary site of the transmission of faith for prayer, rituals, and the celebration of such feasts as Passover. Israel can be called the "house" or "family" of Yahweh (Num. 12:7; Jer. 12:7; Hos. 8:1). Archaeological evidence indicates that the Jewish synagogue too may have begun with Jewish communities in private houses, eventually renovated for specifically or exclusively religious purposes.[54] Similarly, although the Essenes occupy a separate community at Qumran, they also meet throughout Palestine in houses or private homes, where they assemble for meals and instruction. The local house church of the Christians has another precedent in the voluntary clubs and cults of Hellenistic culture, some of which are purely social, others religious or philosophical. Most groups formed around and met in private homes but included members of more than one family.

Since the household is a locus of inclusion, authority, and religious continuity in both the Jewish and the Greco-Roman worlds, it can be expected to play a prominent role in the formation of the early Christian movement. And so it does. The conversion of the household of Cornelius (Acts 10) marks the transmission of the gospel to the gentiles.[55] In four cases, Paul sends greetings to or from house churches, "assemblies of Christians that formed in and around a private household." These are his messages to the Corinthians, written from Ephesus: "Aquila and Prisca with their house church send abundant greetings in the Lord" (1 Cor. 16:19); a message to the same couple, sent from Rome: "Give my greetings to Prisca and Aquila . . . and to their house church" (Rom. 16:3, 5); a note from prison to his friend Philemon, in which he also mentions Philemon's wife, Apphia, and "your house church" (Philemon 2); and greetings to Nympha in Laodicea, also "to her house church" (Col. 4:15).[56]

On the one hand, the Gospels' portrayal of Jesus and his retinue of traveling apostles, disciples, and patrons and the New Testament's account of Paul's missionary activities give us the model of the itinerant preacher as one important form of Christian lifestyle. On the other hand, for many or even most of the early Christians, the church is closely associated with the family and its domicile. Yet not only do "households" include more than just biological kin or kin by marriage, the borders of the house—both architectural and membership—are porous to neighbors and associates. This characteristic is one reason why household conduct is thought to be so formative of social order in general.

The social function of the household, especially patronage, is one factor in defining how the gospel mandate to show love and mercy to the needy is realized. The churches are exhorted to be hospitable to the poor and despised. This does not mean that Christian membership is drawn primarily from the lower classes. Most scholars agree[57] that the majority of early Christians are "ordinary" people, representing all the middle levels of society, as attested by both Christian and anti-Christian writers of the first and second centuries. Although there are some wealthy converts who are able to fund travel and host meetings, they are neither numerous nor of high social status. Christian members of the very upper ranks of society are not in evidence either in the New Testament or in contemporaneous descriptions of the movement. Nor do ancient sources attest to members of the very lowest social levels, although, since they would be less likely to receive specific mention, the omission does not conclusively prove their absence.

Some house churches may meet in poor dwellings or tenements. But private homes of the relatively well-off would form the gathering point for several Christian households, as well as for individuals who convert alone. These households also support and host Paul and other gospel missionaries, helping to form connections among the local churches in cities around the Mediterranean, each composed of a number of house churches. Paul depends on the hospitality of these house churches, linked together as the local church of each city. He sees their members as partners and sharers in his work (Phil. 4:14-18; 2 Cor. 8:1-5) and endeavors to create a sense of larger, more global unity in "the church of God" as including churches in many cities (1 Cor. 15:9; Gal. 1:13). Within these churches and among these churches, inequalities of gender, class, and ethnicity are relativized in Christ, with at least some effect on Christian praxis, not just on internal attitudes.[58] At the same time, the wealthier Christians also function as patrons of those they host, leading to or confirming hierarchies in the community. Although women may gain in equality by participating in patronage, this is at the expense of class inequality with the gatherings they sponsor.

Paul's Letter to the Romans greets several women by name and indicates that they hold positions of leadership. Salient among them is Phoebe, a traveling missionary for whom Paul writes a recommendation (16:1-2). Called *diakonos,* a title denoting an important role as minister, Phoebe worked in the churches in Cenchreae as leader, benefactor, or patron of Paul and others. She is not identified in relation to a husband or male relatives, though she is called "our sister" by Paul, suggesting her full integration into the new Christian family.[59]

The family imagery of communal identity and the spreading Christian movement reinforced each other at the practical and theological levels. Paul refers to other Christians as siblings, advises and urges them "as a father to his children" (1 Thess. 2:11), and even envisions himself as a birthing mother (Gal. 4:19). Although Paul's kinship language in 1 Thessalonians remains androcentric ("brothers," as in 2:1, 9, 17; 4:1, 10, 13, and so on), it does not invoke or describe a hierarchically structured community under the authority of the *paterfamilias* but is instead designed primarily to strengthen the bond of intimacy between Paul and his converts. Nor does group cohesion seal "family" interests off from social concern, for the Christians are urged to love not only one another but all people (3:2).[60] In early Christianity as in later centuries, Christian ideals are not fully exemplified in practice. For instance, status differences even intrude on the eucharistic meal (discussed below).

The Evolving Christian Family

For about a century in the early churches, the household and its dwelling place shape community life and provide an environment in which economic sharing is encouraged, leadership is formed, and missionary work is implemented. It is not until the second half of the second century that some Christians dedicate their homes exclusively to Christian gatherings, modifying the dining room into a larger assembly hall and dedicating other rooms to community functions. Eventually Christians are allowed by the government to undertake building projects specifically for religious purposes, and in 314 C.E., a year after the Edict of Milan affords the new religion state protection, the first basilica appears.[61] On the one side, this transition to churches outside the home may facilitate control of ecclesiastical practice by official leaders outside the household. On the other, the relativization of the authority of household heads within the church communities is also a way of diminishing the influence of wealth and political power in the Christian assembly.

The effects of the close cooperation between the Greco-Roman household and the gospel are controversial from the standpoint of social ethics. As has been discussed above, the Greco-Roman *familia* and *domus* (house) are geared to reproduce economic, class, and gender differences. They are hierarchically arranged and display vast differentials in access to social and material goods. If these households provide the initial, shaping environment for Christianity, to what extent do Christian values transform the family, and to what extent do Greco-Roman "family values" colonize the message and example of Jesus? Does the household model of the early churches modify Jesus' vision of solidarity in the reign of God, or do Christians experience concretely within the family the relationship-transforming power of the Lord's Spirit?

The social realities of early Christian communities are entwined with the patronage system, to which family and household are so key. Patronage is essentially a form of extending family loyalties to "fictive kin"; hence similitudes of patronage can be seen in Jesus' relation to his disciples, in the family rhetoric of Paul, in the financial support provided Paul and other missionaries, in the house-based hospitality of prominent church members, and in the growing concentration of patronal power in church offices in the second and third centuries.[62]

Problematic as the entanglement of Christian house church worship with hierarchy, status, and patronage can be, we are warranted in saying that there is something at the heart of Christian community—as "body" of the risen Lord, vivified by his Spirit—that effectively displaces common assumptions about the purpose and shape of family relationships. This displacement is captured in the baptismal formula of Galatians 3:28 and exemplified concretely in Jesus' many parables of the reign of God.

Corroborating evidence that the Christian ideal of inclusive community was to a significant extent realized in practice can be found in the reports of observers that Christianity is a disruptive cult. Conversion to any cult other than the official religion of the Roman empire was perceived quite rightly as a threat to the convert's allegiance to family and state, and hence as socially and politically dangerous. When new cults attract women, slaves, and other members of the lower rungs of society, transferring their obedience from traditional political and household authorities to the leaders of these anomalous religious groups, reactive hostility can be virulent. Elisabeth Schüssler Fiorenza is convinced that the Christian model of "new family" begins to reconform home, religious community, and world, restructuring the patriarchal household "into a kinship community without clerical fathers and spiritual masters, a community not patterned after the patriarchal family."[63]

The Roman historian Tacitus writes of the Jews that "Those who come over to their religion ... have this lesson first instilled into them, to despise all gods, to disown their country, and set at nought parents, children, and brethren."[64] Pliny and Celsus make similar characterizations of Christians, lamenting the fact that this superstitious new religion attracts stupid members of the underclass, as well as ignorant children and women, and disrupts the proper order of household and society by mixing social classes. Paul's assurance that "There is neither Jew nor Greek, there is neither slave nor free person, there is not male and female; for you are all one in Christ Jesus" (Gal. 3:28), along with his wish that everyone could remain celibate as he himself was (1 Cor. 7:7), must have some hold in reality to evoke outsiders' anxieties about the social implications of Christian conversions.

Family metaphors for community membership serve to strengthen Christian resolve in the face of the obstacles that they could certainly expect to meet, for they were in fact social nonconformists.[65] Indeed, the Beatitudes can be interpreted in reference to the convert who loses status and honor in the eyes of his or her family by converting to Christianity, earning ostracization with dire economic as well as social consequences.[66]

There is also positive evidence that Christians lived by their norms of charity and compassion toward others. The sociologist Rodney Stark offers literary evidence that Christians were admired by friends and foes alike for serving the needy at great personal cost, unlike other ancient citizens of means. In the middle of the third century, during a great epidemic, Dionysius, bishop of Alexandria, commended his fellow Christians who

> showed unbounded love and loyalty, never sparing themselves and thinking only of one another. ... Many, in nursing and curing others, transferred their death to themselves and died in their stead. ...[67]

The heathen, claims Dionysius, "behaved in the very opposite way," throwing the ill into the roads, and abandoning them along with unburied corpses.[68] Confirmatory evidence comes from the emperor Julian, who, in an effort to stimulate similar pagan charities, attributes the growing popularity of the "impious Galileans" to their "benevolence toward strangers and care for the graves of the dead," as well as their willingness to support not only their own poor "but ours as well."[69]

Household Codes

The *haustafeln* or "household codes" of the deutero-Pauline letters (Col. 3:18—4:1, Eph. 5:21—6:9; 1 Peter 2:18—3:7; 1 Tim. 2:8-15; 5:1-2; 6:1-2; Titus 2:1-10; 3:1) provide a complicated and disturbing field on which to display the sometimes conflicting commitments of early Christianity to renew and to radically challenge bonds of family and kinship. These codes prescribe mutual duties of household members and indicate ways in which new norms of Christian identity were incorporated into traditional domestic structures. They have been the object of a great deal of scholarly interpretation over the past two decades.[70] This research has shown essentially that the codes are an accommodationist or realist attempt to give Christian values a practical meaning within the limits of hegemonic social expectations about family, class, and gender. The household codes manifest a double dynamic between the creative values of the faith community and their social context. They can be seen as illustrations of the Christian commitment to engage faith and the new life in Christ with the world, even though such engagement is risky. This does not mean, however, that the *particular* kind of accommodation to society advocated in the codes was *justified* historically, much less that it is still normative today.

Balch provides evidence that the Christian codes are related to standard Greek provisions for "household management," going back to Aristotle, with similar examples in authors like Dio Chrysostom, Seneca, and Cicero.[71] Aristotle sees authority and subordination as natural conditions, necessary to the constitution and welfare of the family and of the state, of which the household is a subunit. The Aristotelian paradigm outlines reciprocal relations of three pairs of social classes (husband-wife, father-children, master-slave), in each of which the dominant member of the pair is the *paterfamilias,* who "rules" over a member of the subordinate class. This structure is paralleled most completely in Colossians and Ephesians. In the Hellenistic precedents, household management was discussed in the context of the order of the city, which the household was to reflect and support (cf. the instruction in 1 Peter 2:13-14 to be obedient to the emperor and his governors).[72]

As already noted, the new Christian religion faced the same slanders as did other novel or anomalous cults in the Roman world. This situation motivated the authors of the Colossian code and its later versions both to encourage behavior in Christian households that was more conformist and to redact Christian teaching and texts so that they could serve an apologetic function for outsiders—Romans fearful that their wives, slaves, and children would be "seduced by bizarre foreign cults."[73] This was a tactic already in use among Jewish and Greek groups whose attraction of converts posed similar social problems.[74] A concern with social stability in relation to marital and household ties is seen in the very same letter in which Paul advises Christian spouses that they have equal rights over one another's bodies and that it is better that they not subject themselves to the concerns of the married state at all. Rather than break up the marriages, it is better that each remain in the state in which he or she was called to faith (1 Cor. 7:24).[75]

If we consider Christian household codes, several points of difference with Hellenistic examples are apparent. First of all, fulfillment of duty is given a specifically Christian or christological motivation, especially in Colossians, where the phrase "the Lord" is repeated seven times, for instance, "you serve the Lord, Christ" (3:24). Since *lord* could be used for any male superior, an association of Christ with the male head of a household is encouraged by this rhetoric, even while a higher framework for construing the relations of household members is proposed. Whereas the "realized eschatology" that the author of Colossians generally advocates, along with the resistance in the letter to the powers and rulers of this world, could have combined into a "message of empowerment" for all those who enjoy the spiritual riches of faith in Christ, the letter works instead to resubmit the gifts of women and slaves to the patriarchal order.[76] Ephesians goes further, four times comparing the male elder directly to Christ as head of the church, as in "the husband is head of his wife just as Christ is head of the church" (5:23).

It is, however, characteristic of the Christian codes that slaves are addressed directly (for example, Eph. 6:7), illustrating that they are incorporated into the community. This would have been highly unusual for Greco-Roman culture, in which directions for household management never treat slaves as subjects of instruction. Ephesians reminds the slave owner that there is a Master in heaven to whom both master and slave are subject—thus undermining the right of the *paterfamilias* over the slave and enjoining a duty to treat slaves justly. Wives and children are also addressed directly in the biblical *haustafeln,* and the duty of the husband to be fair and loving—not unknown in pagan examples—is promoted. As Balch has pointed out, although the Christian household codes require traditional forms of submission, they are also envisioning situations in which slaves and women have departed from the worship of the master's household gods (1 Peter 1:18).[77] The need for these reactionary codes arises precisely in view of the unsettling effects of the household churches' support for this kind of independent behavior of "subordinate" members of non-Christian houses.

The mixed effects of these codes are by now well in evidence. On the one hand, they encourage the embodiment of Christian values in everyday relationships, expecting that even if believers or the community cannot completely change their social milieu, they can still have a significant impact within it. The household codes must be contextualized as instructions for churches whose physical space, worship, and morality were in fact never separate from the whole web of domestic, social, and economic relationships in which believers participated and defined themselves. The house church, parallel to households generally, is in the first generations after Jesus a center for worship, hospitality, religious education, communication, social services, and mission or evangelization.[78]

The codes did not prescribe behavior one went out from Christian community to do, nor did they envision a realm of Christian practice set off from or over against ordinary life. The Christian movement began in the house church as a transformation of ordinary life itself. It was undeterred in its reforming impetus by the fact that some aspects of ordinary reality proved inimical to the gospel. "Christianity recognised that it had perforce to live within an inevitably flawed and imperfect society and sought to live and witness within that society by combining [what seemed] the proven wisdom of that society with commitment to its own Lord and the transforming power of the love which he had embodied."[79] The household codes model a *process* of interpretation wherein the family is constantly challenged and redefined by its Christian identity, even as it responds to other historical and cultural influences in an ongoing dynamic of formation and transformation.

On the other hand, however, this dynamic undoubtedly imports into Christian community the values and structures of the patriarchal household, dampening the freedom of Christian slaves and women, who are sometimes heads of house churches and patrons of Christian activities and are praying and prophesying in Christian communities in socially disruptive ways (cf. 1 Cor. 11:5). Particularly in view of the fact that more revolutionary challenges to family and class were part of the memory of the risen Jesus from the beginning, one could well maintain that the house communities could have and should have been more radical in their reconfiguration of the domestic order.

Schüssler Fiorenza concludes that the problem of social conformity was compounded in the Pastoral epistles (1 Timothy and Titus), because the influence of wealthy patrons, who offered their houses and other forms of support, was eventually added to that of male elders, who were the assumed authorities in the churches. "The ascendancy of the patronage system usurps the more democratic offices of the voluntary association by incorporating the local elite into their own ranks. In so doing, the office of bishop and deacon become patriarchalized to the extent that they are modeled after the wealthy Greco-Roman household." Thus the leadership of women, even of the relatively elite or wealthy women who had headed house churches, is marginalized or redefined.[80] The household patriarchal order invades the charismatic aspects of discipleship and

eventually becomes the model for church order. The transformed, egalitarian, and solidaristic ideal of Christian community is thereby diminished in
its capacity to change the family, household, emerging institutionalization
of church teaching and governance, and larger society.

Osiek and Balch believe that although Christians are originally evange-
lized with an ideology of "humility and unity" (if not complete equality),
the patronage system resurfaces in Christian families and churches once
the church begins to acquire power and privilege.[81] "The church had the
potential through Jesus' disturbing parables and its baptismal ecclesiology
for creating a true equality of discipleship under the unique and sole
fatherhood of God. Ironically, it did not do so, but chose instead to multiply the human symbols of patriarchal authority in the name of God."[82]
This, in turn, reinforces inequalities in family and society by seeming to
give them divine sanction.

Christian Ritual Sacrifice

One of the most important symbolic reinforcements of social relationship
is the meal and the customs surrounding it. For example, traditional meals
in the Greek East required that meals be strictly segregated by sex. In the
Roman West, sexual segregation may have been in decline, as more women
reclined with their husbands at banquets. Romans were adamant about
maintaining status distinctions, however, in the seating arrangements at
meals, as well as in the type of food served to peers or social inferiors (who
were placed at the periphery of the company or even in separate rooms).
"The formal dinner was one of the most important occasions on which
attributed honor might be gained, ascribed honor vindicated, and patronage acquired and exercised."[83] Thus it is not surprising that the ritual meal,
conducted in houses belonging to patrons of the community, becomes
both a symbol of the new relationships Christian belonging creates and an
occasion for the reinstatement or resurgence of older, culturally more typical status relationships.

The central ritual meal of the household fellowships of faith both symbolizes and realizes in practice solidarity in Christ across gender, class, and
ethnic lines. Writing about the Gospel of Luke, Halvor Moxnes correlates
the common meal with the social context of the Mediterranean city in
antiquity. Moxnes calls attention to the disparity between the elite and the
vastly larger numbers of nonelite and to the importance of the quest for
honor within a system of patronage governed by the requirements of balanced reciprocity. The meal is a form of hospitality among the elite that
could serve both sociability and status. The wealthy seek honor by sponsoring festivals and feasting on public occasions and by contributing to

public works, building projects, or cultural events; they are rewarded with public office, statues, or city banquets. Meals are a central part of temple sacrifice and worship, as well as a common activity of clubs and cults.[84] Other voluntary organizations of the time in addition to Christianity— such as professional guilds, devotional cults, and burial societies—also meet regularly around a shared meal and might bring together persons of diverse social class.[85]

The Christian meal, with its Jewish roots, like meals in the traditional religions of Greek and Rome, follows the paradigm of making animal sacrifice to the deity or deities. In Christianity, animal sacrifice is transformed into an "unbloody sacrifice" commemorating Christ's death as a sacrificial lamb. According to Stanley Stowers, animal sacrifice (specifically in Greek religion) can be understood as part of a complex symbolic system in which gender hierarchy and paternal control over children are asserted and maintained. Animal sacrifice typically ties religion to systems of descent, inheritance, and kinship.

> The most fundamental problem in these patriarchal societies is how
> to eliminate, subordinate, or bypass the claims that women might
> represent with the dramatic and bloody rite of childbirth [in which
> women and children often died in the process of bringing forth life].
> Thus, men have employed an equally dramatic and bloody rite of
> their own, animal sacrifice.[86]

Through participation in animal sacrifice, men assert their control over birth and transmission of property by their symbolic control of the body of an animal, its killing, and its redefinition and redistribution as food. The ritual reinforces male definitions of lineage and kinship and male rights in allocation of food and property. Ritual sacrifice sometimes allows women priests but always excludes childbearing women, and it never allows participating nonchildbearing women (virgins, old women, or temporarily celibate women) to wield the knife, cut up and distribute the animal, or partake of specified—especially sacred—animal parts. "Thus, the work of sacrifice creating lineages through men and bypassing rights established through women remained basic" throughout the Hellenistic and Roman empires.[87]

In the Gospels, Jesus is often portrayed at meals as well as accused of fraternizing with riff-raff, ne'er-do-wells, and outcasts (in Luke 19:1-2, Jesus dines at the home of the tax collector Zaccheus). He also interacts directly with women, bypassing what would have been the standard male intermediaries. He advises disciples to include those without honor or the means to reciprocate in their banquet invitations, rather than using meals to cultivate elite group contacts (Luke 14:7-14). At the last supper, Luke portrays Jesus as interrupting the disciples' debate about who was the greatest to remind them that those who would "eat and drink at my table in my kingdom" had to behave as youngest and not greatest, as servants and not leaders (Luke 22:24-30).

Meals are a typical feature of the life of the first Christian community in Jerusalem (Acts 2:46; 10:17-29; 11:3); they successfully break boundaries and create fellowship among Jewish and non-Jewish Christians (Acts 10–11). Paul is outraged to learn that the eucharistic meal at Corinth has fallen prey to the same types of status-motivated divisions and inequities that marked meals of patronage and benefaction in the pagan culture. "When you meet in one place, then, it is not to eat the Lord's supper, for in eating, each one goes ahead with his own supper, and one goes hungry while another gets drunk. . . . Or do you show contempt for the church of God and make those who have nothing feel ashamed?" (1 Cor. 11:20-22). Petros Vassiliadis argues that although the Pauline collection project (2 Cor. 8:13ff.) almost legitimizes rather than destroys the accepted social inequalities of Greek culture, it still forms "an ecclesial (eucharistic) reality that inevitably became the decisive element in creating a new social reality of justice and equality."[88]

Among the first urban Christians, "the ethos of the meal represented a break with the city ideals of patronage, benefactions, and the quest for honor," thus "creating a common identity for a mixed group of Christians."[89] Meals are household events, and Christian assemblies gather a number of unrelated people into family space for a meal. They unite several families in common rituals, while setting aside (at least ideally) the usual expectations about status and prestige. Christian meals, like the meals of other voluntary associations, help bind the fellowship into a sense of belonging and common purpose that transcends the frustrations, exclusions, and disrespect to which some members may be exposed in daily life. The occasion of the meal heightens self-respect and provides collective support for all.[90] The eucharistic meal thus helps configure the family or household setting as a potent base for changes in communal and social roles in general. The symbolic use of family imagery for believers in their relation to one another and to God, focused through the ritual meal, reinforces the intimacy of social relations within a close group and extends the group members' willingness to include new members and to share goods beyond the family, even without the prospect of balanced reciprocation.[91]

Conclusions: Christian Identity's Implications for the Family

Both study of the New Testament and investigation of the social world of early Christianity attest to tensions and contradictions between Christian identity and cultural forms of family life. The families and households of early Christians are integral components of what today would be called "civil society," codependent with other important axes of social identity and agency, including economy, religion, and politics. Jesus' preaching of the reign of God and the disciples' experience of living as the body of Christ call Christians to form new, inclusive families of brothers and sisters in Christ, or of children of God. This alternative differs radically from the strictly ordered domain of the ancient Mediterranean patriarchal family. Not only do converts continue to live, for the most part, as members of their own families and households, but these groups of kin and co-residents also provide the first foundations of Christian affiliation and assembly. Thus the new Christian family, based in kinship and household communities, has the potential to reorient larger attitudes and practices regarding race, ethnicity, religion, gender, class, and economic status.

It may be tempting to read the Gospels' picture of Jesus' iconoclastic behavior as an earlier and more authentic rendering of the nature of discipleship, while seeing Paul's apparent concessions to the *status quo* of the patriarchal family as a later, degenerative layer. Yet such a hermeneutical strategy would be questionable in light of the facts that the Gospels and Epistles are all produced at the end of the first generation and into the second generation of Christianity (from roughly 50 to 110 C.E.) and that, if anything, Pauline teaching reaches written form earliest.

The redaction of the "anti-family" sayings of Jesus as well as Paul's imagery of the new family occur in fairly close historical proximity to the appearance in the deutero-Pauline letters of the codes prescribing submission of women, children, and slaves. Thus it is hard to avoid the conclusion that there is ambivalence toward the family from the beginning of the Christian movement, including: wariness or censure of its exploitative, inegalitarian tendencies and of its potential to subvert Christian commitment; acceptance of the family's importance as a foundation of many sorts of human community, from the church to the *polis*, and acceptance of the legitimacy and even virtuousness of fidelity to family affections and responsibilities; and the unfortunately resilient human inclination to contain prophetic or charismatic threats to the status quo by co-opting their rhetoric of change. Both the Gospels and the letters present us with varied rather than univocal reactions to the family.[92]

The socially radical implications of Christian identity for the family are not to be completely lost in Christian tradition, as will be demonstrated in the following chapter. But ambiguities and contradictions always remain. Purifying the family's internal power relations of any hint of exploitation and preventing family identity from setting a boundary to exclude outsiders are significant challenges. The existence of these particular hurdles no doubt accounts in large part for the appeal of celibacy from the beginning of the Christian movement to those who are seeking a more complete detachment from the hierarchies of power and interest that extend from the family throughout the entire social fabric. Virginity or celibacy gives women and men of all social classes access to lives of spiritual depth, ascetic or charitable conduct, "adherence to the Lord without distraction" (1 Cor. 7:35), and honor among their peers.

The ideal to which Christian faith calls families is a new existence in which marital and kin bonds are the basis for affectionate, mutual, just, and generous internal family relations and for compassionate and sacrificial outreach to those beyond one's own family, especially those who are socially peripheral or powerless. This ideal is not fully accomplished even in the earliest stages of Christian living, as the household codes attest. Nonetheless, we do find a convincing New Testament record of families and family-based communities of faith that begin to transfigure human relationships in accord with Jesus' kingdom teaching of mercy, forgiveness, and compassion. Christian ideals have an impact on institutions like family, economy, gender, and religion.

Culturally, the household is a place where many people come together, associating persons and families of different social classes, even bridging the gap between Jews and pagan converts. The structural openness of early Christian families suggests an inclusive paradigm, in which Christian family identity is focused through commitment and service, not structure or order. As far as the economy is concerned, early Christian families make the patronage system more inclusive and less reward oriented. While classical philosophers regard mercy as a defective, irrational emotion,[93] Christians encourage empathy for sufferers and emphasize the virtues of mercy and charity. Christian families, especially through the sharing of the eucharistic meal, are taught in their ritual practice to overcome contempt for the weak. Regarding gender, Christian women assume leadership roles in family and church, reflecting incipient social trends that are consistent with and amplified by the memory of Jesus' example. The unfortunate capitulation to patriarchy in later church structures does not erase the subversive memory of a baptismal ideology in which women and men are one in Christ. Finally, Christianity as an institutional religion has always to struggle against too close cooperation with other powerful social institutions organized on a grid that marks status and division. But the church is also a global institution in which a multiplicity and diversity of power centers create concrete reminders and requirements of unity within plurality, service and humility within a prophetic mission.

As we examine Christian authors who have reinterpreted the relation between church and family through the course of Christian history, and especially as we ask after the meaning of "the Christian family" today, the central criterion of authenticity to the guiding vision of early Christianity will be the degree to which Christian families succeed in forming members in an ethos of mutuality, equality, and solidarity and in subsuming kin loyalty under compassion for the "neighbor," the "stranger," and the "enemy" as belonging to one's family in Christ. As we shall see, these standards of Christian identity are not always fulfilled in Christian families. Instead, the hierarchical and exclusionary aspects of gender and household structures represented in the New Testament are sometimes used to reinforce and legitimate social inequities.

Chapter 3

Family as Church:
Three Historical Representations

Christian married couples, families, and their homes have always played a major part in the growth of Christianity and the transmission of its values. Yet the effect of family life on Christian identity is not necessarily positive: families tend to create solidarity around their own well-being, although the most distinctively Christian moral virtue is sacrifice for the well-being of others. In every society, family—the institutionalization of intergenerational biological and marital kinship—exists largely to safeguard and enhance status and access to social goods. Families conserve advantages for heirs, in preference to and over against outsiders. Christian families, in contrast, are called to live by faith and love, in their relations to those both inside and outside family boundaries. Historically, however, the families of Christians have served culturally prevalent power structures as well as, and sometimes more than, transforming them.

This chapter will provide an opportunity to examine some examples of Christian teaching about the intersection of Christian family life with church and culture. A critical question guiding the study of these materials will be whether considering the family as church transforms families or undermines the church. The "family as church" metaphor may run the danger of making religion subservient to the values and functions of kinship, especially to the role of kin alliances in the accrual of goods and power. And in cases in which church structures have already been corrupted by anti-gospel social hierarchies, seeing family as church endangers the vitality of Christian conversion by bringing family religious experience into line with ecclesial hierarchies and limits.

As we have seen, the household was important as a locus of conversion in the early Christian movement. Yet the idea that the family actually is a domestic church did not emerge in a direct way from the house churches of the first Christians. In the first place, powerful cautionary elements in early Christianity resisted too close an identification of religious identity and kinship. The worldly concerns and values of the Hellenistic family contradicted the inclusive and eschatological "body of Christ." Christians could not place their trust and hope in the competition for survival and security that was institutionalized cross-culturally in kinship and marriage. The future-oriented nature of Christian hope also diminishes the importance of birthing and educating the young to carry on family traditions and provide parents with biosocial immortality. Christians from the first replaced the family ideology of their cultural contemporaries with the symbol of a new family in Christ. They made virginity available to believers determined to transcend the norms of sexuality and kinship in pursuit of the reign of God.

Moreover, the link between the family and the formation of Christian community that did exist in the early house churches weakened as homes ceased to function as formal places of worship for the Christian assembly in the second century. Indeed, patristic writers of the first four centuries gave relatively little attention to the family, in comparison with the number and length of their treatises on virginity and continence. The virtues of family life received far less emphasis than the glories of virginity and the dangers and tribulations of sex, marriage, and household cares.[1]

Lack of emphasis on a Christian duty of procreation in early Christian writings may be attributable at least in part to the fact that, culturally, such a duty was inextricably tied to the advantage of the patriarchal family and not necessarily to the good or salvation of children in their own right. Nonetheless, the duty of parents to educate the children they do have in a Christian manner has been a consistent matter of concern. Insofar as Christians bear children, those children should be sanctified in the community of faith and become participants in evangelization.

As far as the Christian attitude toward children is concerned, its distinctiveness lies not in holding up a duty of parents to children, nor in affirming that parental commitment is essential to children's or family welfare. Non-Christian ideologies of the family do or did the same, especially in the first-century world of early Christianity. Rather, the distinctively Christian attitude toward children consists in dedicating girls and boys alike to Christian purposes, namely, worship of the God revealed in Jesus Christ and love for neighbor and enemy.

The proximity of church to family is dangerous but unavoidable if the church is to be intergenerational and is to maintain a long-term existence in history and in human society. To overcome the perils that family identity presents, it is necessary for Christian identity to transform the family's self-promoting and exclusionary tendencies and to enhance its ability to teach affection, empathy, and altruism. On the basis of these dispositions, Christian families will be able to cultivate reciprocity and equality internally and to foster the compassionate sharing of goods with outsiders.

A closely related issue is the gendered division of labor institutionalized in families cross-culturally and, by extenuation, in societies. Gender is another line of division marking access to social benefits, and it extends between the family and society as a whole. This division begins with the basic biological differences and cooperation upon which reproduction depends. But gender differentiation virtually always extends beyond a more or less egalitarian sort of reciprocity. The rule is to turn gender difference into role separation by sex, to assign women to less-valued roles, and to reinforce this assignment by ideology and by physical force, both direct and indirect. Gender hierarchy, in short, results in the exclusion of women and girls from social authority, power, and even material goods—another contradiction of the inclusive eschatological community symbolized by Jesus' preaching of the reign of God. Therefore, Christian interpretations of family life must confront the possibility that traditional family structures should be replaced, not reinforced, in the domestic church.

Without having captured every important figure in the tradition, this chapter will consider three theological sources devoting significant attention to the family's Christian responsibilities to form children, to serve the church, to magnify Christian presence in the world, and even actually to transform it. In each of these, the notion that the family functions analogously to the church is given an influential or paradigmatic reading. The three theological representatives are John Chrysostom, Martin Luther, and the Puritans. The next chapter will address the recovery and revival in modern Roman Catholic teaching of the idea that the family is a unit of the church. None of the four theologies discussed in this chapter and the next succeeds completely in meeting these challenges. Yet all reveal in some way the potential of Christianity to exist within and through families, to reorient their values and practices, and to reshape them into Christian enclaves educating for service and change in church and world.

John Chrysostom's comprehensive moral focus is on the greed of the rich and misery of the poor. To Chrysostom, it is essential that Christian families educate children to spurn material possessions and practice charity. Exemplifying a recurrent problem throughout the tradition, however, Chrysostom not only accepts gender hierarchy within the family but uses the New Testament household codes to assign this hierarchy much greater prominence than it is accorded in the Pauline letters themselves. Yet in practice, Chrysostom is able to recognize a potential for mutuality and friendship in marriage that goes beyond cultural norms. He also experiences personal friendship with women and supports a leadership of women in church and family that goes beyond what he endorses in theory.

Martin Luther takes away the early church's option for virginity but raises the status of marriage. More directly than Chrysostom, he accepts the practical equality of spouses in the home. Yet he too holds to a theoretical submission of women. For Luther, the family and marriage are spheres of sacrifice in which Christians bear the cross of Christ; they are not aimed directly at the moral improvement of social relations—for example, equalization of wealth. In fact, his attitudes toward the social order and the hierarchy of roles that stabilizes it are very conservative. On the other hand, insofar as he writes for noble and common audiences alike, calls all to the Christian vocation of love of neighbor and service, and rejects any self-seeking behavior that privileges temporal success over faith, Luther blunts social hierarchies. Since it is the role of the family and of Christian parents to instill the importance of "faith active in love" and since social relations in general are the sphere in which Christian action is carried out, the Christian family has at least an indirect impact on the quality of civil society.

In contrast, the Puritans are aggressively activist regarding social change and the family's agency in bringing it about. Today's citizens of the United States are the heirs of the Puritans' conviction that religious membership is the backbone of civil society and that the family is one of civil society's key institutions. For the Puritans of seventeenth-century England and America, faith is a powerful agent of education and reformation, and the family, above all, is the unit in which dedication to a Christian society is formed and fostered.

But in striving toward their religious utopia, the Puritans insist on patriarchy and rationalize Christians' wealth and prestige as signs of divine favor. They are also determined to enforce Christian behavior among those who do not have the gift of genuine faith. The humble, poor, and unfortunate deserve condemnation, not compassion or a share in the bounty with which their social betters have been gifted. In the Puritan "family as little church" metaphor, the coalescence of patriarchal social order, family loyalty, wealth, and social status, along with an ideology of God's blessing, raises serious questions about whether marriage and family make viable foundations of Christian identity.

John Chrysostom

The early generations of Christians, as we have seen, knew that the family posed grave dangers to faith and faith's morality. They did not present procreation as a duty of Christians or assume that Christian religious identity would be formed in and through kin relationships. To believe in Christ meant to turn to a way of life that could well draw disapproval and rejection from family members. To the extent that the church fathers discussed sex and procreation positively, it was primarily to proclaim the usefulness of procreative marriage in channeling unruly sex drives. When confronted with extreme ascetics, either Christian or non-Christian, who saw all sex and procreation as evil, the fathers offered the containment of sexual desire more often than the procreation of children as a justification for marriage.

The Greek church's John Chrysostom (c. 349–407 c.e.), bishop of Constantinople, is no exception to this generally deprecatory view of sex and marriage. Yet he does see the family as having a positive function in Christian formation. The metaphor of the family as a domestic church that has undergone a revival since the Second Vatican Council of the Roman Catholic Church owes its appearance in the early tradition to Chrysostom. Although originally convinced that Christian children were better off in monasteries than with their families, John learned through his pastoral and episcopal ministry to place the primary responsibility for spiritual and moral training with the family. He encouraged Christian spouses by telling them that "the household is a little church."[2]

On the subjects of sex, marriage, procreation, and family, Chrysostom serves in some ways as a counterpoint to his much more influential contemporary in the Latin church, Augustine (354–430 c.e.), bishop of Hippo in North Africa (then a Roman province). It is helpful to see the two in comparison with one another.

Augustine's views of sex and marriage are well known, widely discussed, and not uncommonly blamed for the major portion of the Christian tradition's bias against sex and marriage, especially its condemnations of sexual pleasure and its insistence that only a procreative intent justifies sexual intercourse, even for married couples. In fact, Augustine wrote about marriage in order to defend it from its Manichean detractors, urging that its three goods—sexual fidelity, children, and sacramentality—made the relationship itself good, secondary in worth to virginity, but not evil.[3] Unlike Jerome, Gregory of Nyssa, and Ambrose, Augustine insisted that sex and procreation are part of human nature, not merely a result of the fall.[4]

Augustine's ultimately positive valuation of marriage, however, is offset by his proclivity to equate sexual desire with lust and shamefulness and to associate sexual intercourse with the transmission of original sin, as well as his speculation that, but for the fall, Adam and Eve would have procreated without sexual desire at all—an improvement he strongly approved. For Augustine, sex without the intention to procreate is a venial sin, unless one is merely complying with the sexual needs of a spouse who would otherwise commit adultery.[5] He spends little time developing the relation between spouses after they become parents or in setting out for Christian families an ideal of parental love for children.

Augustine's own experiences figure hugely in his perspective on sex and family, as he lets us know in his *Confessions*. In this autobiographical account of Augustine's conversion to Christianity, we learn of a childhood in an unhappy household, where his Christian mother's obsessive devotion to this particular son was offset by his pagan father's ill treatment of his wife; Augustine's attraction to Manichean rigorism; his thirteen-year liaison with a concubine or "second-class wife" of lower social status, who bore him a son; his mother's insistence that he dismiss this woman in order to marry a young heiress; Augustine's trauma over both his uncontrollable sexual passions and the loss of his mistress; his intense spiritual friendships with other men; and his eventual choice of celibacy and the priesthood. Augustine's basic approach to family was warped not merely by the occasional and polemical nature of his writings on it as responses to heretics. His personal experiences of marriage, family, and sexuality prompted him to be much more sensitive to their liabilities and painfulness than to their promise as schools of Christian virtue.

John Chrysostom, on the other hand, who tells us much less of his own life at a personal level, seems to have had an introduction to the relative merits of the celibate and marital vocations that ran in the opposite direction. John was a lifelong celibate with pronounced ascetic interests. Yet we have no reason to surmise that his childhood was particularly subject to familial conflict. His mother, Anthusa, was widowed at twenty with two small children. His close relation to her may have contributed to his later respect for celibacy and his appreciation of the advantages it could offer to women especially.[6] Chrysostom was baptized at age eighteen and reports that, as a young man, he was the victim of "vicious passions." Unlike Augustine, he managed to subdue them by avoiding close contact with women.[7] Edified by the self-denying life of hermits in the Syrian mountains, John joined their semi-communal lifestyle for about four years. But unable to stand the rigors of such a harsh monasticism, he was forced to return in ill health to Antioch, the city of his birth, eventually to be ordained a deacon, priest, and then bishop.

At first, avid in his praise of the hermitage from which he has recently returned, John extols virginity by contrasting it with the dangers and degradations of sex and marriage. In his long early treatise *On Virginity,* John, like Augustine, defends marriage from those who would reject it altogether. Yet he identifies abstinence from sex as much more conducive to purity of heart and unity with Christ. In dealing with sexuality, "One must walk on burning coals without being scorched, on a naked sword without being wounded, since lust is as overpowering as fire and steel."[8] At best, marriage prevents the weak from lapsing into "bestiality." Marriage was not included in God's original creative intent, and was made necessary only by the sin of Adam and Eve, to continue the race and provide a lawful outlet for sexual drives.[9] John discouraged the remarriage of young widows, fighting the influence of pro-family Roman laws.[10]

Chrysostom's view of the family shifts, however, in later works[11] that reflect his experiences among the elite of the city of Antioch. He tries to persuade families to incarnate Christian values even while carrying out ordinary relationships and responsibilities in a boisterous Hellenistic city with a reputation for a relaxed approach to morals, entertainments, and pleasures.[12] Both Augustine and Chrysostom lived in the age of Constantine, when Christianity had become an established and protected religion, and its adherents had, proportionately, an investment in the welfare and culture of their cities and the state. Neither saw Christianity as separatist in relation to society, and both adopted a stance toward the status quo that was in some ways accommodationist and in others transformationist. While Augustine aimed his program of critical reappropriation at the government and body politic, John designed his for the sexual body, marriage, and family.

John realized that, while some might succeed in a demanding vocation of virginity or monasticism, the central constituency of the church, in whom lay its hope for social transformation, were Christian householders. This "silent majority,"[13] married and with children, had the means, if they wished, to support frivolous pleasures, like finery, the theatre, and riotous wedding parties—or to devote their resources to the numerous poor who roamed Antioch's streets in desperate misery. While the well-to-do most often spoiled their sons and daughters with too many servants, dainty foods and wine, and luxurious furnishings, the poor resorted to blinding and maiming their own children so they might fetch a few more coins at the beggars' gate.[14]

Chrysostom's major and perduring moral concern, for the sake of which he rattles the security of his congregants about eternal salvation, is not sex but wealth, not lust but greed.[15] In this sense, he reverses Augustine's moral priorities. Augustine makes an alliance between the "City of God" and the "Earthly City," while retaining ascetic, rigorous sexual norms for Christian marriage. John, in contrast, decides to accentuate and influence the positive potential of Christian family life, while remaining stern and idealistic about empathy for the poor and sharing of property. Virginity is not any good as an end in itself, nor sex necessarily bad; what really matters is detachment from worldly interests and ambitions.[16] John hopes to reform the wasteful, selfish, and callous ostentation of Antiochene urban dwellers by reforming the Christian household, disabusing his flock of the idea that self-sacrifice and care of the destitute can be left to monks or other celibate, ascetic philanthropists.[17] Indeed, sharing with the poor is not just a matter of *noblesse oblige;* John veers toward an almost socialist critique of property by suggesting that all wealth has been ill-gotten at some point, since the earth and the Lord's blessings belong equally to all. Those who appropriate the bounty of the earth for their particular use alone—differentiating "mine" from "yours"—do so wrongfully.[18]

Compassion for the poor on the part of the rich requires a sense of common humanity, and John's treatment of sexuality helps establish the body as an axis of common experience and hence of fellow-feeling.[19] Insofar as the Christian battles against the excessive pull of sexual desire and feels the weight of sexual shame, he (or, less acutely, she[20]) knows a common denominator. Lust, like famine or illness, can plague the high- as well as the low-born, the prosperous as well as the pauper. "The medical guild tells us that this desire attacks with violence after the fifteenth year. How shall we tie down this wild beast? What shall we contrive?"[21] Unlike hunger, heat, or cold, desire's danger cannot be warded off by wealth or social standing; in fact, privilege can multiply the occasions of temptation.

According to the customs of the city, the body—its privacy or its availability to the gaze or to sexual use—was a marker of class difference. Wealthy women frequented the baths, attended by their male servants; the reaction of these inferiors to the nudity of the elite was beneath consideration. On the other hand, the bodies of servant girls, slaves, and cheap actresses could be exposed for all to see; even the Roman law regarded their sexual activities or vulnerability to exploitation as unworthy of public concern. "Only John was prepared to see in them a shared human body, subject to shared codes of modesty: 'For say not this, that she that is stripped is a harlot; but that the nature is the same, and they are bodies alike, both that of the harlot and that of the free woman.'"[22]

Chrysostom attacks the self-indulgence of the affluent. He has no patience with women in showy or seductive dress, parading to church bedecked with gold and pearls. He knows only contempt for mansions outfitted with marble, rich carpets, and servants, trumpeting their owners' status for all to admire.[23] He urges parents to bring their children up in a simple, restrained, and modest lifestyle, making them self-reliant[24] and training their sexuality in preparation for a marriage characterized by mutual devotion and respect.[25]

John comes to realize that most children will and should receive Christian education in the home and that the primary responsibility for formation will fall to their parents. Peter Brown remarks that "John elevated the Christian household so as to eclipse the ancient city."[26] John calls the soul of the child a new city, "a city but lately founded and built, a city containing citizens who are strangers with no experience as yet, such as it is very easy to direct. . . ."[27] Far from a mere shelter or retreat from the seductions of the old city, the Christian home is a training ground for practices that resist and disrupt the city's social arrangements, its rules of propriety, and the customary assignment of its denizens' fate. As a prelude to instructing parents on wise direction of the newborn child, John exclaims:

> There is but one kind of place that is shameful, I mean the possession of great wealth, and that is shameful indeed. It brings a man the reputation of cruelty, effeminacy, lazy arrogance, vainglory, and brutality. Place consists not in wearing good raiment but in being clad in good works. . . .
>
> Place does not consist of a well-burnished house nor of costly tapestries nor a well-spread bed nor a decorated couch nor a crowd of servants. . . . The things that concern us are fair dealing, disdain of money and fame, contempt for what the many think honor, disregard of human values, embracing poverty, and overcoming our nature by the virtue of our lives. It is these that constitute good place and reputation and honor.[28]

If the place of Christian instruction and education is the family, John proposes a replacement model of household management for Christians. Marriages are not to be arranged for political or mercenary motives. "You must consider that marriage is not a business venture but a fellowship for life" and "a warm and genuine friendship."[29] John trusts in the close collaboration of wife and husband, praises mutual love and respect in marriage, attends to both men's and women's faults and potential virtues, and concentrates on family stewardship of assets more than on sex and procreation.[30] Yet he does not seriously challenge the hierarchical model of relations in the family transmitted by the household codes of the New Testament. The primary responsibility for the moral and economic ordering of the family falls to the father; John's directives for child raising are addressed to men and speak primarily, though not exclusively, of sons. The husband is to provide moral and religious leadership in molding wife and children as a new cell of Christian society, armed to resist the meretricious allurements of prosperity and ease.[31]

John continues on the ancient Greek assumption of a division of public and private activity, at least within the upper classes. The man manages the affairs of the city council, the marketplace, the armies; the woman manages the household matters, including the supervision of storerooms, the wool-working, preparation of meals, and management of servants, responsibilities for which her husband may be "quite useless." So God "provided for peace," assigning the "more necessary and important part to the man, but the lesser and inferior part to the woman," ensuring by fitting her for "a humbler form of service" that "she would not rebel against her husband."[32] Interestingly, this very description, from *How to Choose a Wife*, envisions a certain autonomy of women in the female sphere, including a superior ability "to raise children well, which are the greatest of treasures."[33]

Wives are to be obedient to husbands but hardly servile. A wife should be chosen neither for beauty nor riches nor social position, but "virtue of soul and nobility of character," so that "we may luxuriate in harmony and lasting love." Marriage binds the couple "in peace, harmony, love, and concord. . . . It exists in order that we may enjoy another's help, that we may have a harbor, a refuge, and a consolation in the troubles which hang over us, and that we may converse happily with our wife."[34] These aspirations are, to modern ears, egregiously androcentric in their expression. Nor, obviously, do John's exhortations to husbands provide structural protection for women whose men are not compliant with his advice.

Yet, compared to Augustine's grudging justifications, John's vision of the friendship possible in marriage is an achievement, even if contained in familiar patriarchal packaging. Augustine too sees friendship as key to marriage, primarily as a development of his theological themes of order and peace; he does not expound this ideal in detail nor express anything like Chrysostom's admiration. Friendship of spouses takes second status in Augustine's concerns, subordinate to the disruptive influence of the sexual drive.[35] But Chrysostom takes the classic Roman ideal of harmony in a well-ordered marriage, sets it within the context of Christian love, and presents a largely, if not wholly, positive Christian reading of sexuality, women, marriage, and parenthood.

John far exceeds Augustine's toleration for sex that is aimed at procreation, for John extols the miracle of sexual union and of parenthood in uniting the couple. When the spouses become "one flesh," "the woman receives the man's seed with rich pleasure." It is "mingled with her own substance, and she then returns it as a child!" Formed from the body of each, "the child is a bridge connecting mother to father, so the three become one flesh." And even when sexual union does not produce a child, the union of the couple is not incomplete. "No; their intercourse effects the joining of their bodies, and they are made one, just as when perfume is mixed with ointment." Anyone who is embarrassed at his frank talk about sex, says John, only reveals their own licentiousness and lack of appreciation of God's gift.[36] "For nothing so welds our lives together as the love of man and woman."[37]

Unfortunately for the contemporary revival of John Chrysostom's domestic church metaphor, however, he does not present it as part of this elegy to sexual love and mutuality. Instead, it appears directly in the context of an interpretation of male headship, in which Chrysostom transfers the authority of the *paterfamilias* to his conception of church governance. Too bad that he did not instead permit the solidarity of Christian community to transmute the hierarchy of household management.

> Govern your wife, and your household will thus be put in order. Listen to what Paul says: *If they want to know something, they should ask their husbands at home* [1 Cor. 14:35]. If we administer our own households in this way, we will be suitable also to govern the church. For the household is a little church.[38]

Of course, John's views of the family and of gender should be evaluated on the basis of the picture drawn from his writings as a whole. But the appearance of this key image at just the point when male mastery in home and church alike is being reasserted provides the reader fair warning as to the resilience of domineering structures and the ease with which the most noble of visions is perverted.[39] Chrysostom wavers on whether subordination is intrinsic to the female sex or results from female fault in instigating humanity's fall from grace.[40] The latter explanation, to which Chrysostom moves later in life, can plausibly be connected with a bad conscience about domination of women and the growing realization that it is not self-evidently "natural" but demands a rationale.

In his own case, Chrysostom's longstanding friendship and collaboration with the propertied but ascetic and devout young widow Olympias belies his theoretical conviction that woman are inferior and in need of male guidance and supervision.[41] The social situation and ecclesial role of Olympias contribute perspective on the relation of gender to family identity, of gender and family to religious commitment, and of the intersection of religion, family, and economic institutions in the patristic period.

If in general virginity provides an escape from marriage for Christians, where lies the value in that fact, particularly for women? And if marriage and family are thought to detract from religious opportunity, can they ever be reconfigured so as to enhance it? The way in which family bonds are to be transfigured by Christian ideals can be better appreciated by comparing family to the ideal state of virginity. The life of Olympias and her relation to Chrysostom provide insight into these questions.

Like Chrysostom's mother, Olympias was widowed as a young bride. Olympias enjoyed aristocratic lineage and connections, had been well educated, was extremely wealthy and, left childless after her husband's death, represented a magnificent potential investment to suitors and their families. The emperor, Theodosius I, tried to force her into a union with one of his relatives. But, professing higher ideals, Olympias vowed herself to religious celibacy and devoted her vast inheritance to church-related projects. Among the most important of these were maintaining both Chrysostom and his predecessor, Nectarius, as bishops of Constantinople; support of Chrysostom and his retinue in exile; the founding of a monastery for women near the Constantinople cathedral; and the furnishing of houses in the capital to host visiting clergy and church dignitaries.[42] Olympias served as advisor to the bishops of Constantinople and was ordained a deaconess at probably less than half the prescribed age of sixty.[43]

In Chrysostom's seventeen surviving letters to Olympias, he extols her modesty, humility, asceticism, and charity, though he leaves out of account (as not squaring entirely with his conception of female virtue?) her direction of the monastery and her self-determination in the face of opposition from the emperor and other authorities.[44] According to Chrysostom, Olympias's concern for the poor is salient among her virtues. Theodosius's later prohibition of deaconesses from contributing their wealth in its entirety to the church might well be a rear-guard action in response to Olympias's steadfast resolve to retain control over her resources and use them to enhance her options and express her own values. Elizabeth Clark suggests that Olympias "enjoyed hosting the great and would-be great as they passed through her city" and that as benefactor "she had the opportunity to associate with those holding power in the church to a greater extent than she could have had in any other role open to a woman."[45] By combining asceticism with generous patronage of religious causes, Olympias and other women like her found a personal independence and a public acclaim that would have eluded them had they remained in marriages or families where their identities and choices would have been subsumed under those of the *paterfamilias*.

Christian teachers and theologians like Chrysostom tended to see women as inextricably linked to sex and procreation and to view the latter as infected by sin and even as a result of the fall.[46] But by renouncing marriage, ascetic virgins and celibate women could ascend to be spiritual equals of men. Women with considerable resources could become men's virtual social equals by renouncing luxury, embracing penance, and utilizing personal assets to support the goals of the church leadership, with whom they become collaborators. Aristocratic contacts and wealth enable a woman like Olympias—whose grandfather and husband both served as prefects of Constantinople, and whose father was among the advisors to the emperor—to exercise considerable real authority among male religious colleagues, even while adopting the commended female style of submissiveness and modesty. Olympias attains this authority by renouncing marriage and family obligations (to marry well and pass on her inheritance) that would typically attend her situation.

In turn, the lives of Christian families can be praiseworthy and salvific if they subvert the standard social order. Instead of conserving and channeling riches and privilege among the social elites, the Christian family should encourage self-denial and service of the poor. And, although Chrysostom uses male preeminence in the family to propose a model for church governance, his attitude toward Olympias shows that this model did not entirely exhaust his ideas of women's leadership. And insofar as Olympias uses resources acquired through her family of birth and her marriage to exercise her ecclesial role, she also presents a contrasting model of women's agency in the family, as not limited to childbearing and not falling totally under the control of men.

It reasonably can be said, in sum, that John Chrysostom's vision of the family, addressed to the affluent classes of Antioch with whose spiritual welfare he was charged, is oriented primarily to forming family members in the virtues of solidarity across class lines, sharing of goods, and simplicity of life. Although he endorses traditional gender roles in theory, his experience and practice open more egalitarian possibilities. Chrysostom presents us with a highly *social* ethic of Christian family life, one that makes the transfiguration of social relationships an important criterion of fidelity to the gospel, as received and lived in families.

Martin Luther

The great church reformer Martin Luther (1483–1546) takes his theological lead in many ways from Augustine, especially in his view that the Christian lives simultaneously in God's kingdom and in the world and that although the "temporal kingdom" is full of sin and woe, the relation between the two realms is dialectical.

What kind of cultural understandings of the family did Luther presuppose or address? The inner framework of feudal society had been determined by kinship bonds. Economic processes were grounded in production and consumption by family units. Family ties, either of blood or of marriage, were important in determining political alliances and in advancing access to benefactors, particularly the king, territorial princes, or other nobility. Identification of a family with the patrilineal descent line became more pronounced in the eleventh century, when regal power was disintegrating and aristocratic families began to establish themselves on their own land, conserved by inheritance of the oldest son. The result was a strengthening of the solidarity of blood relatives. Among the peasants, however, whose access to land was minimal and acclimation to the expanding forms of wealth in urban society proportionately greater, kinship relationships were more flexible and the advantages of many children less impressive.[47] Moreover, delay of marriage due to lack of economic resources reduced the fertile period of a marriage and hence family size among the poor. And since peasant women breast-fed their own children as well as those of others, while women of middle or substantial means were more likely to send their children out to wet nurses, the time between pregnancies was extended for families of scanter resources.

For the wealthy classes, the stem family—an extended group of kin and servants occupying the ancestral house—was more important economically and politically than the conjugal family. The focal point of the extended, co-residential family, however, was the nuclear unit, the *paterfamilias* and his wife, with their immediate descendents. Emotional bonds between spouses and between parents and children were important. The affective quality of family life was of interest to the Reformers but not a wholly original concern. For instance, the expectation of free consent to and fidelity in marriage for both parties had been achieved in the middle ages. Consent rather than consummation as constituting marriage and the immunity of the marriage bond from either the interference of interested relatives or the husband's prerogatives over his wife ("indissolubility") were advanced and juridically recognized by the decretals of Pope Alexander III (twelfth century). Moreover, even within what remained an essentially patriarchal institution, both wife and husband had equal rights to payment of the "conjugal debt." As over against the customs of the Germanic peoples who invaded western Europe in the fourth and fifth centuries, church law came to reflect a practical experience in which the relation of the married couple provided a new center of gravity in defining the structure of the family.[48]

By the time Luther appears on the scene in the sixteenth century, the market economy has emerged in Europe, and family sizes are generally smaller. Members of the nuclear rather than the extended family reside together in the majority of cases, a custom that probably pertains across class lines. Christian humanist authors like the Dutch Catholic Desiderius Erasmus are already defying traditional conceptions of marriage and family—as ordered by patriarchy and for childbearing—by proposing that marriage is more desirable than virginity and by praising the happiness of a companionate union as highly as the fruitfulness of a procreative one.[49] Many commentators of the early sixteenth century had remarked that marriage and family life were in a state of crisis, provoked by exaggerated ideals of clerical and religious virginity that demeaned married people even while scandalizing them with clerical improprieties and by ecclesiastical laws defining numerous and arbitrary restrictions and impediments to marriage, most of which were subject to dispensation for a fee.[50]

Writing in this context, Luther shares some of Augustine's misgivings about sex, seeing it as entangled in the evils of our earthly sojourn.

> Intercourse is never without sin; but God excuses it by his grace because the estate of marriage is his work, and he preserves in and through the sin all that good which he has implanted and blessed in marriage.[51]

Yet Luther's thinking is far from simple. His pastoral concerns dominate over theological and ethical consistency, and his writings—especially on marriage and family matters—are *ad hoc,* passionate, and kaleidoscopic.

While Luther concedes that celibacy is a higher vocation than marriage, he laments the sexual laxity of clerical mores and urges almost everyone to adopt the married state.[52] He denies that marriage is a sacrament or that the church has jurisdiction over it, but he praises it as a God-given blessing and calling.[53] He affirms the authority of husbands over wives in the household; yet he asserts that God created women and men equal,[54] and he commends the firm hand of his capable and no-nonsense wife, Kate.[55] He calls parental authority second only to God's; nevertheless, he upholds the right of young people to have final say in the choice of their marriage partners.[56] Urging fidelity in marriage and reconciliation after a break, he also accepts divorce after adultery or if one partner refuses sex.[57] He demands that a husband be faithful to a sick and sexually incapacitated wife, but he tells women with impotent husbands that they have a right to contract a second, secret marriage in order to have their sexual needs fulfilled.[58]

As does his fundamental theology of "justification by faith," Luther's ethic of sex, marriage, and family reflects the new, modern accentuation of individual experience and the quality of interpersonal relationships—whether with God, spouse, or children. Due partly to the fact that he lives in a time of significant social upheaval and uncertainty, Luther is much more cautious about potential threats to the sociopolitical order than he is about reform of the church. He does not portray the family as a school for the kind of Christian who assaults class, ethnic, or gender structures with radical new virtues. As a community of Christian formation, the family is charged with the duty of leading the young on the path of personal salvation and protecting them from the allurements of worldly values. But in the background, Luther's high view of marriage as one of the fundamental "estates" in which Christians love their neighbor and serve God in this world makes it impossible to say that he is wholly unconcerned with the social impact of the Christian family.

Luther's views of the family and of marriage are highly interdependent, if not to be equated. The background of both is the doctrine of the "two kingdoms," heavenly and temporal, with which Luther maintains a tensive, dialectical relation of the Christian person to the world and of the church to secular institutions. Developing his core insight that we are justified and saved from our sins only through faith in God and in the promises made to us in Christ, Luther locates Christian freedom in the heavenly sphere out of which we live now in faith and in love and service of the neighbor.

In reality, however, our experience of the world is conflictual. Because of sin, true Christians in the world are few; those who do live by faith must carry out their responsibilities in an inhospitable environment. One's duty to uphold the order of God's creation and to restrain evil often requires measures that are of this world, not of the kingdom of God, such as the law courts, imprisonment, or the sword. Just as there is a duality in our experience of the Christian life, so there are two kinds of statements in Scripture about the relation of the Christian to society. While the Sermon on the Mount tells us to love our enemy and "turn the other cheek" (Matt. 5:38-48), Paul's Letter to the Romans advises subordination to the governing authorities and political structures (Romans 13).

Luther concludes from this that the basic institutions of society are ordained by God for human welfare and that, however corrupted by sin and full of suffering they may be, they are to be respected.[59] These forms or "orders of creation" are the church or religion, marriage (including family and the household), and secular authority or government. The last of these, however, was instituted not at the creation but only because of sin. This does not make government itself evil: its function is to limit evildoing and serve the common good.[60] Whenever possible and especially in respect to matters having to do with his or her individual welfare, the Christian should follow the highest demands of faith, bear the cross willingly, and realize that genuine love of God and neighbor will require sacrifice and forbearance. But the Christian can also serve God in and through a worldly vocation, so long as all one's attitudes and actions are imbued with faith and love. The three fundamental estates, vocations, or callings, then, are the ministry, marriage, and magistracy. These vocations are not sacraments, for they are part of the divinely ordained ordering of human nature and human society. As such, marriage belongs not under the jurisdiction of the church but under the secular authority. (Perhaps inconsistently, Luther does not make the same claim about the ministry.)

Because marriage and procreation are natural, even if corrupted by lust and subject to suffering, no one has the power to remain celibate unless given a special grace by God, and that comes only to the very few. Therefore, the church wrongly upholds celibacy as a higher vocation than marriage and contributes to the vice and despair of priests, monks, and nuns by encouraging them to pursue an impossible ideal. Instead, Christians should recognize that marriage provides a sanctioned and even blessed outlet for sexual desire. More importantly, to marry and raise a family is a fulfillment of a command and blessing of God, given to Adam and Eve in their pristine state. "If Adam had persisted in the state of innocence, this intimate relationship of husband and wife would have been most delightful. The very work of procreation also would have been most sacred and would have been held in esteem. . . . For truly in all nature there was no activity more excellent and more admirable than procreation."[61] Moreover, the woman was created to be "the equal of Adam in all respects."[62] Hierarchy is purely the result of sin.[63] Luther tends to see "the blessed living together of husband and wife," though in fairly traditional terms, projected back even into paradise. The woman was created to bear children—free of any pain or suffering—and to provide "a nest and home" for her spouse.[64] On the other hand, on a note of greater equality, the "partnership involves not only their means but children, food, bed, and dwelling; their purposes too are the same."[65]

Luther's own marriage with the former nun, Catherine von Bora, who at twenty-six was sixteen years younger than he, gave him an experiential base on which to test and refine his ideas. Catherine was one of nine vowed religious women for whom Luther had undertaken to provide. She refused offers of marriage until Luther finally and rather suddenly took the step toward which he had long encouraged others, but which he had himself avoided due to his expectation of eventual execution as a heretic. Luther's father had repeatedly expressed a desire for grandchildren to carry on his name, and Luther decided to comply with this wish. At the time he remarked in a letter to his friend Nicholas von Staupitz, "God has willed and brought about this step. For I feel neither passionate love nor burning for my spouse, but I cherish her."[66]

The bond between Martin and "Katie," as he called her, grew deep and strong over the years of their life together. She had a tremendous job in organizing a large household, which often included twenty or more students and guests who would arrive to discuss theology with Luther or consult with him about events of the reform movement. Kate nursed him during illness. He was a sympathetic husband who left remarkably concrete observations about the tribulations of pregnancy[67] and deeply mourned the loss of two daughters among their six children. He writes of their shared grief: "The force of our natural love is so great that we are . . . crying and grieving in our hearts. . . ."[68] Luther made Catherine the executrix of his will, an unusual step in the culture and legal system of his time. She followed him in death six years after, in 1552. Although in defining the human function of marriage Luther emphasizes the natural force of sexual drives and needs,[69] as well as procreation, his personal experience with his own marriage and his astute observation of the marriages and families around him led him to perceive and prize the nature of marriage as a companionship and as a domestic partnership. In a marriage that "goes well," "husband and wife cherish one another, become one, serve one another, and other attendant blessings."[70]

The year before he died, Luther preached a sermon at the wedding of a former priest, dean of the cathedral in Merseburg. This man had lived in a so-called secret marriage for seven years, until the permission of clergy marriage and the strict prohibition of clerical concubinage were formally recognized by civil law and the local ecclesiastical leadership. At the cathedral wedding, Luther calls marriage a "holy estate and divine ordinance," founded at the creation of our first parents and the life for which virtually all men and women are destined.[71] Marriage is intimately connected with family, society, and church, primarily through the Christian education of children. In the divinely ordained and instituted estate of marriage, spouses "not only could but should live godly, honorable, pure, and chaste lives, bearing children and peopling the world, indeed, the kingdom of God."[72] Luther attacks religiously required celibacy and "the impure, filthy, and befouled cloisters"[73] and insists that God wants priests to be married. Any "impurity" in marriage God "covers up," for "it is done in order to bring forth children and God approves of this, for it is his ordinance. . . . Here parents, fathers and mothers, or married people, are excused; God will not consider it impurity on account of inherited sin, nor will he consider it to be a sin. God will rather build his kingdom of heaven over this work. . . ."[74]

The relation among generations defines family, ties the two families joined in the union of a conjugal couple, and allows the couple to found a family through the children they bear. Becoming parents and raising children are roles human beings were all created to fulfill, just as our parents have. "This is a duty which God has laid upon us, commanded, and implanted in us, as is proved by our bodily members, our daily emotions, and the example of all humankind."[75] Bringing up children is in fact "the chief end and purpose of marriage," not only so that they may be our heirs, but so that they may learn "to serve God, to praise and honor him."[76] Luther saw the relation between parents and children as integral to marriage. Married people "can do no better work and do nothing more valuable either for God, for Christendom, for all the world, for themselves, and for their children than to bring up their children well."[77] It is in respect of this relation particularly that we may understand his approach to family, its value, and its duties.

A 1521 letter of Martin Luther to his own father, Hans Luther, is revealing. Luther recalls how he entered the monastery sixteen years previously without his father's knowledge and against his expressed will. Luther now admits that he did so wrongly, since he did not obey "the authority and guidance of the parent," to whom children are made subject by God's commandment.[78] Yet, Luther continues, the authority of parents must yield to "the true service of God," for Christ said, "'He who loves father or mother more than me is not worthy of me.'" If parental commands conflict with those of Christ, "then Christ's authority must reign alone."[79] Luther speculates that God intended to add the ministry of the Word to his monastic vocation, which is why his conscience compelled him to disobey his father in the first place. In respect to the marriage decision also, Luther sees the responsibilities of parents and children as mutual. Engagements should not be undertaken in secret without parental consent. But the rise of secret betrothals and even marriages as a major problem in the European church already suggests a new cultural norm of individual freedom from familial control in making such an important, life-determining decision. It also makes evident the centrality of affective and emotional, rather than economic and political, considerations in the choice of a mate. Thus, Luther warns parents against forcing children into unwanted unions. No parent can command "the desire and love for his [or her] spouse" that God wills to exist between wife and husband.[80]

Luther does not explicitly define the Christian home as a site of structural transfiguration, though his stress on "the freedom of a Christian," even in the family, had radical implications for the family as he knew it. Acceptance of the created order, even in its postlapsarian condition, as somehow divinely ordained is part of Luther's essentially conservative attitude toward society and social relations. He tends to see the Christian home in its mission of child rearing as having a protective role, concerned above all with the child's personal salvation. The father should "regard his child as nothing else but an eternal treasure God has commanded him to protect, and so prevent the world, the flesh, and the devil from stealing the child away and bringing him to destruction."[81]

In a metaphor connotative of the idea that the family is itself a church, Luther continues on this theme, while underlining respect for authority of parents as delegates of God. He asserts that, "Most certainly father and mother are apostles, bishops, and priests to their children, for it is they who make them acquainted with the gospel. . . . Whoever teaches the gospel to another is truly his apostle and bishop." In marriage, offspring, "begotten of its own body," are raised up to worship and serve God. "In all the world this is the noblest and most precious work, because to God there can be nothing dearer than the salvation of souls."[82] Salvation, however, consists primarily in saving faith, not in the world-challenging sanctification of moral relationships. Parents can prepare children for faith, but salvation remains at bottom a matter more of internal disposition and the effects of God's grace on the individual than of communal dedication and action.

In regard to marriage and parenthood, Luther provides a good example of the ethic of the household code, both in its limits and its accomplishments. Yet Luther more self-consciously modifies the traditional subservience of women and the supremacy of the *paterfamilias* in general. For instance, in a marriage liturgy Luther composed to be used widely by pastors, he places the relations of husband and wife firmly under the rubric of the Ephesians code of male identification with Christ and of wifely submission (Eph. 5:22-29 is to be read in its entirety during the ceremony).[83] He portrays women's subordination and pain in motherhood as a cross to be accepted, but he also presents men's toil in earning a living as a corresponding manner of identifying with the salvific sufferings of Christ.[84] The real and practical effects of the mutual love[85] Luther counsels become evident in his discussion of the Christian husband's duties. His depiction of the physically burdensome aspects of pregnancy has been noted;[86] he also contravenes typical gender expectations in the family when he urges Christian fathers to forget peer opinion about masculine honor. It should not be beneath the *paterfamilias* to undertake some of the more trying aspects of infant care.

> Now you tell me, when a father goes ahead and washes diapers or performs some other mean task for his child, and someone ridicules him as an effeminate fool—though that father is acting in the spirit just described and in Christian faith—my dear fellow you tell me, which of the two is most keenly ridiculing the other? God, with all his angels and creatures, is smiling—not because that father is washing diapers, but because he is doing so in Christian faith.[87]

In another example, while commenting on the Fourth Commandment, Luther uses a royal model of God's authority as the paradigm for parental control over children. "God has exalted fatherhood and motherhood above all other relations under his scepter."[88] The *materfamilias* is included, however, and the authority of parents is subject to a still higher law, to which children are responsible above all. Not only are parents forbidden to command marriages, but they are to consider their children's happiness and spiritual welfare above worldly gain, esteeming "neither money nor wealth, great descent, nobility, nor lasciviousness."[89] Furthermore, if a father wants "to conduct himself as a true Christian should, he may forego his rights" and, in patience, permit the child to proceed with what may be an ill-considered choice.[90]

Luther's sense of the Christian family's role in salvation does not amount to John Chrysostom's obsession with forming communities to resist common customs of economic and class distinction. To the contrary, Luther accepts the existing social order and the hierarchical arrangement of its human population. Yet his demand that Christian identity be lived out in very concrete, particular, and daily manifestations of love and sacrifice, foregoing any consideration of political or economic gain, has implications for the institution of family and indirectly for its broader social impact.

Luther's view of the family would in practice change the reality of family as an institution of civil society. Luther elevates the vocation of marriage and exhorts Christian family members to live out the vocation of love in every aspect of life. He criticizes types of parental or legal control over marriage that diminish the free commitment of the couple or that use regulation of marriage as a way of creating revenue for civil, ecclesial, or familial authorities. In this approach, the family as an institution appears as a pattern of life in which married couples and their children can cultivate the Christian ideals of love, sacrifice, and trust in God. This way of life is entered freely and is highly personal, yet it also provides an avenue of social responsibility through which members are accountable to others, support civil society, and live out God's will in the world, influencing customary patterns of relation toward an ethos of mutual respect, service, and forbearance.

Luther's model of family is not unlike the contemporary evangelical-conservative model mentioned in the preface. Although the asset of both is a focus on strong intrafamilial relations dedicated to Christ, both are subject to the criticism that their critique of the social structures defining family life is too weak. In an era of an increasing gap between rich and poor in North America and the globalization of market institutions, it is even more possible and more necessary for Christians and Christian families to take responsibility for unjust structures that affect families and that families can affect. In contrast to Martin Luther, the Puritans take on the project of restructuring society in accord with their ideals. Unfortunately, these ideals are very much tied in to gender and class divisions that the Puritans confirmed and replicated via "Christian family" norms.

The Puritans
Most of the Puritans owe their theological and political heritage to the French reformer of the Swiss city of Geneva, John Calvin (1509–1564).

Calvin shared Luther's view that marriage is a holy estate to which most people are called. Calvin interpreted sex, marriage, and family in less paradoxical terms than Luther, however, perhaps because he was of a more systematic cast of mind than Luther and was more strongly influenced in some aspects of his theological thinking by a humanistic and classical education. In any event, Calvin seemed much less burdened by ideas (or experiences) of the shamefulness of sex and the sufferings inherent in marriage and parenthood. Rather, he presented marriage forthrightly as a covenantal relation in which spouses can achieve true companionship and mutual dedication. Calvin still regarded procreation as the primary purpose of sex, but the relation of spouses to one another is a good in its own right, not just in view of its procreative potential. Sex can be a joyful expression of marital love.

For Calvin, the relation of the sexes is not equal, however. Gender, sex, marriage, and family are all parts of an ordered whole, a society under God that serves humanity's common good in history and is called ultimately to give glory to God now and hereafter. This order is hierarchical in character, with men having authority over women, parents over children, and male householders over all other members. Doing away with the conflict Luther hypothesizes between the created status of woman and her present historical subordination, Calvin holds that woman is the spiritual equal of man but created to be subordinate to him in personal and social relations. This subordination is not just a result of the fall; it represents God's original design.[91]

Similarly, Calvin sees the relation between the church and society as less paradoxical than Luther. This difference was to be significant in defining the ideal of family life developed by the Puritans, both in England and in America. Although worldly society in general is certainly not to be equated with the church, Calvin, and later the Puritan heirs of Reformed theology, were activist in their approach to the possibility of a Christian society. They aspired to a civil association transformed by Christian ideals. Under Calvin's leadership, a "holy commonwealth" took shape in Geneva, a city whose whole pattern of life was dedicated to the glory of God.

In the seventeenth century, the Puritans tried similarly to convert English society to a more pure and biblical form of Christianity. The Church of England was, from the Puritan standpoint, much too accommodating of popery. Puritan revolutionary fervor produced the civil wars of the 1640s that led to the Commonwealth and Protectorate under Oliver Cromwell. The Puritans did not succeed in permanently unseating Anglicanism as the national church; Charles II became the head of a restored monarchy in 1660, and with him the Church of England regained its monopoly. But Puritan separatists were able to reinvigorate their vision of an ordered society under God in the colonies of New England. Although the designation "Puritan" includes some Congregationalists and Baptists, all Puritans share Calvin's zeal for a converted common life, a covenantal commonwealth uniting believers in obedience to God's revealed commands.

In the Puritan communities of the new world, the church, made up of voluntary believers, takes up again the mission to govern every aspect of life. In an era in which the establishment of a national church had been an unquestioned tradition throughout Christendom since the fourth century, English "Anglicans and Puritans both exhibited a sense of destiny, of being the chosen people, of special mission," and aligned this destiny with that of the nation.[92] This sense of divine favor, guidance, and ultimate triumph was to imbue culture in the United States for centuries to come, manifest in the resilient hope of "a Christian America," and, in later more secularized terms, the assumption that America is entitled to international moral leadership.

Central to the Calvinist and Puritan sense of social mission is a theology of covenant. God's covenant with Abraham is fulfilled in Jesus Christ, but the heirs of this covenant are not by any means identical with those professing belief or claiming church membership. Rather, genuine "saints" are those whose hardness of heart has been healed by God's grace, who worship God truly, and who live according to God's commandments.[93] John Calvin had put much more emphasis than Luther on the moral sanctification of the believer already justified by faith; hence the former's distinctive stress on the pedagogical "third use of the law." According to Calvin, those who have been elected by God and saved by Christ's grace will show their redeemed status in word and deed, guided by divine commandments. Although faith is bestowed by grace alone, conduct (including family relations) may be guided and improved by obedience to the moral and religious laws contained in Scripture. The law and commandments direct believers to "complete perfection." Likewise, the Puritans aspire to the complete reform of spiritual and social life.[94]

The Puritans envision themselves as God's chosen people, blessed by God in both a spiritual and a temporal sense. Through righteous behavior, believers glorify God, bring God's temporal blessings on themselves and their communities, and confirm their justified state. Yet, while Luther places strong emphasis on the conversion of the individual believer, both Calvin and the Puritans see salvation as a highly communal affair. Hence the key role of the church in salvation, of the family as a cell of the church, and of faith in transforming every sphere of life in which believers associate. Calvin's "entire object was to bring human life in its totality under common obedience to God in Christ."[95]

Because he draws a distinction between the visible (earthly) and invisible (true) church, Calvin realizes that the church in history will not be perfect, nor will all ostensible members be truly saints. Perhaps for this reason, he is willing to regard the children of believers as church members by heredity. Puritans were subsequently to develop a key role for parents in occasioning the conversion of their children, though election remains ultimately dependent on God's favor. Calvin himself anticipates the characteristic and frequently expounded Puritan ideal of a family united in true worship of God and so constituting the basic unit of church and commonwealth. He writes, "What a wonderful thing to put on record, that the name 'church' is applied to a single family, and yet it is fitting that all the families of believers should be organized in such a way as to be so many little churches."[96]

The Puritans make the family a vital and indispensable center of religious training. They organize domestic religion under the authority of the husband and father. Yet women have a key, if secondary, role. Both parents have an obligation to give children, apprentices, and servants religious instruction and to educate them in patterns of life consistent with godliness. "This duty to enforce good behavior in the family was the germ of all political and ecclesiastical authority."[97] Proper governance of the family is essential to the well-being of the state, since the group covenant enjoyed by family, church, or state is not the same as the covenant of grace God makes with every redeemed individual. A group covenant necessarily includes the nonelect with the elect. The enforcers of the external aspects of the collective covenant, by securing external obedience, also gain the reward of temporal prosperity for the whole community, even if not salvation for all.[98] Family training and discipline are key to this goal. The English Puritan Thomas Taylor summarizes well the expectations of his contemporaries when he exhorts,

> Let every master of a family see to what is called, namely, to make his house a little church, to instruct every one of his family in the fear of God, to contain every one of them under his holy discipline, to pray with them and for them. . . . The way to frame a good servant is to make him God's servant. . . . How many men go back to their estates and marvel things thrive so ill, and see not this to be the cause; that suppose themselves be not wicked, yet they suffer their sons or servants so to be, through whose hands the work goeth, and all is in a wante and consumption? . . . Many complain of evil times and general corruption: and many talk of want of discipline in the church, or good laws in a state, will not mend things till thou mend thy family. If

all families, where reformation must begin, were brought in to this
discipline, our eyes should see a happy change.[99]

Other sixteenth- and seventeenth-century English clergymen who
alternately draw analogies between family and church and between family
and state are Richard Greenham, who writes that the godly must bring
"the church of God . . . into our households and nourish it in our families";
John Downame, who calls the family "a seminary of the church and the
commonwealth"; William Gouge, who sees the family as "a little commonwealth . . . wherein the first principles and grounds of government and
subjection are learned"; and Richard Braithwaite, who, like Taylor, warns
that a man's family is "a private commonwealth, wherein if due government be not observed nothing but confusion is to be expected."[100]

These voices are echoed in New England by the likes of Cotton Mather,
who agrees that if families are subject to "an Ill Discipline, all other *Societies* being therefore *Ill Disciplined,* will feel that Error in the *First* Concoc-
tion"; Eleazer Mather, who calls families "the Seminaries of Church and
Common-wealth"; and the governors of the Massachusetts Bay Company,
who try to place every single individual who is not the head of a family
under the governance of some other head of household.[101] This is, they
believe, necessary not only for the fulfillment of religious duty but so as to
root out social disorders before they have a chance to do real damage. It is
remarkable how readily these authors assume that church and commonwealth should be structured according to one model, the model of obedience to the *paterfamilias.*

The family's role in educating for the hierarchy of civil society as well as
for Christian duty presents at least two key problems for later Christian
social and family ethics. The first is the hierarchy of husband over wife that
the Puritans do not merely take for granted but repeatedly assert to be central to effective Christian family governance. Reinforcement of family
hierarchy is an overriding concern in Puritan presentations of the Christian family. Certainly, the Puritans make household hierarchy and gender
subordination much more central to their self-understanding than these
principles are in the New Testament or the writings of Chrysostom and
Luther.

The second problem is the Puritan emphasis on the domestic sphere as
the originator *par excellence* of religious devotion and good citizenship.
Again, this emphasis is certainly stronger than in Chrysostom, who leaves
open the option of virginity, or in Luther, who puts more stock in the
direct relation of God to the believer. For the Puritans, the flourishing of
the family is virtually equated with the welfare of the church. But family
well-being is closely associated with worldly prosperity and peer respect,

on which Puritan families focus much of their energy and in which they take great pride. And it is just these values that are inimical to a form of community that embraces the poor, despised, and outcast.

It can and has been argued that the exaltation of Christian domesticity produces a kind of familism that undermines the inclusiveness of the gospel and its orientation toward the poor, as well as the commitment to the common good of all so necessary to a just society. Janet Fishburn defines *religious familism* as "the use of religious language and rituals to express and reinforce family commitments. There is a kind of *folk religion* or domestic religion in which believers use God as a means to achieve their own ends." Under religious familism, the beliefs and symbols of the religious tradition are manipulated in order to give divine sanction to the particular desires and objectives of a family or of those families exhibiting the structure, values, and social status of the kind of family that serves the social goals of the religious group providing the endorsement.[102]

Puritans saw the family primarily as a vehicle of the salvation of themselves and their children, both for this world and the next. Puritan gentry and merchants arranged marriages suitable to conserve or augment family wealth and position and to guarantee the security of children. And strictly controlled families and households were regarded as essential to the economic and social welfare of Puritan communities in general. The dubious premise of these practices is that Christianity affirms family cohesion and welfare as a fundamental value and that Christian views of family life are well geared to the temporal success of the state. Seeing the family as domestic church in such terms can hardly avoid domestication of the church.

Anthony Fletcher has argued that indeed the very purpose of the Puritan family was to supply an institution of civil society that could reinforce patriarchy and reestablish it when necessary. "The crucial issue was the protection of monogamous marriage as the linchpin of the social order."[103] This social order, as we have seen, is arranged around a chain of authority from divine to civil and ecclesial to familial authority. In *Gender, Sex, and Subordination in England 1500–1800*, Fletcher analyzes the Puritan ideal of household governance using the same sociological categories of "honor" and "shame" that have been applied to Greek and Greco-Roman society of the Mediterranean and ancient Near East. Maintaining male honor is essential to prosperity, since prestige guarantees access to material and political goods. Male competency is tested and proved by mastery over the household. The defenders of a tightly controlled system of male honor are in effect safeguarding their place in the hierarchy of social beneficiaries; the welfare of the society or state actually amounts to the welfare of the controlling elite, and the honor-shame system defines one place in or in relation to that elite. As in ancient Greece, Fletcher argues, male honor among the Puritans is attached to control over women, especially women's sexual behavior. In the patriarchal family, women's chastity and fidelity betoken their subservience to husbands or fathers. Daily symbols of controlled sexual behavior are found in respectful speech and demeanor, as well as in obedience to all commands from their husbands.

In the Puritan case, however, women and men are spiritual equals, in that both are saved by God's grace and called to a pious life. Both, likewise, are obliged to educate and correct children and servants. This means that mutual love, trust, and friendship are portrayed as intrinsic to the marital ideal to a vastly higher degree than in ancient cultures. Moreover, male command of women's sexuality does not mean that sexual experience is never considered from the female point of view. Sex and sexual pleasure for both parties are valued in marriage and are seen as important constituents of love. Also, for the Puritan man, virtues such as honesty, hard work, and decency toward others in the community are as important as sexual control (although to be made a cuckold, especially a witting one, seems to loom as the largest personal disgrace[104]). But as concerns the personal relationship of husband and wife, the wife is to obey the husband in all things, follow his initiative, and conduct herself with modesty and humility.

The need for and means to proper order of the holy household are expounded in sermons, advice literature, and conduct books of the seventeenth century. Christopher Hill observes that the Reformation, by reducing the authority of priest and institutional church offices, enhances the responsibility of Christian laypersons, especially those in positions of authority, to ensure that religious duties are fulfilled by subordinates.[105] For the Puritans (as for Calvin), the interlinking of the church and the commonwealth means that religiously designated authorities in family and community also bear responsibility for upholding the social practices requisite to the smooth function of political and economic affairs. William Gouge is an eloquent, representative, and influential guide to such instruction, especially in his treatise, *Of Domestical Duties* (1626). In Gouge's own household, children and servants are catechized by means of prayers twice daily and three times on Sundays, as well as the reading of the Bible. Parents and heads of families have a fearsome obligation to ensure that all in their care follow a godly way of life.

To this end, the power of the father reigns supreme, exercised not only by exhortation, education, and example, but by strict discipline and punishment when necessary. It is unquestioningly accepted that "that person, who by the providence of God hath the place of an husband, a father, a master in his house, the same also by the light of nature hath the principality and sovereignty therein" to rule over wife, children, and servants.[106]

Parental duty demands that great care be taken in educating children in the fear of God with all due discipline, training them in a suitable profession or trade, and arranging marriage to a partner who can help advance their spiritual and temporal good. The guiding assumption is that the child in its natural state is a wayward and sinful creature who must be trained up by reversing inborn instinct.[107] The means of correction should be proportionately harsh. According to the unanimous opinion of the Puritan clerics, parents must follow a program of child rearing that includes "the demand for outward marks of deference and obedience, the religious education of the young, and the control of their behavior by admonition and beating."[108] Evidently, all children, both boys and girls, will require physical punishment at some point, if not on a regular basis. According to Gouge's *Of Domestical Duties,* "stripes and blows [are] a means appointed by God to help the good nurture and education of children," as he attempts to demonstrate from extensive biblical citations.[109] Gouge, nonetheless, writes with pained emotion in grieving the death of his little daughter, "my sweetest child."[110]

Perhaps because the bonds of parental affection inclined to interference in the strictness of the prescribed disciplinary regimen, Puritan families entrusted their boys at a young age to the more rigorous demands of schoolmasters and often sent their young children, both boys and girls, into apprenticeships or domestic service, even when this does not seem to have been economically necessary.[111] The regularity of beatings of servants in private households no doubt varied widely, but the brutality of English public school masters is legendary down almost to the present day.[112] The education of girls who remained at home centered on preparation for a subservient role in marriage and the accomplishments necessary to excel in domestic life. This might include learning French and dancing, playing a musical instrument, reading creative literature, and writing; it certainly included study of the Scriptures and devotional works, as well as the arts of housewifery.

Parents also had almost absolute discretion in selecting vocations and mates for their children, in regard to both of which religion and wealth were the prime considerations. Though they could establish the parameters for marriage choice, however, parents were not to force their children into marriage against their will.[113] Children retain the prerogative to reject aversive prospects, since love of spouse is an essential component of a pious and righteous life.

If we turn to the spousal relation itself, we find that the hierarchy of the household codes patterns the advice books. Richard Baxter considers that the "natural imbecility of the female sex" will require a great deal of patience from men.[114] Somewhat more moderately, Gouge's commentary on Ephesians 5, in *Of Domestical Duties,* notes that submitting to one another is "a general mutual duty appertaining to all Christians" and that "subjection" can have many motives, qualities, and consequences. To wives, he commends a subjection that, though "necessary" due to the inferior place of women in the natural order, may still be "voluntary" when dutiful respect causes a willingness to yield to the authority of the husband. Gouge endorses the civil law by which women are denied property rights to the "common goods of the family." Like other Puritan divines, however, he also denies the right of husbands to beat their wives, even if they are not obedient.[115]

The rule of husbands does not go uncontested, in both subtle and overt ways. In fact, a rise in preachers' and teachers' attention to certain traditionally valued codes of behavior corresponds to a proportionate rise in frequency of practical contradiction. One should not assume that the advice books reflect reality, so much as a utopia to which their authors aspire. Some evidence suggests that, in fact, women manipulate, ignore, or openly resist some of the clerical pronouncements about their status and its constraints. Some women may even step outside the roles that are officially prescribed for them. As in the case of Chrysostom and Luther, actual practice among the Puritans seems not always to conform absolutely to espoused ideas.

Sometimes women could reshape their familial and maternal roles to better advantage. For example, Fletcher notes that the custom of following childbirth with four weeks of seclusion of the new mother and child among other women, concluded by a churching ceremony, is "a collective social event in a reserved female space" that offers support to women and attracts male appreciation for women's domestic labor, sexual services, and reproductive contribution.[116]

Women's special piety provides another route to respect and power. Spiritual purposes justify private devotions, meditations, and self-education through reading and study.[117] Both men and women are encouraged to reflect upon and recount their experiences of conversion, and a particularly dramatic or miraculous account lends special status to its subject. Especially at the time of the English civil war, women pray publicly for political changes, organize prayer meetings in their homes, and publish pamphlets. "Though most female authors deprecated their own abilities and described themselves as 'instruments of God's power,' they clearly intended their works to be read by men and felt no limits as to subject matter, delving into complex theological and doctrinal matters and directly challenging the actions of the King or Parliament."[118]

Fletcher also recounts nine case studies of Puritan marriage, gathered from private documents, such as diaries, letters, and memoirs. In five of these, the level of intimacy and interdependence that Puritans consider to be desirable in marriage erode the subordination and obedience that is expected of women. Letters by these couples manifest love and devotion in fond and informal terms, but even so, most of the wives most of the time maintain a rhetoric of humble submission through which they profess obedience, even while giving their husbands advice and asserting their own opinions, goals, and decisions. For example, Lady Brilliana Harley is selected for marriage by a member of the English gentry some two decades her senior. Among her attractions are her family's wealth, court connections, and Puritan lineage. Never overstepping the bounds of wifely respect, she begins correspondence to her husband (a friend of William Gouge) with "Dear Sir," and ends it with "your most faithful affectionate wife." Yet, when her husband, Sir Robert, is away sitting in Parliament in 1643, Lady Brilliana is left in the countryside "to defend the castle . . . against the royalists."[119]

Other women help their husbands to conduct business affairs and even stand in for them in negotiations, sometimes to the annoyance of their male counterparts. Joan Thynne and her daughter-in-law Maria each manage things at the family's estate while their husbands remain in London for many consecutive months. "Joan's legal expertise was considerable. . . . Maria was strong and independent; she arranged the movement of her husband's livestock, told him what should be done about cutting woods and selling timber and warned him about leases that needed revision."[120] In 1607, one woman writes to her father that in order to gain success in a dispute with a neighbor, "I have answered his letter like a woman, very submissively, if that will serve, for I perceive that they cannot endure to be told of their faults."[121]

Although patriarchy and misogyny limit women's independent access to the marketing opportunities that are emerging from 1500 to 1800 or gradually exclude them from traditionally female occupations such as brewing, women do avail themselves of the chance to trade in food and small wares. Some keep shops or hire market stalls; others peddle in the streets. Some retain a hold in the livestock and dairy businesses.[122]

In summary, there are several factors militating against the actual subordination of women on a par with that to which the conduct books and sermons of the Puritans admonish couples. The Puritan ideal of marriage includes intimacy and affection, both personal and sexual. Intimate friendship and cooperation on a daily basis tend to disestablish assumptions about natural superiority and to replace them with practical reciprocity and mutuality. In addition, the subordinationist reading of Ephesians 5 contains the premise of spiritual equality, as well as the exhortation to modify subordination with mutual love, respect, and reverence.

The fact that young people are accorded some choice in selection of a marriage partner also helps to establish a basis for mutual devotion and support by encouraging the positive commitment of each to the success of the relationship and the welfare of the household. This trajectory is deepened by the fact that the education of girls for household management comes increasingly to include topics of learning traditionally reserved for boys and assists women to give astute advice to men or to act on behalf of men who are away from home for prolonged periods. Unlike Chrysostom's friend Olympias, however, the Puritan woman does not have the option of a professed celibate vocation in which she can exercise authority on her own, either spiritual or economic. Prudent and providential management of a male-headed household is proclaimed as the female path to salvation. It is also a woman's access route to social status and repute and to the respect and trust of her husband, who may then delegate responsibility to her.

The iconoclastic and subversive examples of Puritan women's behavior show that the modern ideal of equality is making some inroads in marriage, even under the patriarchal ethos. Economic and class distinctions are another matter. For the Puritan gentry especially, wealth and status are essential to personal and familial honor. Class distinctions in order and authority are not only accepted but aggressively maintained. Landowning families consider themselves to have a right and duty of civic and religious leadership, extending from control over their own lineage, heirs, domestics, apprentices, subordinates, and tradesmen, to influence in the local economy, church, politics, and government.

Generosity to the poor, a biblical virtue, becomes for the Puritan gentry part of the ideal of civility and sociability; it is just as important a part of honor as the maintenance of household order.[123] Christopher Hill has remarked that this sort of tradition is "at once ostentation and a form of social insurance."[124] Support of the poor by the ruling class reduces the numbers of vagabonds, paupers, and beggars, who come under the authority of no family or church, cause social unrest, and threaten local government. The Puritans, who see charity as a duty to the commonwealth, seek to combat poverty by providing labor as well as direct relief. Richard Stock writes in terms familiar today: "This is the best charity, so to relieve the poor as we keep them in labour. It benefits the giver to have them labour; it benefits the commonweal to suffer no drones, nor to nourish any idleness; it benefits the poor themselves."[125]

In worship, class and gender distinctions are reinforced so as to give religious validation to the reciprocal order of family and commonwealth. Seating arrangements in church are designed to display both the familial hierarchy and the ordering of families in the local community. Janet

Fishburn has written of "the family pew" as a space in which church members could display the piety, conduct, cohesion, and social standing of gathered household members. Some wealthy Puritan families erected ostentatious pews, which sometimes had to be cut down because they obstructed the view of the altar. Congregations devised various ways of marking and respecting differences in gender, landownership, contribution to parish rates, and roles in parish affairs. In some parishes, servants and masters sat together, and in others, domestics and apprentices sat at the back of the church building, along with the poor, or along the sides. Where church architecture was suitable, gender and wealth distinctions could be reinforced on parallel tracks, with men seated in the center aisles, in descending order of importance from front to back, while their wives sat similarly arranged on the side aisles. "Family order mirrored public order: public seating symbolised family order."[126]

Over half a century ago, Edmund Morgan concluded his study of *The Puritan Family* with a chapter titled "Puritan Tribalism."[127] His judgment on the Puritans is harsh: "They translated 'Love thy neighbor' into 'Love thy family.'" They did not completely neglect the surrounding sinners, since they punished every breach of the law possible, striving to bring all under the external observance of God's commands. But in the end, the church "was turned into an exclusive society for the saints and their children. Instead of an agency for bringing Christ to fallen man it became the means of perpetuating the gospel among a hereditary religious aristocracy."[128]

The genius of the Puritans, however, is to see that society can be transformed, that civil institutions at the grassroots can be enlisted as agents of change, and that cultural symbols, especially religious symbols and narratives, are necessary and powerful enablers of change. This active, aggressive approach to the transformation of society is strikingly modern and crucial to the revolutionary atmosphere of seventeenth-century England and America.

Conclusions: Christian Views of Family and Children

The praise of family as a form of church carries with it, in each of the theologies studied, both assets and deficits. A brief review of what has been accomplished and lost with this metaphor will be instructive for contemporary attempts to reclaim it. Compared to the Puritans, Chrysostom envisions a much less powerful role for Christian identity in society as a whole. Nonetheless, he shares their conviction that Christian faith brings practical obligations. Key among them are asceticism and care of the poor. Part of Chrysostom's vision of family is gender hierarchy, a cultural assumption that he and other Christian teachers underwrite with the Pauline "household codes" and a reading of Genesis that blames woman for Adam's fall. The option for the poor, however, does modify internal family relations also, in that marital friendship and mutual parental duties of spouses are acclaimed. Chrysostom also praises vowed virginity, a way of life that allows women to function outside of the usual familial constraints.

Luther, like the Puritans, is familiar with a well-established Christendom and hence equally aware of the church's immense potential influence in civil society. The price of such influence may always be the perversion of Christian identity itself, as it makes compact with secular goals. But different concerns lead Luther away from an activist social approach to the family. These concerns are distinctively Protestant. Like Reinhold Niebuhr, Luther is acutely conscious of entrenched sin and is therefore not optimistic about far-reaching social change. In an era of violent unrest, he is afraid of change and backs off from it. He looks at suffering and sin as the cross to be carried and not as the enemy to be conquered. The central human moral problems are pride and the quest for autonomous self-fulfillment, denial of sinfulness and avoidance of self-abnegation. Living in the world requires of Christians sacrifice, above all else, even in their divinely ordained vocations, including marriage and family. Family life too exists under the sign of the cross and demands constant sacrifice and the acceptance of suffering. A similar sensibility about morality and society is present in modern family authors, who find the solution to family problems in more sacrifice from parents rather than in working to change the social conditions that create the problems and make the sacrifices necessary.

Still, Luther's image of the family is revolutionary. It is not an inferior state to virginity but an estate established with God's blessing. Family members should be respected as individuals in their own right and should make a marriage commitment freely. And family relations can be transfigured by Christian love, sacrifice, and service. Luther's hope for concrete effects of "faith active in love" nourishes contemporary authors who trust that loving sacrifice of family members will in fact work changes in family life. But one can question whether this approach neglects the intrinsic rewards of family life that come to loving parents and spouses and are necessary to attract or convert people to new patterns of behavior. It may also be too accepting of realities like gender inequity, oppressive social structures of labor and economics, and conflict between Christian ideals of family life and cultural norms.

The Puritans, in contrast, are confident that Christians can control family relations, and enact broad reforms in family, church, and Christian civil society. For Calvin, likewise, Christianity can reform the commonwealth. In his view, the primary moral function of the Christian family is to educate members, especially children, for renunciation of wealth and compassion toward the poor. But for the Puritans, family life according to Christian norms brings not only personal satisfactions but also worldly prosperity. Puritans are of a temper both more belligerent and more visionary than either Chrysostom or Luther, perhaps especially in the New World, where the social setting is novel and unstable. The Calvin-informed Puritan vision of a dedication to the will of God ranging across the whole of life carries forward radical conversionist motifs from the New Testament. But the limits they place on communal inclusiveness and their vigorous insistence on enforcing hierarchy and social distinction within the community of believers place them at odds with Jesus' illustrations of the character of God's kingdom. They reestablish family loyalty to serve precisely those ends that Jesus sees as most inimical to God's reign and presence and in view of which both he and Paul seem to see the family as a potential threat to Christian faith. Still, their strict conceptions of family order and their respect for wealth and status are modified in practice. And their positive, active vision of Christian faith in church and world gives much to be learned.

In conclusion, we can lift up positive Christian attitudes toward children that resonate through all three theologies. Although perpetuating one's lineage is not a specifically Christian obligation, when Christian couples do have children, they bear a serious responsibility to nurture and educate them well. Joint and mutual care for all of a couple's children is one important equalizing factor in Christian views of gender relations in the family. For Chrysostom and Luther especially, the object of nurture is not glory, security, or any other earthly reward for the parents or even for the children themselves. It is the conformation of children to Christian virtues consistent with salvation. Only in Luther do we find heavy stress on the suffering and self-denial that are required of parents. The duty of steadfastness in providing children with adequate spiritual and moral guidance is pronounced in all three.

Christian education of children does not focus on parental abandonment of other responsibilities and rewards so as to concentrate solely on the child. It does require patient and consistent parental attention to the child's gradual acquisition of traits of character that will allow him or her to express God-given faith through moral action, especially compassionate action toward the neighbor, stranger, or enemy. Through family belonging, a Christian child is inducted into a way of life modeled by parents and members of the extended family. Through family, the child learns how a Christian participates in church and world. The child grows to share in the larger community of religious experience and moral service that the family represents in miniature.

This Christian vision of family life is often in reality distorted by gender and class divisions that prevent the Christian family from being a catalyst for compassion, generosity, and justice. The next chapters will propose the Catholic metaphor of family as domestic church, as reinterpreted ecumenically in light of African American family experience and theology, as a possible vehicle for renewing the social mission of Christian families.

Chapter 4

Domestic Church:
Families and the Common Good

The Domestic Church Metaphor

A gospel identity should convert families to love the neighbor and serve others. Yet historically, the so-called Christian family has often been co-opted by existing social structures, especially those that reproduce economic and gender inequities. Therefore, an important task for the church's mission to Christian families today is to discover or create a family identity that is genuinely countercultural. While examples from the tradition carry liabilities, they also manifest certain strengths. John Chrysostom, for instance, was clear in his demand that Christian families serve the poor; Martin Luther called families to embody Christian love in their internal relationships; the Puritans actively established a Christian presence in the world that was capable of remaking the institutions of civil society and even government. Christian family evangelization today, however, must improve upon these models by refusing to capitulate to any hierarchies of sex, class, and wealth that contradict the essence of Christian social ethics: to embody the reign of God in human society by including the neighbor, stranger, and enemy in a new family of sisters and brothers in Christ.

The recovery by recent Roman Catholic authors of the metaphor of family as domestic church can serve as the catalyst for an ecumenical and critical reappropriation of a family ethic that is socially transformative. A Christian family ethic for contemporary culture will need to be responsive to the relevant cultural realities of gender, economics, class, race, and sexual orientation. In North America today, many families are not only excluded from economic prosperity but also deprived of access to other basic social goods such as education, health care, and adequate housing. Many long-standing inequities are built on gender, race, and class differences. Yet traditional American individualism colludes today with a new moral relativism that resists public judgment on any economic, racist, sexual, or familial behavior of individuals and groups. This climate makes it very difficult to reach social consensus either about what structures of marriage and parenthood best serve the well-being of family members or about the importance of families taking responsibility for one another broadly across society—not only in social groups made up of similar families of similar socioeconomic standing.

Families laboring under disadvantage to become participating members of American society need the support of other families, civil society, and government. Yet these families also have a contribution to make in defining what family is, how families carry Christian identity, and how the church is built up in and through families. Therefore, the ideal of family as domestic church must begin from three important premises: (1) Christian families structure their internal relations according to Christian ideals of spirituality and reciprocity; (2) Christian families serve others in society to build up the common good by transforming society itself; and (3) Christian families struggle, survive, and thrive together, despite economic, racial, and ethnic differences or differences in family structure.

Catholic families from many ethnic groups, like their counterparts in other religious denominations, have often been slow to take up the mandate to seek social justice by overcoming racism and sexism and by redistributing wealth. Recent decades have seen renewed attempts in official Catholic teaching documents and the writings of Catholic theologians to shape families around religious faith, loving relationships, the common good, and a preferential option for the poor.

Of course, this agenda is not uniquely Catholic. It reaches back to common Christian sources, such as the New Testament and patristic authors, and reflects shared concerns of Reformation authors like Luther and Calvin. Unfortunately, like the nineteenth-century Protestant Social Gospel movement, modern Catholic social teaching has tended to adopt a top-down approach to social change. The social responsibilities of governments and the privileged classes are accentuated, while the poor are seen primarily as the recipients of action for justice. Both liberation theology and the civil rights activism that changed American society in the 1960s have challenged this perspective. Formerly "marginal" communities are producing more grassroots leaders, as well as educators, politicians, social scientists, legal theorists, historians, theologians, and creative artists.

The Catholic church, an originally immigrant and largely lower-class church in the United States, has had experience in empowering socially disadvantaged groups through education and advocacy for religious rights and social services. The Hispanic or Latino Catholic presence is especially visible today in the United States. On issues of family, African American Catholics in particular are active. The African American theological voice links the Catholic vision of the domestic church with a broader interfaith discussion that intersects with historical and social-scientific research on families in America.

Recent Catholic Themes

Since the publication of John Paul II's *On the Family*[1] in 1981, the Roman Catholic Church has seen a resurgence of the domestic church metaphor. In recent usage, the family is called a "church" in order to encourage church participation by all families, to foster prayer and religious catechesis in the home,[2] and to promote family dedication to the common good.

The family's social mission is thought to derive from Christian identity. "Christian families, recognizing with faith all human beings as children of the same heavenly Father, will respond generously to the children of other families. . . . With families and through them, the Lord Jesus continues to 'have compassion' on the multitudes."[3] But responsibility to the common good is also part of human nature and natural morality, which, like Christian morality, demand that families rise above egotistic familism. "Thus, far from being closed in on itself, the family is by nature and vocation open to other families and to society and undertakes its social role."[4]

These points will be expanded below, and criticisms will be discussed. For the present, it is sufficient to stress two aspects of Catholic teaching about domestic church. First, it addresses economic inequities and holds Christian families responsible for just distribution of material and social wealth, not limited to almsgiving but demanding structural change. All families have both a right and a duty to enhance and benefit from the common good of the whole society.

Second, and on a truly novel note compared to Christian family teaching of centuries past, the domestic church is a sphere of relative gender equity. As recently as 1930, Pope Leo XIII was still calling for the subordination of women to men in a scheme that placed the family as a civil institution within an equally hierarchical model of society. Now, according to John Paul II, it is important to underline "the equal dignity and responsibility of women with men. This equality is realized in a unique manner in that reciprocal self-giving by each one to the other and by both to the children which is proper to marriage and the family."[5] Unlike contemporary proponents of male headship, John Paul II does not advocate the submission of women to men in the family.[6] (That this defense of gender equality should not be received with a wholly uncritical attitude will be demonstrated below.)

These two aspects owe much to our late modern cultural ethos, prizing individuality and individual freedom. This ethos has encouraged expanded roles for both sexes and greater social consciousness of the unacceptability of great disparities of advantage among classes and races. Hence, a socially transformative approach to family is not unique to the Catholic tradition. It is a general characteristic of modern Christian ethics. Walter Rauschenbusch, writing just as the papal social tradition was emerging around the turn of the century, likewise saw the family's emotional bonds as a school for other-concern.[7] Recent Roman Catholic symbolization of the family as domestic church, however, will provide the focus of this chapter, since it is in this tradition that the metaphor has been most extensively developed and most explicitly linked to social justice concerns.

The next chapter will consider how African American experiences of family expand the vision of domestic church. Catholic social teaching converges with and supports the insight of African American scholars that successful institutions of civil society, including the family, must be linked with larger national and federal institutions in order to represent broad public accountability for the common good. The U.S. Catholic bishops relate the domestic church metaphor to gender, race, and class in the United States in their pastoral letters on economics, on family, and on welfare reform. Their pastoral statement "Always Our Children" encourages families to accept and support their gay and lesbian children, even when they do not fully affirm their identities.[8]

Family and Catholic Social Teaching

In the original Catholic social encyclical, *On the Condition of Labor (Rerum Novarum)*, authored in 1891 by Leo XIII, the subject of family arises in relation to work and the right of a workman to support his dependents. This encyclical is a response to industrialization, the exploitation of the working classes by capital owners, and the rise of atheistic socialism. According to Leo, capitalists may own and accumulate property but must provide workers with decent conditions and pay them a living wage adequate to support a family.

The encyclical co-opts the socialist critique of greed and exploitation, while still maintaining that "private ownership must be held sacred and inviolable."[9] It is a duty of property owners and of the state, if need be, to ensure that workers are adequately paid. Yet the essential acceptability of capitalism remains untouched. Distinctions of class and wealth are assumed by the encyclical and presented as the natural concomitants of the social roles essential to an organically functioning society. Workers are counseled to be industrious, honest, and modest, so that their employers and social superiors will be "won over by a kindly feeling toward" them.[10] Marxist class struggle is definitely out.

Workers are supposed to be male.[11] "Women . . . are not suited to certain trades; for a woman is by nature fitted for home-work, and it is that which is best adapted at once to preserve her modesty, and to promote the good bringing up of children and the well-being of the family."[12] Women remain within the domestic sphere, providing traditional female services for the welfare of the family and of society. These services are not to be remunerated in any direct way; women and children are economically dependent on the male workforce. According to the 1931 encyclical of Pius XI, *Reconstructing the Social Order (Quadragesimo Anno)*, "the wage paid to the workingman should be sufficient for the support of himself and of his family.... It is wrong to abuse the tender years of children or the weakness of women" (71).

Christine Firer Hinze provides a trenchant critique of such assumptions and their impact on Catholic social teaching. She deplores not only the gendered assignment of social roles and the division of domestic from economically productive labor but also the lack of common social accountability for children. In the end, she argues, the notion of a family wage is viable and worth retrieving, but only if domestic work is included in the definition of repaid labor. She commends John Paul II for placing domestic labor in the category of family wage-deserving work and mentioning measures such as "grants to mothers."[13] Unfortunately, as Hinze realizes, it is still presupposed that mothers will be primary parents, responsible for family and domestic labor.

Hinze also draws attention to more fundamental questions about the economic system beneath the public-private and wage-labor framework. "The institutions and ideology of the capitalist, free market economy that have underpinned the notion of a family living wage must be subjected to more thorough critique and reconsideration."[14] For instance, the "logic of capitalism" might corrupt the domestic sphere itself and even undermine the institution of marriage. These larger questions will receive further attention at the end of this chapter, in response to recent proposals for welfare reform.

If we look at family order in earlier encyclicals on marriage, we find much the same scenario as in those on labor economics. Leo XIII, the initiator of the modern social tradition, portrays the family as the basic cell of society. In a passage that could have been written two or three centuries earlier by a Puritan divine, Leo declaims:

> This is a suitable moment for us to exhort especially heads of families to govern their households ... and to be solicitous without failing for the right training of their children. The family may be regarded as the cradle of civil society, and it is in great measure within the circle of the family that the destiny of States is fostered. ... If in their early years [children] find within the walls of their homes the rule of an upright life and the discipline of Christian virtues, the future welfare of society will in great measure be guaranteed.[15]

In an 1880 encyclical titled *On Christian Marriage,* Leo specifically employs the Christ-church analogies of Ephesians 5 to insist on male headship, even while espousing mutual love and companionship. "The husband is the chief of the family and the head of the wife. The woman . . . must be subject to her husband and obey him. . . ."[16] Children, meanwhile, are to "submit to the parents and obey them," although "the power of fathers of families" is limited by the "rightful freedom" of children to choose spouses and marry.[17]

Half a century later, Pius XI likewise proposes an "order of love," in which the "primacy of the husband" grants him authority over wife and children. As for the wife, household order requires "ready subjection" and "willing obedience."[18] She is the "heart" of the family, who acknowledges her husband as its "head." Nonetheless, the gender picture in Catholic teaching is beginning tentatively to change. Pius warns that good family order does not mean the woman should be treated as a minor or deprived of the liberty that "fully belongs" to her "in view of her dignity as a human person."[19] Unfortunately, this does not include the right to be the principal authority even in the home, to reject maternal and domestic roles, or "to conduct and administer her own affairs."[20]

The place of the family in the larger society is also slowly changing in these encyclicals. First of all, class divisions and economic disparities are less taken for granted. Secondly, the family becomes more than a separate cell within the social hierarchy. David Hollenbach has argued that the writings of Pius XI, for instance, imply an organic view of society, in which subsidiary parts cooperate in a solidaristic, not merely hierarchical, way. Institutions that meet essential needs and responsibilities of persons are harmonized and integrated in the well-functioning and just society.[21] Already Pius XI is demanding that large or poor families who are not self-supporting should be provided for jointly by public and private funds, for "it is incumbent on the rich to help the poor." The common good and "the very life of civil society itself" demand that the State take necessary action to relieve poor families and parents of children, whether married or unmarried.[22] While moving toward a vision of solidarity in the common good, however, this tradition tends to underplay the intransigence of human selfishness and sinful structures, and so to trust that moral persuasion can motivate social change without the need for serious conflict.

In the middle of the twentieth century, the popes adopt an increasingly international view of socioeconomic justice and become more critical of global economic trends. They begin to see the situations of families in poor nations as integrally connected with the patterns of consumption and expansion of the wealthier nations. A landmark encyclical is Paul VI's *On the Development of Peoples.* Insisting that no one has an absolute right to own and dispose of property, Paul rejects an economic ethos ruled by competition and urges that aid to developing countries is a duty of human solidarity and justice.[23] "At stake are the survival of so many innocent children and, for so many families overcome by misery, the access to conditions fit for human beings; at stake are the peace of the world and the future of civilization."[24]

John Paul II and Families

The social teaching of John Paul II develops this trajectory. Specifically, he takes an international view of social justice, is critical of global capitalism without repudiating the market, sees families as interdependent agents within civil society, and terms the Christian family a "domestic church" dedicated to the common good and rightfully participating in the benefits social belonging bestows.

In his 1988 encyclical *On Social Concerns,* John Paul II expands on the international outlook of the Second Vatican Council and on the themes of *On the Development of Peoples.* He urges Christians to adopt "the option or love of preference for the poor."[25] A key principle of social relations in this encyclical is solidarity, to which structural sin is identified as the principal obstacle. The materialism and consumerism that often propel market relations undermine the "authentic liberation" of all peoples.[26] The pope targets problems that affect poor families, especially children, such as unemployment, homelessness, and lack of clean water, hygiene, and health care.

In a later encyclical, authored not long after the disintegration of Communist societies in Eastern Europe, the pope gives qualified support to free enterprise as an effective means of maximizing human resources to meet human needs. The injustices of market systems still come in for strong criticism, however, including their tendency to deprive some families of the means to live, while fostering a consumerist attitude toward children and family relationships, not to mention social commitments in general.[27] Human society can be built up properly only if "each person collaborates in the work of others and for their good. Man works in order to provide for the needs of his family, his community, his nation and ultimately all humanity."[28]

John Paul II has addressed family issues repeatedly during his pontificate. The most important statement remains *On the Family* (1981); subsequent pieces include the *Charter on the Rights of the Family* (1983) and his *Letter to Families* (1994) in observance of the United Nations' International Year of the Family. The latter pieces reveal somewhat different orientations. Whether this is more due to shifts in the papal perspective, to forces and questions that at the time had a high ecclesial or social profile, or to the character of the advisors and drafters upon whom the pope relied is difficult to say. In a sense, the perspectives are complementary and may be addressed to different though not mutually exclusive audiences.

The *Charter* defends family social rights as entitlements but seems most concerned about state policies that interfere in family self-determination. *On the Family* seems more concerned about engaging society in general and families in particular in serving the poor by supplying basic needs. The *Letter* spends proportionately more space than either defending the "norm" of the two-parent family and showing why contraception and divorce are incompatible with papal teaching about marital love. Perhaps the *Charter* intends to assert the basic social claims of families living under conditions of widespread deprivation, especially the Third World, where families lack basic material goods and where social policies are geared to limit population. The *Letter,* on the other hand, reproaches the wealthier inhabitants of industrialized cultures for capitulation to individualistic liberal values, perceived to lead to family "breakdown."

Among these, it is *On the Family* that contains the flagship exposition of family as domestic church. It also forwards a defense of the social and familial rights of women. It does not address global economic inequities and their impact on families at any great length. The mission of the domestic church is construed in such a way, however, that the plight of society's less-fortunate members is kept in frequent view. Outlining problems facing families today, the pope mentions consumerism, deteriorating family relations, divorce, abortion, and a "contraceptive mentality." But he also calls to mind the fact that many Third World families "lack both the means necessary for survival, such as food, work, housing and medicine, and the most elementary freedoms."[29]

A keynote of the document is the exhortation, "Family, become what you are."[30] Families are by nature intimate communities of love, basic cells of society,[31] and participate in, contribute to, and benefit from the common good. This means families must be guaranteed the necessary material and social preconditions of participation. It is the social responsibility of those who are able to contribute to the welfare and full participation of others to do so. Christian families make a "'preferential option' for the poor and disadvantaged."[32] Families naturally educate members in empathy and altruism, expanding care for the common good to ever larger circles of society. John Paul II is advancing not just an evangelical ideal but "an authentic family humanism."[33]

The family is defined as domestic church in light of this calling:

> The Christian family is . . . called to experience a new and original communion which confirms and perfects natural and human com-

munion. . . . The Christian family constitutes a specific revelation of ecclesial communion, and for this reason too it can and should be called 'the domestic church.' . . . [The Christian family is] 'a school of deeper humanity.' This happens where there is care and love for the little ones, the sick, the aged; where there is mutual service every day; when there is a sharing of goods, of joys and of sorrows.[34]

Families should "devote themselves to manifold social service activities" that cannot be met adequately by "the public authorities' welfare organization."[35] They also should take the initiative in ensuring that laws and other institutions support families well. While the state should not needlessly usurp the autonomy of families, neither should families be abandoned to hostile social forces or left without effective institutional links to the assets their society can offer.

In the conviction that the good of the family is an indispensable and essential value of the civil community, the public authorities must do everything possible to ensure that families have all those aids—economic, social, educational, political and cultural assistance—that they need in order to face all their responsibilities in a human way.[36]

As noted at the outset of this chapter, *On the Family* makes headway against traditional patriarchal headship by presenting marital love as in principle a relationship of equals. John Paul II nowhere advocates women's submission and in fact concludes not only that women should not be limited to domestic roles alone but that "the equal dignity and responsibility of men and women fully justifies women's access to public functions."[37] There is an important caveat, however. Women's advancement in family and society should in no way erode their "femininity" or reduce the recognition given to "the value of their maternal and family role, by comparison with all other public roles and all other professions," which ought to be "harmoniously combined" with maternal duties.

An irreducible ambivalence in the papal approach to gender owes to John Paul II's firm espousal of a complementarity model of equality. The liabilities of such models have been frequently noted. They tend to devolve in practice to less socially valued roles for women, with a smaller sphere of freedom, self-determination, and social leadership than is allotted to men.[38] For example, the pope urges men to fulfill their responsibilities as fathers in cooperation with mothers, but envisions only the parental role of *men* as revealing divinity, to wit, "the fatherhood of God." On the other hand, discrimination against women and "machismo," or "a wrong superiority of male prerogatives which humiliates women" are ruled out.[39] At the very least, this is a long way from the views of Leo XIII and Pius XI, writing less than a century before.

More recent papal writings exhibit even stronger advocacy for women, especially in view of women's low status internationally. The pope's theory of complementarity, however, also gets reinforced. Positions on women's ecclesial, social, and sexual roles that depend on complementarity and define women's nature as maternal are continually reemphasized: women are not allowed access to contraception, abortion, or divorce under any circumstances; they are not to be ordained priests. Hence, John Paul II's assertion of women's equality in principle is partly but not fully supported by the kinds of institutional practices he envisions as serving the common good at the concrete level (in marriage, family, church, and civil society in general).

Violence and discrimination against women in heavily patriarchal societies, extensive populations of which too frequently suffer under the additional burden of poverty, are rightly higher on the papal agenda than the equal rights of women in developed nations. Celebration of the dignity of the maternal role may be a useful instrument to enhance women's standing in the former situations. Expansion beyond this role, however, is key in the latter ones, and justice for women is a moral mandate in *all* societies. Yet, when addressing women, parents, and families in prosperous societies, the pope's concern about the permanency of marital commitments and responsibility for children can overshadow his commitment to women's social advancement. A deeper and more troublesome issue is whether women's advancement requires more flexibility on some of the magisterial sexual norms (especially the absolute ban on contraception) that go back to a time when women were directly and vehemently asserted to be subordinate to men, destined for domesticity alone, and ideally fulfilled as mothers.

To many North Americans, the papal eulogization of mothers sounds regressive. North American and European Catholics are well aware that the exclusion of women from the ordained priesthood, justified on the same theory of complementarity that is elsewhere used to promote women's well-being, is at odds with the education of girls and the vocational expectations of adult women that most modern societies take for granted. To some Catholics, the pope's countercultural views on women's full equality in the church represent a bulwark of tradition against cultural flux. To many others, his notion that women are by nature maternal; that, even when not literally mothers, their "special genius" consists in nurturing, maternal behavior in all other relationships; and that the "special" feminine vocation to love provides a rationale for exclusion from the church's most respected leadership roles, are simply incredible. Beyond that, these views undermine the ostensible sincerity of papal statements about women's equality in family and society.[40]

Justice for women must include just relations in family *and* church. A complementarity model of justice for women, advanced under the aegis of "domestic church," can endanger women's hard-won growing equality in the family by suggesting that family relations ought to emulate the unequal status of women within church structures. Margaret Farley has aptly argued that most families in the world today, including most Western families, are still essentially patriarchal in structure and that this structure needs to be changed. She questions whether the Catholic church can serve as a prophetic voice in this regard unless and until it "can model in its structures the coequal discipleship which was part of the original vision of Christianity."[41]

These criticisms find their target. They may explain why the domestic church metaphor has not met wide acclaim among laity in the North American church. Yet the pope's writings on women, their parental and familial roles, and the compatibility of such roles with public professional roles are best seen in larger perspective. Putting the pope's writings on women and family in a broader view will not silence fair observations of a lurking gender inequity under the defenses of women's dignity. But it can at least bring John Paul II's genuine accomplishments and the legitimate priority he tends to give to global social concerns into focus. The two factors important to an adequate perspective are the primacy of John Paul II's concern for the most oppressed women among the cultures of the world and the advance represented by the remarks of this pope about gender and family in relation to recent predecessors. A good example of his perspective, its genuine novelty, and its notable limits is his *Letter to Women,* written in preparation for the 1995 United Nations World Conference on Women in Beijing,

This letter opens by thanking women in different walks of life, most of them defined in reproductive and familial terms—mothers, wives, daughters, sisters, and "consecrated women" (virgins). On a new note, however, the pope also thanks "women who work"—not because of unfortunate economic necessities that draw them regrettably away from home but because women in the "social, economic, cultural, artistic and political" areas "make an indispensable contribution to the growth of a culture."[42] The pope laments the fact that women still suffer discrimination, that "they have often been relegated to the margins of society and even reduced to servitude," and adds that if "objective blame" belongs to the church in contributing to these situations, "for this I am truly sorry."[43] Referring to "the great process of women's liberation,"[44] he upholds "real equality in every area," including "equality of spouses with regard to family rights."[45] He denounces abuses such as sexual violence against women.[46]

Again, the pope admires the "genius of women"; women's vocation is to give of themselves, since "more than men," women "see persons with their hearts."[47] There are differences "specific to being male and female." Christ has chosen men to be "icons" of himself, through the ministerial priesthood. Women should imitate Mary the mother of Jesus. Men and women have different roles, considered of equal value, in the economy of salvation.[48]

In the *Letter to Families* composed just before the *Letter to Women,* the family is defined as the fundamental community in which persons learn how to be truly human and how to build up in the world a "civilization of love." Again, the pope insists that the civilization is neither utopian nor exclusively Christian. It is part of the human ideal of family life; family love can educate for and inspire social change. But the Christian family, as domestic church, is specially graced to nourish communities in which persons are recognized and valued in themselves.[49]

Given the pope's view of women's unique role in recognizing the individuality of persons and in making a loving response to all, the special vocation of the family would then seem to rest especially with women. Women, it would seem, are more closely associated by nature than men with the upbuilding of a "civilization of love." Strikingly, in the *Letter to Families,* the fatherhood of men is interpreted precisely in relation to and by virtue of the maternal role of women. Both the civilization of love and the successful raising of children will depend on the father's "willingness . . . to become willingly involved as a husband and father *in the motherhood of his wife.*"[50] The family structure primarily indicated by the wording of the *Letter* is the nuclear family, since it presents the family as constituted by and beginning in marriage and especially in the sexual relations of the couple, in which love is expressed and a child conceived. A substantial portion of the document is devoted to abortion as a violation of the welcome to life that families should provide.[51] The principle of subsidiarity is applied to the family to support needed public assistance to parents, but even more to limit outside interference in the right of parents to bear, raise, and educate children according to church teaching and in observance of the norms the pope believes to express genuine human well-being.[52] All of this amounts to a vision of women in the home, a private, autonomous sphere of love, in which the mother is constantly prepared for the arrival of another birth, and where she above all others exemplifies empathy and devotion.

The Holy See's 1983 *Charter on the Rights of the Family* presents a somewhat more balanced picture: states, nations, and societies are called to responsibility to offer supportive institutions so that families may flourish.[53] It is asserted without doubt that the family as an institution is based on marriage and exists, with "inalienable" rights, prior to any state. But society, particularly "the State and International Organizations, must protect the family through measures of a political, economic, social and juridical character." Poverty and the well-being of children—before or after birth, in or outside of marriage, with parents or as orphans—are among the concerns of the *Charter*. The preponderance of articles, however, still addresses the rights of families over against social interference in religious, marital, reproductive, and child-raising decisions. Despite significant and admirable advances, the official Roman Catholic approach to family matters is still overly concerned with reproductive issues, not sufficiently attuned to gender and race as intersecting causes of economic inequities that affect families, and too quick to assume that an audience of ecclesial and political rank-holders will endorse and effect wide-ranging changes.

The Practicality of the Message and a Grassroots Response

While Catholic teaching in the modern period is increasingly concerned with equality and participation for society's excluded members, including women, it still usually appeals to those who already occupy positions of social power to remedy the situation. This approach is appropriate insofar as the power-holders who are best positioned institutionally to bring about change are likely to be proportionately loathe to relinquish privilege. Conversion is in order. This approach is not adequate in itself, however, for three reasons. First, conversion is not always effective, which requires that pressure must be brought to bear from other quarters. If energy for change is to come "from below," then church leaders should work to empower and cooperate with underrepresented groups and must be willing to loosen their own claim to power to aid that process. Second, pressure for change from below will need to be channeled not only through stronger social and religious expectations about just and unjust behavior but also through the more coercive means of legislation and court decisions. Third, the ethos and institutional patterns of a just society backed by a genuinely Christian social ethic cannot be defined and determined only from the perspective of the traditional power-holders, however sincerely they may aim to become more just. There must be a more visible and adamant presence of women and of underrepresented ethnic and racial groups. Christian social ethics in general, and Catholic social ethics and the image of the domestic church in particular, must be better informed by those who until now have been largely outsiders to the formation of the domestic church vision.

Feminist criticisms of the notion that the Christian family is a domestic church come from the fact that women perceive practical liabilities in this teaching, because it is contextualized by glorification of motherhood and the assumption that men have primary roles in the public sphere. This perspective suggests that women are somehow more responsible than men for children and for the quality of familial love and that, therefore, they are more closely tied to the family's social mission and less suited for social roles in public and professional life. The converse side of the idealization of women's nurturing virtues is the delineation of a female sphere devoted primarily to domestic duties. From within this sphere, women are able to perceive that the traditional family ideal needs revision.

Another line of response to the ideal of domestic church comes from those whose socioeconomic circumstances are not easily reconciled with the middle-class model of the nuclear family. Some of these same critics may have found other patterns of family life to be viable, rewarding, and perhaps even superior contexts for engendering Christian identity.

For example, Ernie Cortes, an experienced Hispanic community organizer, inquires whether the social character of the Christian family's mission has been envisioned in radical enough or practical enough terms by today's teaching church. Perhaps this teaching has been too influenced by and focused on the nuclear family of the middle classes in Western, industrialized societies. Cortes proposes that Catholic social teaching about the family move from the "entitlements" and "family autonomy" posture of the *Charter* to a highly activist engagement in creating new mediating institutions in which families can participate and that, in turn, support families.

Cortes is a member of the national staff of the Industrial Areas Foundation (IAF), a multi-religious and nonpartisan coalition of over six hundred congregations, primarily in Texas. The organizations of the IAF educate families in poor and minority communities to collaborate in order to interact more effectively with the "power centers of the community" toward the improvement of daily living conditions for thousands.[54] Cortes also was instrumental in organizing the San Antonio Communities Organized for Public Service (COPS), one of the most powerful organizations in the Southwest and one of the earliest associated with the IAF. COPS draws its members from twenty-six low-income Catholic parishes. Under IAF-trained leadership, COPS "won over 750 million dollars in new streets, drainage, parks, libraries, and other improvements, reversing a long history of disinvestment in the inner city."[55] Cortes was named a MacArthur Fellow in 1984.

Like some of the other participants in the civil-society debates, Cortes thinks mediating institutions in the United States are in decline, at least among the urban poor. But he considers a vital yet underrated part of Catholic social thought to be the role the church in the United States played in providing support networks to an immigrant population striving to integrate with the larger society while preserving its own ethnic, cultural, and religious identity. Catholic parishes and schools and the labor movement provide instances of civil society in which Catholic social teaching is implemented at the concrete level. They enable marginal "outsiders" to influence collective efforts to produce and distribute social goods. In so doing, the church transmits its cultural and religious values in both public and private spheres and enhances links between the two.

In a recent work on Catholic charitable organizations between the Civil War and World War II,[56] Dorothy Brown and Elizabeth McKeown argue that the extensive network of church-sponsored services for Catholic immigrants became during that period the most visible face of the church's public presence. The church's role as advocate for the poor and partner in government programs positioned Catholics to shape social legislation for families and children.

> Religious congregations and lay volunteers developed a collection of local institutions that eventually included schools, hospitals, foundling homes, orphanages, settlement houses, industrial schools, remedial institutions, and shelters for women. Catholic charities workers also initiated noninstitutional service programs that included housing and employment registries, probation and recreation services for youth, outdoor relief, family casework, and home nursing services.[57]

In the early days of Catholic charitable work, Catholics "took care of their own," preparing and encouraging recent arrivals to the United States to become productive citizens, thereby also upholding the reputation of Catholic culture. Care for the poor was seen as part of the charitable mission of Catholics, especially of religious congregations. Prior to the Second World War, the aim of charitable work was not to give a voice to the poor as such but to equip them for emergence into the middle class, where, of course, they would soon come to enjoy economic and political power. As Catholic immigrants underwent class transition, the poor served by Catholic charities were increasingly no longer Catholic. Federal legislation in the 1960s encouraged state welfare agencies to purchase services from private organizations. This meant both that Catholic charitable services have become directed toward a much more pluralistic clientele and that its local and religiously based entities cooperate closely and regularly with national infrastructures of government and economics.[58]

Today all families, including poor families, need institutions through which they can become political and economic agents and not merely recipients of services. For example, families can and should take an active role to pursue their right to a living wage, decent housing, and good education for their children. The church can and should help supply practical access to families and local communities seeking greater social participation and should work in cooperation with federal, state, and local non-Catholic organizations.

Christian families today are in fact engaged ecumenically in every area of civic life. For Cortes, the Christian family is the activist family, and the role of the church is not only to protect but to empower families. Obviously, this implies some corollary transformations of the structures and practices of the church.[59] Brown and McKeown confirm this view with their own observation that Catholic charitable organizations have become "top-down" imitations of the institutional church and that the sense of distance between the bureaucracy and the churchgoer may account in part for the relatively low proportion of individual charitable contributions by Catholics.[60] Religious institutions, more properly political institutions, and families need to function reciprocally, with the educational and transformative dynamic moving in both horizontal and vertical directions.

In the last two decades, collaboration of Catholic agencies with other social institutions has become an increasingly widespread and pluriform reality. Several documents from the National Conference of Catholic Bishops have encouraged this engagement. These include *A Family Perspective in Church and Society* (1988); *Putting Children and Families First: A Challenge for Our Church, Nation, and World* (1992); *Follow the Way of Love* (1994); "Moral Principles and Policy Priorities for Welfare Reform" (1995); and "USCC Statement on Political Responsibility" (1995).[61] In 1994 the University of Dayton held a national symposium to address shared responsibility for family life, documenting the need and reality of partnerships among families and other civic institutions.[62] In the proceedings of the symposium, Robert Bellah asserts that marriages and families can be sustained only in the context of multiple communities, not in isolation. Citing the 1994 episcopal message to families he affirms that the opportunity for political participation will strengthen family life. According to Bellah, government should cooperate with citizens through effective public-private partnerships, controlled by the principle of subsidiarity and focused primarily on local community.[63] Nevertheless, as James Healy notes, a genuine "Catholic family perspective" must challenge those representing families in the legislatures and courts to ensure that state and federal policies and funding include all families equitably, even families considered to be "outside the norm" in form or function.[64]

An effective future role for the Catholic church, Catholic organizations, and Catholic families, combating poverty and supporting family life will be contingent on grassroots interest and commitment of Catholics as well as the willingness and ability of Catholic agencies to foster broader public accountability for the poor. Notably, Catholic leadership at the popular level is also speaking on its own behalf. Increasing numbers of articulate spokespersons are prominent in public life and academia.[65]

Families, Welfare, and the Bishops' Response

The U.S. welfare reform debate is about poverty and about families—two realities that often meet in households headed by young single mothers. Controversy over the future of welfare reveals that family is interdependent with other institutions and that families cannot be reformed without a deep realignment of surrounding institutions, practices, and values. The welfare reform debate is, then, at its deepest level about the accumulation or redistribution of economic resources and of the social capital that follows money (like good schools and pro-social neighborhood associations). Where economic and social resources are abundant, "illegitimacy" declines, and welfare dependency all but disappears. These correlations should be obvious. Yet some participants in the welfare debate still seem persuaded that the answer both to single parenthood and to economic independence can be found in the moral conversion of the poor, sparing the better-off any drastic changes in the economic and employment structures to which they presently entrust their own needs.

Although the term *welfare* can refer to any state or federal means-tested program to help the poor, such as Medicaid, Food Stamps, and public housing, most of the recent debate has focused on the long-term dependency of female-headed families on AFDC (Aid to Families with Dependent Children). Many analysts on both sides of the political fence agree that childbearing by young, unmarried women is a key component of the problem of poverty. To recall that the majority of welfare mothers are white, that a disproportionate number are African American, and that many ethnic and racial groups are represented among families on welfare can serve as a reminder that the well-being of these families, and especially their children, is everybody's problem.

Although AFDC has cost the federal government some $5 trillion over the past forty years, that amount makes up only about 1 percent of the federal budget. Nonetheless, public opinion in the United States holds that decreasing welfare benefits is an important component of a balanced national budget and that welfare provides disincentives to positive social behaviors like work, economic self-sufficiency, marriage, and joint parental responsibility for children.[66] Some social conservatives like former Speaker of the House Newt Gingrich and social scientist Charles Murray[67] see the poor as responding to economic incentives not to work. Their solution is to take away incentives by cutting off welfare benefits. This kind of argument appeals to the working poor and struggling middle class who seek a scapegoat for their own economic woes and want to better their situation without being asked to make further financial sacrifices for others.

Despite a middle-class consensus that welfare costs too much money and traps the poor in dependency, Americans have failed to generate political support for successful welfare reform, defined as the movement of welfare recipients into the adequately paid labor force. One reason is that such reform costs more money than welfare benefits themselves, albeit modest amounts relative to other social programs. Providing realistic employment opportunities for all those who can and want to work will require more jobs, as well as education and job training, child care, and health insurance. As Gary Bryner points out in his moral and political analysis of the welfare debate, a full-employment policy may demand that some middle-class entitlements be shifted to low-income recipients. But this unpopular prospect is in conflict with the "welfare cheat" myth motivating the so-called reform agenda in the first place. Contrary to popular demand, true welfare reform will require commitment to a whole host of "collective tasks such as improving public safety, education, housing, transportation, and urban infrastructure," which are all "part of the solution to reducing poverty and creating a more sustainable society."[68]

These tasks were not part of the welfare reform policies enacted in the United States in the late 1990s. In 1996 Congress passed and President Clinton signed the historic Personal Responsibility and Work Opportunity Reconciliation Act. Gary Bryner terms this legislation "welfare devolution" rather than welfare reform. Senator Daniel Patrick Moynihan predicts that it will "substantially increase poverty and destitution," cause "2.6 million persons to fall below the poverty line," pose work requirements that cannot and will not be met, and be "the first step in dismantling the social contract that has been in place in the United States since at least the 1930s."[69]

The new welfare law replaces AFDC with the program Temporary Assistance to Needy Families (TANF). The new program in effect ends welfare as a federal entitlement and converts benefits into block grants from the federal government to states, which are then free to devise and experiment with their own welfare programs. The 1996 legislation mandates cutting $55 billion in federal welfare spending over the next six years and requires that remaining funds ($16.4 billion to fiscal year 2003) be used by the states within certain constraints. States must spend on welfare at least 80 percent of what they spent in 1994. Recipients may receive assistance for only two consecutive years, with a lifetime maximum of five years. States may not provide cash benefits to children born to women on welfare, to noncitizens, or to unmarried teenage mothers not living with their parents. States must ensure that a certain percentage of recipients participate in work for a specified number of hours per week. If recipients are not moved off the welfare rolls, the states will be subject to cutbacks on federal money.

In 1997, Congress modified the 1996 law, increasing grants to states to extend benefits for legal immigrants who were living in the United States before the bill was passed, for disabled children, and for able-bodied, childless adults who had lost Food Stamps in the 1996 bill. Whether this welfare reform legislation represents an effective public response to urban poverty is highly questionable. Gary Bryner is not alone in regarding urban poverty and its attendant ills as "America's most pressing social problem" and as having been left virtually unaddressed by the legislation of the 1990s.[70]

Recent data suggests that while welfare reform may be moving people off the welfare rolls, it may not be moving them into decent jobs or out of poverty.[71] End-of-welfare rhetoric often stresses ending "dependency," rather than ending poverty. Not all those who cease to depend on welfare find jobs or comparable means of support. Many of those who do become employed are so poorly paid that they are on the whole worse off than when receiving welfare benefits. Welfare offices often do not inform potential recipients that they can receive Food Stamps and Medicaid immediately. Most states also put the emphasis on getting people off public assistance and into jobs before they receive adequate education and without adequate support services, like transportation and child care. By far the majority of recipients still lack medical benefits. Thus newly employed former welfare recipients may have poor prospects for job longevity and promotion.

Strangely enough, states now have more money to spend per welfare case than they did under the old law. This is due to the fact that levels of federal financing to the states have, by law, remained fixed since 1994, while the welfare rolls have dropped. Some states, like Wisconsin, Illinois, and New York, have turned some of this money into job training, transportation, and child care benefits or wage supplements to low-wage workers. In Chicago, one of the most intensive and innovative programs for introducing former welfare recipients into the workforce interfaces with local employment needs and offers extensive support services, including a mentoring program for those with poor work records. As a result of the Greater West Town Development Project, dozens of people have been

trained for and hired by Lyon and Healy Harps, the country's largest man-
ufacturer of the instrument. Employees receive benefits and health insurance, have opportunity for advancement within the company, and have
performed well to date.

But other states, like Idaho, Wyoming, Mississippi, Florida, and Texas,
have offered little or no new services to the poor.[72] According to Peter
Edelman, a law professor at Georgetown University who resigned as Assistant Secretary for Planning and Evaluation at the Department of Health
and Human Services to protest the 1996 welfare law, "States are sitting on
large surpluses of unspent federal welfare money while welfare-to-work
needs—child care, transportation, literacy, mental health services and
drug and alcohol treatment—continue to go unmet." The number of
"extreme poor" living at less than half the poverty line has increased, and
one child in five in the United States is poor. The real issue is not welfare
reform but poverty, and poverty is still keeping many families in misery,
despite new welfare and employment statistics.[73] The fact that states are
hoarding federal money while seeing residents on assistance move from
dependency to poverty shows that enabling greater and more positive
social participation by poor people was not the genuine aim of changes in
the welfare law. Rather, it was simply to rid taxpayers of the economic burden that welfare was perceived to entail, as if the common good did not
require mutual responsibility for families and children.

A dominant approach to welfare in the rhetoric surrounding and promoting the legislation is to see both dependency and self-sufficiency as
contingent primarily on individual sexual and reproductive behavior and
on the will to work. But it is too narrow to ponder the profound moral
issues at stake only in light of personal and communal disenchantment
with the "traditional" nuclear family. Disregard for or distrust of the institution of family as centered on the married couple owes partly to the general individualism and relativism promoted by consumerist culture. But
this is not a sufficient explanation of the "crisis" of marriage and family
today, especially among the socially disadvantaged. Humans are, after all,
like other primates, a community-forming species. Despite an ethos of
individualism, humans rarely in fact live in isolation. Therefore, before
calling for more and stronger community, we must recognize that humans
typically *do* live in communities; the question is what kind of communities we create and who is accepted within them. Theorists of the African
American family in America have shown how at least some families are
strong along consanguineous lines even as the importance of the conjugal
bond diminishes; this is not only true for African American families. And,
to look at the broader picture, one must also ask about the other, perhaps

newly configured communities and institutions against which families define themselves. The dismantling of welfare is symptomatic not of a blunt disappearance of communities and institutions but of a shifting and narrowing of what were once public allegiances and communal identities, so that the least well-off are no longer considered by the privileged to be deserving and participating members of the polity. Worst, it is a refusal of communal responsibility for the welfare of children, a refusal to see fathers as equally responsible for the plight of "welfare mothers" and their children, and a stigmatization of women as sexually feckless and idle, undeserving of public support.

Welfare as a national entitlement for poor families was an important symbolic commitment to "a national ethic of fairness, justice, and common concern," and of "our commitment to each other." Gary Bryner warns:

> We may be sacrificing a great deal in order to gain the advantages of devolution, and in an era when many decry the collapse of collective values and ideals, we take a risk when we reject one example of a collective commitment.[74]

Although Bryner, professor of political science and director of the public policy program at Brigham Young University, writes as a secular author, his book's concluding sentence alludes to American religions' "warnings about judging the poor, against claiming for ourselves that which belongs to God, and about failing to share the resources we have been given with those who lack them."[75] His diagnoses and fears share much in common with Catholic social teaching, especially as it has been brought to bear on the welfare debate by the U.S. Catholic bishops.

Catholicism, Economics, and Families

In a thorough book on the Catholic church's contribution to public discourse about welfare reform, Thomas Massaro, S.J., distills from the bishops' position five guidelines: focus on the *struggle against poverty* as such, not merely welfare dependency; acknowledge some insuperable or at least appropriate *barriers to employment,* such as the crucial role of mothers in caring for small children, and accommodate these realities; respect some absolute *moral prohibitions* for policy, such as the abandonment by federal government of a safety net for vulnerable children and their families; recognize *"carrots and sticks"* in an atmosphere of human dignity and mutual accountability; and *avoid the demonization* or marginalization of recipients of public assistance, which means including them in policy formulation and empowering them for full social participation.[76]

The primary document in which these principles are expressed is *Moral Principles and Policy Priorities on Welfare Reform.*[77] Issued in 1995 and aimed in great part against proposals that children be denied benefits if their mothers are on welfare at the time of their birth, this document was widely noted but little heeded in 1996. Stating that the bishops believe "our society will be measured by how 'the least of these' are faring," the document asserts that "real welfare reform . . . will require new investments in a family tax credit, education, training, Women, Infants, and Children program, work and child support. . . . Our everyday experience in helping families leave welfare suggests that hope, opportunity and investment are essential to this transition."[78] Although the bishops believe that "subsidiarity and solidarity" require responsive "community institutions," they also demand creative public programs and public-private partnerships.[79]

This perspective draws strongly on the vision of the 1986 pastoral letter on the U.S. economy, *Economic Justice for All*.[80] This pastoral letter affirms economic participation as a human right; advances a preferential option for the poor and vulnerable that requires structural change; applies subsidiarity both ways to local ventures and to government, to public and to private efforts; addresses the impact of the economy on families; considers gender, ethnicity, and race in relation to economic opportunity; and begins to put the consequences of an adjusted U.S. market economy in global perspective.

Of special note for present purposes is the bishops' acknowledgement that although two-thirds of the poor are white (no. 193), the burdens of poverty and unemployment fall disproportionately on African Americans, Hispanics, Native Americans, young people, women who are the sole support of their families ("the feminization of poverty" [no. 178, n. 33]), and children, "the largest single group among the poor." "That so many people are poor in a nation as rich as ours is a moral and social scandal that we cannot ignore" (no. 16). The impact of economic and cultural deprivation on families is a serious national threat and challenges all to build "a more just society" (no. 19).

The bishops see the family as "the basic building block" of society and call for renewed sexual responsibility and fidelity in marriage, as well as for economic arrangements that support rather than weaken families. They note that although the results of family and marital disintegration may be more visible among the poor, they do not affect only that one segment of society nor are more prevalent there. "In fact, one could argue that many of these breakdowns come from false values found among the more affluent—values which ultimately pervade the whole of society" (no. 344). Thus, economic reforms and social welfare programs must avoid stigmatization of and a punitive attitude toward the poor (no. 194).

The reforms and remedies proposed by the bishops are aimed at prefer-ential inclusion of the disadvantaged in a market economy modified to end discrimination and to promote equal opportunity. "The first line of attack against poverty must be to build and sustain a healthy economy that provides employment opportunities at just wages for all adults who are able to work" (no. 196). Those who are unable to work should receive "adequate levels of support" (no. 212). Women with small children should not be forced to work outside the home, but "parents" who do take on out-side employment should have access to good-quality day care (nos. 207, 208).

Although the bishops are very concerned about structural adjustment of the U.S. economy to ensure more equitable access, they only tentatively raise questions about the ethics of a market system as such. Such questions are implied as soon as the bishops recognize that even a "healthy" U.S. economy must be measured by a standard of international justice that takes into account its impact on developing countries, countries who lack market access, countries whose labor is exploited to produce U.S. imports, countries who are heavily in debt to the industrialized nations, and coun-tries whose economies are manipulated by the Bretton Woods institutions (the World Bank and International Monetary Fund) in whose construc-tion they had no voice. The bishops realize that the preferential option for the poor applies internationally, that families worldwide suffer from poverty, and that "the Christian ethic is incompatible with an exclusive focus on maximization of profit" (nos. 274, 280). The solution envi-sioned, however, seems to be economic growth based on market relations, in the future shared more equitably through enhanced participation by marginal nations and groups (no. 292).

To some critics, this solution is not radical enough, either nationally or internationally. The premise that the market economy is a moral and effective vehicle for social justice is in need of more critical scrutiny. In a clever essay in *The Atlantic Monthly,* Harvey Cox compares American trust in the market to a new religion, complete with myths of origin, legends of the fall, doctrines of sin and redemption, sacraments, a calendar of saints, an eschatology (a teaching about "the end of history"), and even "a post-modern deity—believed in despite the evidence."[81] Although Cox finds the disagreements in worldview between the traditional world religions and the "new dispensation" to be basic, he doubts the old religions will rise to the occasion and challenge its doctrines. "Most of them seem content to become its acolytes or to be absorbed into its pantheon, much as the old Nordic deities, after putting up a game fight, eventually settled for a diminished but secure status as Christian saints."[82]

Less witty but more blunt, John Cobb proposes that "the new dominant force in global history is 'economism.'" Cobb judges economism to be "the global religion of our time," whose god, namely, wealth, Christians should name as idolatrous.[83] Joerg Rieger introduces the book in which Cobb's essay appears by advising that

> living in relationship with those who have not benefited from the vic-
> tory of capitalism can teach us much about the radical distinction of
> God and Mammon. . . . A look at the underside of Mammon's shiny
> surface is inevitable if we want to understand the false god.[84]

The gap between rich and poor is widening even in the United States, in which the wealthiest 1 percent increased their share of assets from 20 percent to 36 percent between 1975 and 1990.[85] For both rich and poor, the market is displacing other centers of value and other ways of structuring personal and social relations.

Mary Hobgood, a Catholic social ethicist, takes the radical, neo-Marxist, and utopian view that the only path to economic justice is to take control of capital away from private owners, who exercise immense influence on government. Her goal is to make the economy a democratic institution and to initiate a democratic process of decision-making about economic priorities, along with a thorough restructuring of work.[86]

According to Hobgood's systemic analysis, the economy of work and poverty in the United States is part of the global expansion of capitalism, in which investors are "roaming the planet for the best business deals," in the process destroying "massive amounts of above-poverty wage work" to maintain competition for low-paid work, maximize further profits for owners, and increase the gap between rich and poor.[87] Welfare reform and "workfare" not only flood the low-end labor market, according to Hobgood, but also stigmatize women who deviate from a "family values" ethos for which there is no longer economic incentive, and ensure that poor women will "endure work that denies conditions of human dignity."[88] Targeting the "immorality" of unmarried mothers permits "the basic dynamics of an economic system that is destroying the material basis for family life to remain invisible and unchallenged."[89] Meanwhile, government and politicians, whose campaigns are subsidized by corporations, provide corporate subsidies by decreasing taxes on business. The only way out credited by Hobgood is the creation of local, national, and international networks and coalitions to "challenge the status quo of white supremacist, male-dominant, global corporate feudalism."[90]

Hobgood rightly calls on the bishops to make a global, systematic analysis of the economic realities they decry and is also rightly cynical about economic and family "reforms" that ultimately serve the market elites. Whether it is possible or even desirable to abolish capitalism is questionable, however, in light of the fact that self-interest is not limited to market economies but is found fairly universally in human nature. All human relationships, economic and otherwise, can be and are perverted when self-interest is unrestrained. This does not mean that self-interest either can or should be entirely eliminated. The popular "democratic" processes for which Hobgood calls are certainly ideal, but no theorist, including Marx and Hobgood, has yet devised concrete political and economic structures that are immune to corruption by concentrations of power in the hands of individuals and groups for whom self-interest overrides considerations of solidarity and equality.

Ultimately, the moral issue is the organization of the market, where "growth" becomes an absolute imperative without a deeper analysis of whom growth benefits. The assumption that global economic growth will work to the general benefit is erroneous, as demonstrated by the effects of the "structural adjustment programs" that international monetary institutions have demanded in debtor nations. Economic growth eliminates poverty only when it is accompanied by policies that direct economic benefits toward the least well-off. Yet such policies are dismantled for the sake of maximizing growth, and more wealth accumulates in the hands already wealthy.[91]

Thomas Massaro cautions the bishops that their aim of full employment may not have taken adequate account of the imminent economic realities of a post-industrial age. Although Massaro does not discredit the market as thoroughly as Hobgood, some of his concerns about its current functioning are similar. Citing the United Nations' *Human Development Report 1993*, he suggests that the introduction of labor-saving technology, like the expansion of corporate production into a global labor market, is an attempt to keep labor costs as low as possible so as to increase and protect profits for "elite capitalists and managers."[92] Despite economic growth, the prospects for poor workers worldwide are declining, and yet in a market economy, the only route to material well-being and social participation is through waged labor.

Massaro is forced to conclude that a work ethic based on market logic "is perfectly compatible with a caste system which locks a large percentage of the population out of any reasonable hopes for a decent life."[93] While he does not advise the wholesale dismantling of markets, he does propose a "new logic of distribution" based on the renewal of social concern for the plight of the least well-off, a concern that can be advanced in religious idioms but is not limited to them. Distributive justice derives from the fact that all human beings have a natural and God-given right to share in the

material resources of the earth. If waged labor in a post-industrial era cannot provide access to these resources for all, then distributive justice
requires alternative means of allocating reasonable shares to individuals
and families. Even if full employment is not possible in this era, public
authorities must be accountable for basic human needs.

This line of argument is supported by Catholic social ethicist Daniel
Finn's view that the play of market forces must be contained and limited.
Finn does not accept that self-interest (as embodied in markets) must be
abolished for a moral economic system to exist.[94] Seeking one's own welfare and that of one's family or close associates is natural to human beings
and part of what constitutes human fulfillment. The problem lies in disproportionate self-interest, pursued without consideration of consequences for others and outside of the moral and structural limits necessary
to prevent abuse. "Fences" can and should be constructed around markets
to limit the inequities exacerbated by the concentrations of economic control in a post-industrial era or to counteract the exploitative behavior
Hobgood faults in the corporate profit-making imperative. Christians can
give "conditional moral endorsement" to self-interested market interactions, so long as they are structured within boundaries that limit their
scope and effects, and protect certain goods or spheres of life from the rule
of market exchange.[95]

Both Massaro's critical assessment of the bishops' assumption that
employment for all is an accessible goal in a post-industrial era and Finn's
requirement that market behavior be fenced in could fruitfully incorporate Hobgood's stronger view that labor itself needs to be restructured. In
an age of globalization, the expectation that the market is in general a sat-
isfactory way of distributing goods is more and more problematic.
Although welfare is designed to be a compensatory mechanism for redistributing goods in market economies, welfare too becomes ideologically
and practically distorted. Instead of compensating or equipping the poor,
welfare can serve the self-interest of employers who want a guaranteed
low-wage workforce or protect the "family values" of the more advantaged
middle class. Welfare reform also must build fences around self-interest.

Despite their criticisms of episcopal teaching on welfare reform, Massaro and Finn, and to a notable extent even Hobgood, share the hope typical of Roman Catholic social ethics that social injustice can be overcome
by persistent, collaborative reform of social structures. Their proposals are
more worldly wise versions of John XXIII's 1968 call to rebuild international social relations toward the universal common good in an atmosphere of mutual trust and cooperation (*Peace on Earth*, nos. 113, 142).
Niebuhrian critics of this tradition might well express skepticism that self-
interest can be overcome sufficiently to permit the reconstitution of civil

society and the global economy around principles of compassion, solidarity, and equal respect, especially if that means serious redistribution of material goods and control over social capital.

A key criterion of *bona fide* welfare reform is whether it incorporates the political, institutional, and financial support necessary to empower recipients to become full participants in society and the common good. As usually stated, this criterion is meaningful, long-term work opportunity commensurate with the worker's ability and skills and backed up by adequate preparation and benefits. Work so defined is more than mere market exchange, for it requires and symbolizes social solidarity and accountable investment in the futures of individuals and families. In the words of the Catholic bishops, "the measure of welfare reform is whether it will enhance the lives and dignity of poor children and their families."[96] Such enhancement virtually requires that education, training, and work opportunities be integrated with civil institutions and initiatives at the local, community level (albeit reliant on government funding). But it also demands national accountability in the form of laws and policies regarding fair employment and housing practices, good education and health care for all children, and a tax system oriented to the benefit of those who have command of the least, not most, economic resources.

In a provisional analysis at century's end, Mary Jo Bane offered that the 1996 reforms had indeed changed the culture of welfare in the United States in some unexpected ways.[97] Welfare workers concentrated much more than previously on the short-term nature of welfare and on what could make recipients more self-sufficient. Moreover, the number of single mothers with children who were employed had risen eight percentage points between 1994 and 1998, up to a level of 80 percent working. This increase in labor force participation, however, accounted for only about half of those single mothers who left welfare, indicating that some had replaced welfare with reliance on family "or other resources." Decreased reliance on Medicaid and Food Stamps was even more significant, leading Bane to conclude that "many families are not receiving the health and food stamps to which they remain entitled," either because they are discouraged or put off by the "hassles" of the changed system, perceiving a greater stigma attached to reliance upon it.[98]

According to Bane, poverty rates among families headed by a single mother were down 5 percent from 1994, partly because of a good national economy. But poverty rates (annual household income below about $13,000 for a family of three) in such families "remain at a shockingly high 39 percent," based on 1998 figures. Many had only moved from welfare to low-paying jobs without benefits or advancement opportunities. "By and large, the welfare poor have become the working poor."[99] Bane thinks this

shift may have contributed to a changing climate surrounding welfare politics, since most Americans find it easier to sympathize with workers than
welfare recipients. Although rage may in many cases have been merely
replaced by indifference, Bane hopes that a more receptive hearing will be
found by policies to provide child care, health insurance, and income supplements and to invest in the most disadvantaged places and groups of
people. Poverty, not welfare, is the real moral issue, and poverty is what the
next political battles ought to be about.

> They ought to be about working families who are not making it in the
> globally competitive low-wage labor market, about workers who lose
> their jobs in the next recession but who are not covered by employ-
> ment compensation, about multiply disadvantaged men and women
> with serious barriers to work, about children whose parents have nei-
> ther time to spend with them nor resources to purchase high-quality
> substitute care. They ought, in short, to be about our brothers and sis-
> ters who are trying to be responsible workers and parents, but who
> are unable to succeed in spite of their efforts.[100]

The churches have a role to play in enhancing a climate of compassion
and in building up practices of unity and cooperation that can alleviate
poverty by creating a more inclusive society.

Catholic social ethics has in recent decades reflected a "preferential
option for the poor" that helps to address the economic and social conditions that make family life difficult for many. If, as the modern papal social
encyclicals have maintained, the common good requires the mutual interdependence and participation of all members of society, then all families
are in justice owed the support necessary to make their social contribution
possible. Moreover, while government must assume some responsibility
for the macroallocation of resources, local ventures and mediating institutions must reflect the perspectives and priorities of those that policies will
affect, giving them a voice in defining reforms. Catholicism employs the
metaphor of family as church to signal that families have a right and duty
to educate their members in a Christian spirituality that includes compassionate accountability for the well-being of their neighbors. This accountability requires more than private charity. It requires the creation of
effective, just, inclusive, and participatory social institutions enlivened by
the spirit of solidarity.

Chapter 5

Lessons from African American Families

An Important Perspective

Several African American theologians have addressed the history of the black family in the United States. Their reflections are instructive for the general debate and especially for the identity of Christian families. Toinette Eugene has assessed the dynamic encounter of the African American family with Catholic family ministry focused through the domestic church metaphor.[1] Other theologians whose writings are relevant are Robert M. Franklin, a Protestant participant in the Religion, Culture, and Family Project and co-author of *From Culture Wars to Common Ground*, and Sylvia Ann Hewlett and Cornel West, co-authors of *The War against Parents: What We Can Do for America's Beleaguered Moms and Dads*. West is a radical African American theologian and social ethicist. Hewlett is a white economist, frequent author on family matters, and a consultant to the Religion, Culture, and Family Project.

The work of three social scientists will augment a black-informed Christian social perspective on the family: Andrew Billingsley, who writes eloquently of the assets African Americans bring to family life; William Julius Wilson, who spells out with equal eloquence the plight of urban ghetto families; and Donna L. Franklin, who argues that mother-only families need more support both from the government and from civil society at the local and state level. These authors illustrate the dialectic that must necessarily occur between social experience and Christian ethics if Christians are to develop a normative ethics of family for the North American setting. Such an ethics relates family structures and individual families to the interplay of family and other institutions of civil society.

Toinette Eugene begins one of her essays with a quote from another African American scholar, J. Deotis Roberts. I take their agreement on an emblematic depiction of the black Catholic family as a propitious aegis under which to begin the present discussion.

> The church in the black tradition has been an extended family, while the family, in many instances, has been in fact a "domestic church." Church and family together have nurtured our suffering race and preserved us through all the ordeals of our history.[2]

Eugene maintains that black families not only support family members and other black people under oppression but also are structurally "open" and socially active toward *all* who are in need, up to and including positive, reconstructive engagement with their own oppressors. Theologically and ethically, the black family, whether amid successes or from within fierce struggles, provides a paradigm of Christian family identity that incorporates kingdom values of mutual sacrifice, inclusion, patience, endurance, and hope and trust in God.

I do not aim to treat theories of the black family in America comprehensively nor claim anything like a full and true appreciation of the realities behind the theories that I do treat. I certainly do not presume to speak for African Americans in relation to family matters. My aim is, rather, to begin to absorb the lessons about family life that African American experience can teach those of us who come from other segments of America and who tend to approach the situations of families in this country primarily from the standpoint of the "traditional," middle-class nuclear family, relatively privileged by class and socioeconomic standing.

Toinette Eugene has written, "White feminist theologians who wish to contribute to an inclusive feminist theology that respects and reflects the diversity of women's experience need to learn from the experiences, moral values, and feminist theology articulated by black women."[3] The late Sr. Thea Bowman, consultant for intercultural awareness for the Catholic diocese of Jackson, Mississippi, in introducing a readings and resource book for black Catholic families, invites whites to read it. She hopes that they may be better able "to walk and talk and work with Black families and to listen sensitively and persistently so that they can engage in a true mutuality of ministry and evangelization; so we can change and grow and be community and Church together."[4] This chapter is an attempt to listen to black women and men who are expressing a vision of families in America. It is but one moment in a multicultural theological conversation about experiences of family.

Some History

Partly because African American families were for so long afflicted by slavery and its effects, and partly because the ravages of poverty have disproportionately affected them, critics of American family life today have placed the ills of black families under a magnifying glass. A frequently cited problem for urban and rural families is the number of children who lack two parents in the home, especially poor children whose fathers are not consistent parental figures. Single parenthood and father absence are indicators of childhood disadvantage,[5] though these factors alone do not guarantee a troubled childhood.[6]

Donna Franklin has argued that the roots of the single-parent black family lie deeper than recent social causes such as ghettoization and joblessness.

In the years following emancipation, staying together was a priority for most black families. But they were kept in a state of poverty and indebtedness by a system of sharecropping that subjected their labor to the tyranny of the same plantation owners in the Cotton Belt for whom they had toiled as slaves. Also, during this time, having borne a child out of wedlock was not a deterrent to a girl seeking marriage, since a future spouse would likely view the children she brought as a sort of dowry that would augment his efforts at tenant farming.[7]

When the Freedman's Bureau of the federal government took over supervision of sharecropping contracts and labor, it protected the advantage of the planters first and foremost and furthermore conferred patriarchal authority on the black male by giving him the right to sign contracts for the labor of his entire family.[8] These policies, according to Franklin, harmed families by discriminating against women and creating greater rates of abuse of black women in the family. During World War I, a new pull of jobs in the North and a series of floods and droughts that destabilized crop productivity in the South led to a wave of northern migration. The fact that "urban areas were the land of opportunity" for black women who were single or were unable to "live amicably with husbands on a tenant farm" is "the clearest explanation for why mother-only families were more prevalent in urban areas." In addition, says Franklin, adolescents were discouraged from marriage because their labor was valuable to the family. Marriage as an institution was valued but unmarried childbearing was not stigmatized, for children were valued as commodities by men and families and for their emotional rewards by women.[9]

In the 1930s, further northern migration uprooted blacks from their institutions of communal support, including kin. New Deal policies offered women and children some relief services without providing either assistance to agricultural workers or domestic servants or any lasting social programs to improve the economic opportunities of blacks. By failing to outlaw racial discrimination in housing and lending, these policies began to create the urban ghettoes that have proved so inhospitable to family life today.[10]

Black families are, of course, diverse.[11] Although within a generation after emancipation 80 percent of black families were headed by a married couple, slavery had enduring effects on black family structure, whose precise nature is still a matter of debate. What is not in doubt is that black families survived with many strengths.[12] Eugene recapitulates the work of social scientists in claiming for black families strong kinship bonds and nurturing family ties, strong work and religious orientations, adaptability of family roles, and support from community figures and role models.[13] Robert Franklin and colleagues include high regard for both the consanguineous and the marital family, reciprocal enrichment of families and church, a relative equality of sex roles in the family, and symbolic and social resources for overcoming male alienation from families.[14]

Despite these deterrents to "nuclear" family formation among the veterans of slavery and their descendants, *most* black families until about 1980 have been two-parent, "intact" families. Most wives and mothers in these families have undertaken paid labor outside the home by necessity, and child care has often been shared by extended families, especially grandparents. Sociologist Andrew Billingsley warns that the idea that "unwed mothers and their households" are "synonymous with the black family" is a myth.[15] Many black families did manage to survive together on the margins of society, and many others have climbed into the middle class. It is both factually and rhetorically important to celebrate the strengths of black families, including their adaptive flexibility in the face of often hostile social forces, before the difficulties they face today are realistically confronted.[16]

Current Factors

Andrew Billingsley, William Julius Wilson, Donna Franklin, and others have amassed considerable evidence showing that the formation of single-mother families is encouraged by social and especially *economic* factors that originate beyond black communities. The historical pressures noted by Franklin have been exacerbated by recent economic conditions. According to Billingsley, in the 1950s a technologically driven economic transition drove millions of black men out of a stable blue-collar workforce, taking mothers out of the home and into the service sector and white-collar labor. The "devastating" impact of this transition into a post-industrial era has been "expanding black joblessness, expanding black single-parent families, and an expanding sense of hopelessness."[17]

Corporate profits and huge compensation packages for managers, newly abetted by government policies, have contributed to an ever larger and growing gap between rich and poor in this country. Benefits are purchased by policies of industrial relocation, "outsourcing," and "downsizing" that have radically changed employment and wage patterns and enlarged the inroads of poverty in the former middle class. The major culprit, in the eyes of Hewlett and West, is not just an impersonal technological revolution that seems historically and scientifically "inevitable," but something quite deliberate, even if habitual: "managerial greed." Longer workweeks, lower wages, or joblessness is the result for all but a tiny elite. The impact on black men and black families has been disproportionate and dire. The declining presence of black males in the home, West and

Hewlett argue, is partly due to welfare (AFDC) policies that have systematically excluded men for three decades, but it is also the result of the disappearance of many blue-collar jobs as well as racially biased "crime
control policies that target young black males."[18]

Wilson correlates social and structural causes of the emergence of "the
new urban poor" with cultural factors in poor communities. Urban poverty
is primarily due to changes in the nature of available work and the retreat of
employers to more profitable areas, exacerbated by racism. But also a factor are "values, habits, attitudes, and styles" that predominate in communities left behind by changing, race-sensitive structures of employment.
While liberal analysts tend to emphasize the structures, conservatives
stress the subculture of the poor, calling for a change of heart and greater
resolve on the part of individuals and communities as the key step in
improving their lot.

Wilson shows how attitudes and behaviors of the poor are interdependent with economic and employment structures, a correlation that seems
to go unrecognized by many white critics of welfare, who are complicit in
creating these structures. For example, residents of a neighborhood are
able to maintain social control and realize common goals only if they have
strong resident participation in formal institutions, voluntary associations, and informal networks and if they take personal responsibility for
collective supervision of neighborhood problems.[19] By undermining such
institutions, joblessness and poverty produce other forms of organization
that harness individual and collective energy around strategies that in
other settings would amount to "anti-social" behavior. Wilson thus illustrates brilliantly that so-called cultural factors are largely derivative from
socioeconomic ones.[20] The culture of poverty may be maladaptive to consistent employment, but employment is not a consistent option in settings
like the abandoned urban ghetto.

Children who grow up in families with a steady breadwinner and in
neighborhoods where most adults are employed will more likely emulate
the habits of those adults, including "attachment to a routine, a recognition of the hierarchy found in most work situations, a sense of personal
efficacy attained through the routine management of financial affairs,
endorsement of a system of personal and material rewards associated with
dependability and responsibility, and so on." Unsurprisingly, children
from jobless neighborhoods emulate the means of acquiring advantages
and assets that are presented in their life-world, thus perpetuating what
Wilson terms "weak labor-force attachment."

For instance, a "major local drug dealer," interviewed by a Pentecostal
minister trying to keep other kids from going down the dealer's path, was

asked why youngsters were so often lost to churches' efforts. The trafficker did not explain his magnetism in purely material terms but replied, "When the kids go to school, I'm there, you're not. When the boy goes for a loaf of bread or wants a pair of sneakers or just somebody older to talk to or feel safe around, I'm there, you're not."[21]

A twenty-five-year-old father of two from Chicago's West Side, who works two jobs to make ends meet, presents the difficulty of many other black males by explaining that

> the society that they're affiliated with really don't advocate hard work and struggle to meet your goals such as education and stuff like that. ... They don't see nobody getting up early in the morning, going to work or going to school all the time. . . . Well, that's been presented to you by your neighborhood.[22]

These young men are not simply passing up work and education because illegal routes to money seem easier; work and education do not exist among their reasonably available options. An "unemployed" drug trafficker makes this point: "I been working since I was fifteen years old. I had to work to take care of my mother and father and my sisters. See, so can't, can't nobody bring me that bullshit about I ain't looking for no job."[23] In turn, drug activity in a neighborhood triggers other problems of social organization, like crime, prostitution, and gang violence. Conversely, when unemployment rates fall and a higher percentage of young, less-educated black men are working, crime rates decrease.[24]

For overwhelmed men in impoverished communities, "lack of meaning is the axis in a cycle of idleness, demoralization, and abandonment that is also debilitating to the commonweal," concludes a study co-authored by another African American scholar, June Gary Hopps. Many men and women in such circumstances will turn to "anti-social" coping strategies in order to garner a share in life's rewards and to establish efficacy and self-respect.[25]

In urban poverty zones, the types of social and economic association that spawn mistrust and violence in the larger community can be seen as compensatory efforts to recreate channels of access to social goods. In truth, they serve neither the long-term good of individuals who participate in them nor the common good of society, whether local or national. Yet what is often overlooked in the civil-society debate is that these enterprises are at least to some degree pro-social for their members.

When the more constructive institutions of civil society languish and die—often because what once seemed vital local institutions were actually subsidiaries of a larger socioeconomic system not genuinely designed to serve or include the now-abandoned residents—the poor will turn to or invent other institutions that seem to meet their needs. The short-term benefits of such "solutions," along with the absence of any long-term rewards that might plausibly be offered by any other forms of social organization, explain their hold on the urban poor.

Racial and ethnic groups that have been systematically excluded from economic opportunity suffer disproportionately from inability to sustain lasting two-parent families, a fact stressed by Wilson as well as Donna Franklin. Although the rate of *all* births outside marriage increased nationally by 54 percent between 1980 and 1993 (to a total of 27 percent), in 1993, 57 percent of black children were living with a single parent, as compared to 32 percent of Hispanic and 21 percent of white children.[26] Thus, while the actual number of white single mothers on welfare is larger than black mothers similarly situated, since the white population is so much larger than the black, black single mothers are disproportionately represented in their own racial category. According to 1993 statistics, the mothers of 31 percent of black children had never been married, again a proportion higher than in other racial categories.

Certainly poverty correlates with unwed motherhood; a disproportionate number of "persistently poor" households are headed by young black women.[27] But in contrast to family theorists who assert that "illegitimacy" *causes* the poverty of children, Wilson and Donna Franklin marshal evidence that poverty is the cause of single-parent families. Poor education and joblessness are disincentives to marriage. Data shows that marriage rates are significantly lower among unemployed young black fathers than among those with jobs. From the woman's perspective, not only is there no economic incentive to marry a jobless co-parent, but a woman (and her extended family) may have strong disincentives. Marriage can mean long-term attachment to and even financial responsibility for a male who brings to the union and to parenthood few assets and many probable liabilities. For the female sexual partners of poorly educated and jobless males, non-marriage is a reasonable choice. "From the point of view of day-to-day survival, single parenthood reduces the emotional burden and shields [these mothers] from the type of exploitation that often accompanies the sharing of both living arrangements and limited resources."[28]

Unlike some middle-class or professional women, for whom the choice not to marry or to divorce may reflect individualism or lack of commitment, nonmarriage may actually be the best alternative for these urban women and their children. The young women who are most likely to have children under such circumstances are those who have the least to lose.[29] Society at the level of their own neighborhoods offers so few other paths to peer recognition and to adult status that teenage childbearing becomes much more attractive than it is to girls who can look forward to education, steady employment and advancement, and marriage to a reliable, financially secure mate.

Adding to these problems is the alienated youth culture that began to affect both blacks and whites in this country after World War II. In recent decades, the family has lost influence on teenagers to peer groups and schools. Contributing factors have been greater economic autonomy of teens, less adult supervision, and, in the post-war nuclear family, a pattern of father absence from the home, coupled with the housewife's overinvestment in a small number of children in an isolated domestic space. The resulting reduction of social controls on and social affiliation of young people has resulted in more premarital sex and more out-of-wedlock births.[30]

Expanding on Wilson's analysis, Donna Franklin terms the never-married black mother the "truly disadvantaged" and outlines how her status leads to the reproduction of poverty. Such a mother is likely to have been born to teenaged parents, to have borne a child as a teenager, to never have completed high school, to live in the central city in public housing or a poor neighborhood, to have more than four children, to have the weakest attachment to the labor force, and to be on welfare and thus to have a low income. She concurs with Wilson that such mothers (and their daughters) are "more likely to perceive public assistance as a more attainable means of support than marriage."[31]

In a much-cited work, Mary Jo Bane and David Ellwood conclude that welfare begins in the formation of single-parent families, that prevention is better than cure, and that the elimination of unmarried teenaged motherhood would also signal the elimination of AFDC (now TANF). Bane and Ellwood, however, are not optimistic about changing patterns of family formation or even significantly discouraging single motherhood among teens. The only plausible—and not easily achieved—solution is to help single parents move off welfare.[32] The reliance on welfare by young black mothers corresponds at least in part to the erosion of job availability for young black males, but it is not an effective alternative toward independence for these women. It does not enable them to escape the same structural exclusions from the national economy that are represented in male joblessness.

Another contributing factor to the halting pace of change for black Americans is the shape of the U.S. political tradition. Wilson proposes that the institutional base of social rights (to employment, economic security, health, and education) has historically been weak in the United States. Segregated inner-city populations are particularly vulnerable to economic restructuring and consequent social dislocations, since there is little broader social interest in or institutional base for renewing access to rights that deepening poverty has threatened.[33] This is even more the case when the poor are seen as members of an "other" and even "inferior" racial group, an identification that is more likely to be made when the fact of their disenfranchisement appears to make a claim on the assets of the more privileged. Rationalizations for the status of the powerful are sure to follow.[34]

Wilson's integrated social explanation of the "decline" of families in the urban desert pushes us toward a Christian ethical analysis that looks for explanations and solutions linking individual choice to structures and the dynamics of group belonging both inside and outside the ghetto. Unfortunately, as Wilson registers only too well, Americans tend to see the causes of poverty and the solutions—welfare, for instance—in individualistic terms. The tragedy and social roots of unemployment and poverty are lost in the American belief system, and "truly disadvantaged groups" are deemed responsible for their plight.[35] Even middle-class, two-parent, and economically secure black families, increasingly occupying the suburbs and enrolling their children in the same schools as whites, still suffer vestigial racism and the feelings of inferiority it spawns. Generations of exclusion from the culturally central sources of social capital and from denigration of the kinds of moral and social capital potentially offered by African American subculture have lasting effects. These factors can sometimes impede the ability of newly middle-class black children to perform well in school, to enter into mainstream economic and cultural life, and even to form stable, secure families.

Billingsley's assessment of the situation aligns with the Christian social ethics of Reinhold Niebuhr, who saw social dynamics as unavoidably corrupted by self-interest and power.

> The challenge is to make this society more responsive to, and supportive of, all its members. Without vigorous, organized, and persistent advocacy on the part of the collective African-American community, however, it is not likely that the society will abandon its hegemony over the resources and amenities largely enjoyed by the wealthiest, most powerful, and most privileged elements of the nation. Frederick Douglass said it well: "Power concedes nothing with a demand. It never has. It never will."[36]

Community Solutions

The African American community has hardly been quiescent toward its economic and social difficulties. Billingsley documents many black self-help initiatives. These include the custom of parenting other people's children within an extended family or adoptive family network, the founding of black schools and scholarship funds, and promoting black-owned businesses and economic development in the black community. In 1984, the NAACP and the National Urban League, the nation's two oldest and largest black national organizations, sponsored a national black family summit, at which all national African American organizations were represented. A few months later, the leading black women's organizations assembled to develop a nationwide program for the prevention of teenage pregnancy.

Donna Franklin offers ways in which local and federal or state initiatives can cooperate to enhance the prospects of black families. Teens should be encouraged to delay childbearing until adulthood and preferably marriage. Nonetheless, never-married mothers will continue to need services focused on parenting education in support groups and childcare and family preservation efforts involving the extended family, as well as education and job training. Franklin discusses an Infant and Health Development Program that intervened with parents of premature, low-birthweight infants in eight cities. Through parenting support, this program was able to produce significantly higher IQs and fewer behavior problems in those infants than those in a control group, with greatest gains for children of the most disadvantaged mothers. Such interventions can aid young mothers to develop the sense of agency and "self-efficacy" of which their environment may have deprived them. While structural changes need to be made, the individual's competencies and the support of her immediate family and community can and should be enlisted to develop her human capital and break the cycle of poverty.[37] Franklin follows other black leaders in affirming that, while a government role is indispensable in providing support, "the black community must take the lead in defining the new and continuing problems it faces, in communicating the urgency of these problems, and in both prescribing and initiating solutions."[38]

The core ethical and social issue to be confronted here is the erosion of the civil institutions that *together* are needed to support labor, schools, and families and that disintegrate together as unemployment and poverty rise. The family is one of these institutions. Interlinked, practical, local institutions are necessary to support families, and the vitality of such institutions often requires coordinated efforts beyond the immediate communities they serve. In other words, the importance of efforts to change cultural attitudes and to build strong families and local communities does not absolve those interested in the health and viability of marriages and families from working to develop national economic, educational, welfare, and social services policies that are truly supportive of all families. All of the analysts of family life discussed in this chapter agree that both initiatives from within the local community as well as supportive national policies and funding need to work cooperatively to rebuild or strengthen families in trouble, no matter the races to which they may belong.

Black Church, Domestic Church

Perhaps the most important institution of civil society for black families and for their communities as a whole is the black church. In 1984, the ten black Catholic bishops of the United States issued a pastoral letter on evangelization, *What We Have Seen and Heard*.[39] While offering the resources of the church to black families and calling families to renew their Catholic identity, the bishops also affirmed that the black Catholic church has now "come of age" in America and has a critical role to play in serving as a witness of the gospel. The bishops appropriate a message of the pope to Africans for African Americans as well, declaring their belief that "the Holy Father has laid a challenge before us to share the gift of our blackness with the Church in the United States."[40] Key to this gift is the African American experience of family, which builds on an extended family "related by kinship or strong friendship."[41]

> The sense of family in our own African American tradition can easily be translated into a richer sense of Church as a great and all-embracing family. . . . In a word, evangelization for black Catholics is a celebration of the family, a renewal of the family, and a call to welcome new members into the family of God."[42]

Andrew Billingsley devotes a chapter to the role of the church in the African American experience, viewing it as "the strongest institution" in the black community, one that is "prevalent, independent, and has extensive outreach."[43] African American Baptist and Methodist reform programs include thwarting drug traffickers by rebuilding abandoned houses into apartments; sponsoring a nationally recognized child development center; creating a mentoring program between male church members and boys; mounting an AIDS education and counseling program; and, in the case of the 141-year-old Concord Baptist Church of New York City, providing a square block of church-run institutions and annual awards of $75,000 to community agencies offering social service programs. Virtually all of these church initiatives serve families, from pregnancy counseling and early childhood education to elderly housing.

In Billingsley's estimate, no other institution "is as completely accepting of black families in all their complexity, nor as supportive," as the black church.[44] Black Catholic psychologist Edwin Nichols agrees that African Americans can hold up an ideal of marital and parental faithfulness while rallying around families and individuals in difficulty, especially to help nurture children:

> As Christians and as blacks, we are not judgmental of others. . . . Whereas, in predominantly white communities, the unwed mother causes so much scandal that she is out, I think that one of the major focuses of our Christianity as blacks is that we love our neighbors as ourselves. I think perhaps that is the most important facet of black Christianity and specifically black Catholic Christianity.[45]

The extended family has provided a coherent but open-ended structural base for intimacy and mutual support. This structure has been well-suited both to foster the identity of family as church and to provide a hospitable environment for the gospel vision of a "new family in Christ." Undoubtedly, the pressures under which black families survive have rarely permitted them to be tempted by complacent, self-satisfied prosperity or to distort the Christian family message by using family identity to conserve wealth and prestige. Likewise, the traditional gender roles dominant in most cultures were surmounted during slavery, when blacks banded together in the domestic sphere. There they enjoyed their only opportunity to approach other human beings as equals, to cooperate in sharing tasks and responsibilities. After the Civil War, black men still had little economic power; women shared the breadwinning role. In order to meet basic needs, everyone in black families had to earn as much as possible and to share in family chores.[46] Living under duress, slaves and their heirs put the gospel into action in a creative reinterpretation of family ties and family order.

Using Wallace Charles Smith's *The Church in the Life of the Black Family*,[47] Robert Franklin highlights the role of the church in binding families into supportive community and compares both individual families and the black church to the kind of inclusive community called together by faith in the early days of Christianity. The black church has always been a home for "families in whatever form," for whom it has been a source of encouragement and practical helpfulness. Finally, the church and pastor become a new, larger, metaphorical family, not replacing kinship families but drawing on their energies to create a spiritual family of mutual respect, support, and renewal.[48]

It is just these qualities of black families that Eugene brings into convergence with the Roman Catholic ideal of domestic church. As "little church," the family must in an intimate way be "the Sacrament of God and Christ."[49] The black family as domestic church mediates the compassionate love of God through its family spirituality and catechesis, but this love does not reach its limit with a closed family circle. "The spirituality for the black family is not a spirituality for the family alone, but it must articulate and announce to society and to the world in which it lives the Kingdom of God and the Good News of Jesus the Liberator."[50] Eugene identifies "black love" as the chief attribute of the black family, an attribute that provides a natural foundation for the revelation of God's grace. The black Christian family announces to the world that the reign of God is present, by acting with "*effective* compassion and *affective* justice." In Eugene's words, the love of the black domestic church shows

> willingness to include prodigal children, outcasts, the pariah, the stranger, and even the oppressor within the folds of its embrace. Historically, black love has enabled the momentarily crushed spirits of black folk to look beyond the immediacy of present suffering to a God who has never forsaken them in the hour of anguish and despair.
>
> It has been the religious aspect of black love that has prompted black Christians always to consider the worth of all human life: born and unborn, legitimate and "illegitimate"; single or several times married; old, unemployed, young, and inexperienced—all in terms of the accomplishment of God's will expressed in the here and now.[51]

As has been argued throughout the present work, however, another conception of family relations, deriving from the New Testament household codes, has been repeatedly championed throughout Christian tradition as a way of ordering family relationships. This model is patriarchal and historically has been amenable to the importation into Christian families of cultural values prioritizing economic and political standing. This model has, in fact, been most in evidence when the members of Christian communities have been relatively successful in worldly terms.

In some evangelical denominations today, this model is being reinvigorated in reply to the "breakdown" of the family, especially as a means of persuading men to fulfill paternal responsibilities by promising them family authority and the submission of their wives. Not surprisingly, this model has also enjoyed popularity in some current-day black circles in which male fidelity to mate and children has been under siege in the ways elucidated by Wilson, Billingsley, Donna Franklin, and others. These men's spirituality and fidelity movements are essentially revivalist efforts to reawaken commitment within an emotional atmosphere of male bonding and restored energy for the future. What reality of spousal and parental relationship lies under the rhetoric of groups like the Promise Keepers and the Nation of Islam is still a matter of debate. If judged from the standpoint of "fatherlessness," the reconstitution of the male role in the family may be a major advance over the status quo of father absence for children and lack of emotional, social, and financial support for women.

One way to look at these fatherhood movements is to see them as complementing admittedly necessary social measures to support families with a moral appeal to men's own aspirations for better, more intimate family relations. This appeal, suffused with biblical imagery, aims to give men the means to rise above social and cultural conditions that militate against family investment. They are attempts from within formerly alienated groups of men to take concrete, personal action to reconstitute civil society. New associational forms are produced to combat the individualism plaguing middle- and upper-class families and to give moral·support to poor families, in which fathers face a real world of social disinvestment, disinterest, or even hostility.

Hewlett and West tend to view such movements in a benign light, as calling and actually enabling men to assume greater accountability in family matters, even when propitious social circumstances (more economic advantages and less racism) have not yet been pulled into place. West and Hewlett blame slavery (and what they call its latter-day version, welfare) for having demolished the black man's "male protector" role, destroying pride and self-respect. In this light, they sympathetically view religiously-affiliated male movements, such as Promise Keepers (which includes an appeal for racial unity among men) and the Million Man March of the Nation of Islam. These movements can shore up the cultural symbol systems that will enable members to surmount the effects on families of joblessness and poverty. Such movements "create the conditions that allow many more men to become loving, attached fathers, . . . anchor men much more firmly in productive lives, and greatly enhance our store of social capital."[52]

Hewlett and West interview one man who attended the Million Man March. He expresses wonder at the sight of so many black men gathered together in strength, "trying to hold themselves to different standards . . . to their god, to their women, to their children."[53] The interviewee affirms that African American men have to fight against employment practices and government policies that harm their role in the family. Yet they also must look inward to "self-discipline." This is the message of the Nation of Islam: "When you join the Nation, you have to stop all kinds of bad behavior: drinking, smoking, fornication. When I was rootless and confused, this helped ground me."[54] Nevertheless, Wilson's economic critique of the conditions that must be presupposed for strong families cannot be forgotten in the evaluation of these movements, for blacks or for whites. Being a faithful and effective husband or father requires more than moral determination and more than male *esprit de corps;* it requires that necessary conditions be present for actual fulfillment of what one has determined to do.

Some black women are, in my view, rightly concerned about sexism, both within and outside the black community. (These concerns are echoed by critics of white men's participation in groups like Promise Keepers.) Never absent in human history or in any racial group, sexism seems to have made inroads among African Americans as a result of the hostile social conditions that drive black men to assert their identity over against one of the few other groups over whom they consider themselves able to exercise power.

Womanist (distinctively black feminist) authors define their program of sexual equality in much the same terms as the domestic church. It is inclusive, not separatist. It locates sexual and gender cooperation within a full assessment of and confrontation with the socioeconomic factors that inhibit the human flourishing of black women and men together. In Eugene's words, the domestic church is for womanist Christians the "home base for liberating praxis." What this base furnishes is "a legacy of perseverance and self-reliance, a legacy of tenacity, resistance, and insistence on sexual equality—in short, a legacy of love spelling out standards for a new womanhood."[55] Womanist theology draws on prophetic and redemptive strands in biblical traditions, over those reaffirming existing structures and lines of order. "Womanist moral values are expressed through radical healing and empowering actions in company with those who are considered the very least in the reign of God."[56]

I believe one can conclude from this manifesto that the healing and empowering of black (or white or Latino or Asian or any other) men cannot be achieved in Christian terms at the price of further exclusion from the praxis of God's reign of female companions, who also struggle for recognition of their full humanity and distinctive gifts. The authority of men as such over women as such is not an appropriate standard for relations within the Christian family today.

In their pastoral letter, the black Catholic bishops acknowledge gender tensions among blacks but summon "black men to become what their fathers were—even when an evil institution sought to destroy their individuality and their initiative—that is, models of virtue for their children, and partners in love and nurturing with their wives." This is followed up quickly with words of appreciation and respect for the burdens borne by black women, whose role they see as "complementary" but not "subordinate" to black men. Reinforcing examples they mention are Sojourner Truth, Harriet Tubman, and Mary McLeod Bethune, and the Catholics Elizabeth Lange, Henriette Delille, and Mother Theodore Williams, who founded black women's religious congregations in the face of hostility and opposition.[57] It would be naïve to think that African American Catholic bishops have completely overcome the patriarchal forms that affect church structures as a whole. Nonetheless, they resist adopting a model of male headship in order to entice men into greater family involvement.

Racial Equality, Civil Society, and Catholic Social Teaching

The link of healthy civil institutions, including families, to broader social networks and to centralized government authority is a theme of Catholic social teaching, one much in evidence in teaching about the domestic church. African American analysts of families and society agree that local institutions need broad-based support from beyond the immediate communities they serve, especially when they are dealing with the effects of attitudes, practices, and policies that are themselves wide, even national, in scope.

A recent issue of *The Brookings Review* is devoted to the questions of whether civil society is in decline and whether its health requires integral partnership with national institutions. The issue includes an article spotlighting a group of black inner-city ministers in Boston who joined together to promote local economic development, strengthen families, and resurrect "the civil life of their jobless drug-and-crime infested neighborhoods" by tackling everything from summer recreation programs to faith-based, individualized drug treatment.[58] Their impressively successful venture eventually drew a $75,000 grant from a New England philanthropy, the Institute for Civil Society, to mobilize interventions in half a dozen other cities. But church-related efforts still experience difficulty in attracting state and federal funds. The author John DiIulio Jr. argues that churches alone cannot fill the gaps left by government withdrawal from assistance to the poor. The civil-society sector and the state need to work in tandem to provide social services and welfare programs.

In Roman Catholic social teaching, ever guided by the principle of subsidiarity, the domestic church and the church as a community institution, along with the other institutions of civil society, have always been interlinked with bigger structures. In the words of Pope John XXIII's 1961 encyclical, *Christianity and Social Progress (Mater et Magistra)*:

> where . . . appropriate activity of the State is lacking or defective, commonwealths are apt to experience incurable disorders, and there occurs exploitation of the weak by the unscrupulous strong, who flourish, unfortunately, like cockle among the wheat, in all times and places (no. 58).

It is the links among institutions from the family to the federal government that allow communication, mediation, and allocation of resources among all the members of society. Without some institutions that stretch across society, it would be impossible to aim for coordinated and equitable participation in the common good.

Despite the many successful initiatives sponsored by black community groups and national organizations, few theorists are convinced that efforts from within the African American community will in themselves be sufficient to address the ingrained racism that still hinders black efforts to participate fully in American society. For Wilson, Billingsley, Donna Franklin, Robert Franklin, and West, like virtually every other African American family theorist, the state of civic institutions is key in defining the health of families, and these institutions have a national dimension.

Billingsley identifies no fewer than twelve systems of the larger society on which all families depend and to which families in turn contribute. Beyond the obvious economic, political, and educational systems, these include the housing and health systems, social welfare system, criminal justice system, military system, and transportation, recreation, and communications systems.[59] Clearly, black families neither enjoy full social inclusion in these institutions now nor have the power to bring about full participation without much broader cooperation from the majority population. The authors here considered understand civil society to be interdependent with federal and national coalitions, policies, and laws, as well as with market and business interests that more frequently exploit or abandon the "underclass" instead of enlarging its windows of opportunity. Although some authors note that racism has nowhere near the organizing power that it had in this society a generation ago or a century ago[60]—a claim it would be hard to deny—this kind of assertion can obscure the "cool racism"[61] that still pervades many, most, or even all of our social structures.

This is why government and some centralization of economic reform efforts must be the top side of the principle of "subsidiarity." This principle has been long championed in Catholic social encyclicals as upholding the right of smaller or subsidiary groups in society to operate autonomously, insofar as possible, within their appropriate spheres. Schools, churches, business, and certainly families have a limited right of self-determination, a realm in which they are and ought to be protected from state control. The operative word here, however, is "limited." The limits of autonomy are set by the requirements of social justice. The vertical as well as horizontal integration of civic institutions is essential to subsidiarity.

In *Christianity and Social Progress,* John XXIII reinterpreted the principle of subsidiarity introduced by Pius XI by noting that, although the state or public authorities should never "absorb" private economic initiative, it is still their responsibility to moderate economic fluctuations and to avoid "mass unemployment." It is within the power and the duty of public authorities "to reduce imbalances, whether these be between various sectors of economic life, or between different regions of the same nation, or even between different peoples of the world as a whole" (no. 54).

As we have seen, when community-building institutions disappear, they do not leave a vacuum for long. In socially or economically marginal circumstances, the decline of some structures of civil society can permit more pernicious varieties to take root and flourish. Just and effective intervention must combine interpersonal and structural support from local institutions in proximity to the affected community with more comprehensive policies that redistribute national resources more equitably. For instance, Wilson urges a national jobs-creation initiative, parallel to Franklin D. Roosevelt's 1935 Works Progress Administration. He believes a new public works program would offer a variety of forms of local and regional employment under a federal umbrella, at slightly below minimum wage, to every American adult who wanted it, backed up by child care, health care, and Social Security.[62]

Donna Franklin stresses the importance of inner-city revitalization and job creation through federal financial support for activities in local communities. For example, in the creation of "enterprise zones," local state governments receive money from the federal government in response to proposals encouraging low-income residents to start new businesses or rebuild housing in designated areas. Taxes and regulations can be decreased in such cases to support resident ownership. An effective means of organizing the poor for such ventures is community development corporations that address affordable housing and neighborhood safety.[63]

Hewlett and West are backers of a spectrum of pro-family social measures including more stringent marriage, divorce, and child support laws, child care, parental work leaves, a shorter workday, family health coverage, federally funded work-support programs for students and ex-convicts, tax relief for families with children, and housing subsidies. They also place a high priority on value formation within communities of belief and commitment, which can then become pro-active and persistent in striving for civil institutions that incorporate their needs, abilities, and priorities. These problems and solutions are not unique to black families, of course.[64] Black families and other "minority" families may be harder hit when economic losses strike a community or the nation, since economic exclusion is so often defined by racial or ethnic criteria and by demographic criteria in turn dependent on race and ethnicity. But the kinds of solutions required to resolve economically driven family losses and frictions are comparable across racial groups.

To understand families as domestic churches means to see them not as the recipients of external initiatives alone nor as confining their spiritual affiliation or their self-generated social efforts to their own kin or to a subset of families that all resemble one another structurally or ideologically. The life of families in the black churches provides a moral and social witness to the obligatory character for Christians of support for all families, especially when the welfare of children is at stake. The key task for Christian churches and families is not to define the criteria by which some are excluded from the Christian scope of concern but to support all persons and families in finding human well-being and in living the virtue of compassion that defines Christian discipleship. That this will require difficult sacrifices by the privileged should come as no surprise.

Conclusions: Learning from African American Families

The keynote of the last two chapters has been the metaphor of domestic church as used in Catholic teaching to advance a social view of families. The social nature of the family means both that families are interdependent with other civil institutions and that families participate in the common good through an open-ended commitment to other persons and families, especially the least well-off of their society. Catholic teaching emphasizes the importance of permanent marriage and two-parent families nurturing children as family forms most conducive to family well-being and social contribution. The domestic church in recent papal and episcopal teaching, however, has been understood to include all families committed to fulfill the social mission of compassion and service in a spirit of Christian love. The example of the black Catholic domestic church illustrates that families under duress can often imitate the inclusive generosity of the reign of God more faithfully than privileged families.

Turning to the recent debate about welfare reform in the United States, we have seen that Catholic episcopal teaching is optimistic—perhaps overly so—about whether a public sense of social solidarity can be created to overcome inequities and exclusions in the nation's market economy. Nevertheless, important contributions of this line of thought are its emphasis on the preferential option for the poor, empowerment of the poor, and the importance of linking local and national institutions, public and private, in meeting the needs of families more adequately. Although part of the mission of the family as domestic church is to cultivate Christian virtue in its members and to form a spirituality of love, sacrifice, and fidelity, the domestic church is also linked to the common good of society as both a contributor and a beneficiary. Thus, to call the Christian family a "domestic church" ties families into the larger systemic agenda of Christian social ethics, including the transformation of oppressive and exclusionary mediating institutions.

Chapter 6

A Christian Family Vision

A biblical text that begins to define what is required for a family to be domestic church is the so-called parable of judgment in Matthew 25. In its resounding lines, "the Son of Man" proclaims "to those on his right hand":

> "Come, O blessed of my Father, inherit the kingdom prepared for you from the foundation of the world; for I was hungry and you gave me food, I was thirsty and you gave me drink, I was a stranger and you welcomed me, I was naked and you clothed me, I was sick and you visited me, I was in prison and you came to me. . . . Truly I say to you, as you did it to one of the least of these my brethren, you did it to me." Then he will say to those at his left hand, "Depart from me, you cursed, into the eternal fire prepared for the devil and his angels, for I was hungry and you gave me no food, I was thirsty and you gave me no drink. . . ." Then they also will answer, "Lord, when did we see thee hungry or thirsty or a stranger or naked or sick or in prison, and did not minister to you?" Then he will answer them, "Truly, I say to you, as you did it not to the least of these, you did it not to me. And they will go away into eternal punishment, but the righteous into eternal life." (Matt. 25:31-46)

The disciple finds and serves Christ in "the least of these" by recognizing them as Christ's true family, to whom he refers as "my brethren." To be one in the family of Christ is to "welcome" compassionately those whose suffering is within our reach, taking care of their basic needs for food, clothing, and assistance in time of sickness and travail. The family of Christ includes not only the "stranger" but even the criminal—the one who stands convicted of wrongdoing.

If the family is a school of intimacy, empathy, and love, then the family as little church schools these virtues in attentiveness to the least of Christ's brethren. The virtues of compassion, mercy, and service are not merely held up as distant ideals or supererogatory forms of perfection. Those who fail to find Christ in active love of neighbor must "depart from" him on the day of his glory. Moreover, the text operates on the assumption that those to be cast out are "the righteous," who have not seen that being upright includes active identification with the miseries of those whom they consider less worthy.

Although the passage from Matthew underwrites the preferential option for the poor that provides the social framework for the lives of all Christians, its examples are personal. Its direct appeal to personal response and responsibility gives this parable its moral impact and motivating power. Modern Christians will understand the commanded virtues to result in structural change, empowerment of the poor, and ecumenical cooperation in a public forum and in civil institutions, none of which were very realistic possibilities for disciples at Christianity's point of origin in the first century. In her book on virtue, Diana Fritz Cates makes the case that friendship is a school for compassion and that moral virtue consists in choosing to develop, expand, and extend compassion by training our cognitive, affective, and imaginative capacities appropriately. Moreover, compassion can and should take institutional form, because mediating institutions enable us to recognize and respond to the situations of other persons with whom we are not in immediate, personal contact.[1] Thus, a Christian ethic of compassion and other-concern must be fulfilled through an institutional component, in which sacrificial altruism is extended to distant persons and communities. This institutional extension of co-responsibility with and for other human beings in concentric and overlapping communities from local to global is the essence of social ethics.

Empathy in the face of need is a fundamental human response, learned in the intimate associations of family first of all, then educated toward a wider range of further recipients.[2] Sometimes the needs of family members and of nonmembers will conflict. As Stephen Post poignantly illustrates with instances from his own family life, it can be difficult to know when and how to exercise the preferential option for the poor in the concrete.[3] But the point of the parable of judgment is that Christians must always be aware of neighbors and strangers who suffer as making real claims on them. It is the distinctive contribution of Christian ethics to define prophetically and redefine the identity of the "deserving poor." The religious symbolism of Christianity (and of other religions) that evokes identity with and compassion toward those who suffer has potential to stimulate the imagination and widen the moral outlook of all persons and groups so that natural human emotions are trained toward a generosity that can temper, if not entirely overcome, egotism and fear.

The needs depicted as objects of Christian other-concern in Matthew 25 direct our attention toward the kinds of essential goods that all persons and cultures experience to be necessary. Precisely because the needs and goods identified in the parable are basic to human well-being, our common human condition makes recognition of another's deprivation a human and not only a Christian possibility. Therefore, Christians can cooperate with others in civil society, politics, and government to pursue ends recognizable by all as good and worthy. The gospel text does present Christian virtue as embodying a radical and distinctive orientation toward these universal needs and goods. Those who look upon the needy in Christian faith will see them as Christ and as members of one's own family in Christ. Thus the preferential option to seek goods for kith and kin becomes the preferential option for all those wanting for the material and social necessities of human well-being, including stranger or wrongdoer. Christians have the obligation to heighten the visibility of these priorities in the public domain, making social structures more just.

Ecumenical Christian Commitment to Families Today

In their book about the family debate in North American culture, Don Browning and colleagues offer a vision of family as domestic church that distinguishes what they take to be Protestant and Catholic features of this analogy.[4] Their definition provides a way to recapitulate some themes of the present work, while offering an opportunity to examine how different conceptions of the Christian family are at variance or are complementary.

Browning et al. identify prayer and religious catechesis in the home as one of the most crucial characteristics of family as "little church," practices that they allow have not been consistently pursued in mainline Protestant families of recent decades. Importantly, they note that Christian prayer together can and should lead to the sort of transformation of family hierarchies that they surmise to have occurred when inclusive eucharistic rituals were practiced in the house churches of Christianity's first generations.

The key difference that these authors see between Catholic and Protestant understandings of domestic church is that the former is *sacramental,* while the latter is *covenantal.* By this they mean that Catholicism holds that the presence of God in the family is mediated through the sacramental system of the *institutional church,* while Protestantism sees God as present in the family through the parents' own *personal relationship* or covenant with God and God's covenant with the family, existing in dialogical relation to God's covenant with the church. This definition reflects and builds on the Reformation prioritization of individual faith and the responsibility of conscience over ecclesiastical structures. It also represents the biblical and Reformation insight that persons' relations to God and to others in God require and are founded on personal decision and conversion (covenant).

From another angle, however, the emphasis on choice and personal commitment does not completely capture the importance of parental responsibility to children that Browning et al. want to stress. Part of their agenda is to clarify the duty of fathers and mothers to care for their off-spring (and co-parents) whether or not that particular responsibility is one parents (especially fathers) would prefer to choose. In other words, biological parenthood morally constitutes a responsibility and morally demands a commitment on the basis of a preexisting, natural reality. The idea that moral relationships arise in important and compelling ways from biological and material forms of human interdependence ("creation") is captured more explicitly in the incarnational view of human existence symbolized in the Catholic sacramental system.

This system not only gives sacramental events an institutional orienta-tion, but also equally importantly identifies human experiences like birth, death, and marriage as occasions of the inbreaking of the divine. God is incarnate and redemptive in nature and natural realities, including nat-ural human relationships and associations that are capable of being sanc-tified and raised into communion with God. Since persons are by nature social, their family relations are also socially extensive or extenuating, making the family interdependent with other institutions, all of which open out onto the common good. Thus participation in the family as a social institution interwoven with the other institutions of civil society is also an opportunity for divine presence. Browning and co-authors move on in subsequent sections to discuss very perceptively the importance and possibility of ecumenical cooperation for the transformation of civil insti-tutions that support family life.[5] But the coexistence of Christian families with other families in the common good is a more integral and founda-tional theme of Catholic teaching about families, as is the service charac-ter of the Christian family. Human relationships and institutions, in Catholic perspective, are not so corrupted by sin that they scarcely func-tion as mediations of divine presence unless explicitly disciplined by Christian norms that reject ordinary human values. Sin, in fact, is identi-fied in terms of violations of human nature, not so much as capitulation to human drives and desires.

From the Protestant, covenantal side, however, returns the equally necessary caution that nature is corrupted by sin and fails to serve as a ready norm for human behavior. On the issue of family specifically, a covenant perspective holds up prayer in the family as a way of cultivating personal sacrifice as part of a relationship with God. Family spirituality is also important in Catholic teaching about the family as domestic church. But a Protestant, biblical approach will be acutely aware of the difficulty of enacting the relationships of human empathy and sharing that our genuine and natural interdependence would demand. It refuses to be as sanguine about the healing of social life and institutions as recent Catholic social teaching about the common good, including welfare reform. Protestantism identifies a family covenant with God over and above or outside sinful human relationships and worldly structures and tends to stress that personal commitments are prior to and more important than the reformation of social structures. Thus the covenant model of family can help advocate reconfiguration of the natural family to meet Christian ideals. Within this model, a strong critical stance toward Christian family values will be essential to ensure that family ideals and aspirations are genuinely Christian, not just cultural or "natural" familism justified in religious terms.

The Christian family and its family values are not the same as the natural family with its often exaggerated values of family security and advancement; nor is the Christian family the same as the family of modern liberal individualism, where commitments are decided and defined by individual choice. Understanding the family as domestic church requires understanding "church" properly. The primary values defining the Christian family are the same values that define the "new family in Christ": other-concern and compassionate love that overlooks socially normative boundaries and is willing to sacrifice to meet the needs of others. These values are more important in defining the Christian family than is a particular family structure. This does not mean that all structures are equally valid, since some more than others—especially long-term fidelity to mates and children—will serve human growth and happiness and contribute to a more humane society. But it does mean that structure alone is not the key criterion of Christian identity, and it opens up the possibility that even "nontraditional" families may exhibit the most important Christian family values, and for that reason be authentic domestic churches.

Today, in the era of globalization of media, economics, education, politics, and legislation, concern and sacrifice for others take institutional forms, extending personal commitments into consistent social support and allowing broad-based collaboration in marshalling forms of support that include the poor and empower the poor themselves to realize a more humane existence. Certainly civil institutions that support all members of society to realize their potential, meet their obligations, and fully participate in both the domestic and public spheres of the common good must take shape at the local level, tailored to meet local needs and to capitalize on local opportunities. But solidarity as a social virtue also requires that resources be collected and redistributed in regional, national, and international networks, both private and public, so that individuals and families can exercise their responsibilities even toward those to whom they do not feel a close personal tie or with whom they do not enjoy a mutually beneficial immediate relationship.

There are certain family structures and relationships that would serve individual, family, and social well-being in virtually every culture. These include the faithful, long-term personal commitment of sexual partners; their mutually respectful cooperation in domestic life, including participation in institutions such as religion and the economy that link families to society; the equal dignity of women and men; the permanent commitment of parents to nurture and educate children together; sharing material and social resources in the family so that the human needs of all are met; and care for the elderly, the sick, and other vulnerable members. Christian identity confirms these relationships, roles, and values, at least to the extent that they do not overshadow the Christian's duty to extend empathy and care beyond family membership and to support social institutions that serve the needs of other families, groups, and individuals.

But the ultimate tests of a distinctively *Christian* ethics of family life go beyond the well-being of family members and the successful accomplishment of family roles. The Christian family defines *family values* as care for others, especially the poor; it appreciates that truly Christian families are not always the most socially acceptable or prestigious ones; it values and encourages all families who strive earnestly to meet the standard of compassionate action; and it encourages both personal commitment to and the social structuring of mercy and justice.

A Program for Christian Families

We may conclude with five constructive recommendations for Christian family life, along with a word about the likelihood, even inevitability, of failure to follow them fully. The first two of the five address the natural, human functions and importance of families; the latter three address the Christian conversion of family bonds and roles.

1. Christian families should be grounded in the kinds of human relations that promote family well-being in general. Key among them are sexual relationships characterized by faithful commitment and responsible procreation, including long-term shared dedication to the welfare of children; equality, dignity, respect, and reciprocity among adults and between adults and children in ways appropriate to their age and maturity; affection, intimacy, empathy, and mutual support among family members.

2. Family roles should promote social well-being by educating for economic and political participation, including respect for the rights and fulfillment of the responsibilities to others that are part of the common good.

3. The kinship family's well-being is for Christians integrated with and to some extent relativized by the inclusive nature of the Christian community as "new family in Christ." Christ's new family potentially reaches out to all those who are weary and heavily burdened, whether Christian or non-Christian.

4. The natural pro-social role of families is shaped for Christians by a *preferential* option for the poor. In institutionalizing just treatment and just access to goods across society, those who have been previously excluded must be first included. Although justice in its own right may be interpreted as having such a preferential or remedial component, the Christian imagination will be formed to highlight this priority in a special way and to sustain its importance in the face of conflicting practical claims.

5. Christian families will place their moral commitments in the context of a relationship to God and will train the moral imagination to see human relationships in the light of the reign of God. Adults should serve as models to children, including them in the life of a faith community, through liturgy, eucharist, social events, and service activities. Such practices form Christian identity within family life, embodying the meaning of Jesus' command to love God and neighbor in practical relationships in the church, in a circle of family and friends, and in the larger community and society. It must be acknowledged that while it is simple and obvious to state that Christian families will incorporate Christian "spirituality" and prayer, it may well be difficult to re-create a contemporary Christian family spirituality in culturally available, meaningful, and powerful symbols and rituals. This is a place in which the churches can learn from the experience of families and in which the white middle-class families typifying mainline Protestantism and Catholicism can learn from Christians of other ethnic groups and social classes.

As all of us who aim to be Christian families struggle to achieve even one or two of these goals, we realize that the Christian life is truly the way of the cross as well as a journey to redemption. Sometimes our aspirations are ridiculed or rejected by our culture or simply considered unrealistic or irrelevant. Worse, the process of trying to live as Christian families makes us all too acutely aware of sin and failure in our own lives and in those of persons whom we love. Every family experiences situations that cause fear, anger, grief, guilt, and shame. Few continue for long without developing hurtful patterns of insensitive, manipulative, or angry behavior; few parents can honestly say they have loved their children unselfishly and with wholehearted acceptance of their children's independent needs and identities. Many marriages and families break apart; sex is often exploitative, even within marriage; violence and abuse break out more frequently than we will openly admit. Children do not receive all the care and under-standing they deserve from parents; elderly parents do not receive the patient devotion and respect their years, if not behavior, have earned them. Christian parents too often fail in attempts to pass on their faith in a vital way to children; children, in turn, cause parents pain by abandoning or betraying their most treasured moral and spiritual ideals. Even without notable disasters, family life over the years invariably brings with it stresses and strains, hurts and disappointments, that too often become hardened into bitterness and alienation.

Even when family life seems rewarding and successful in itself, the social concern of Christian families can be very hard to sustain. At most, it seems, we can teach ourselves and our children to look with greater under-standing on different kinds of families undergoing their own trials and seeking their own rewards and to offer our time and resources rather spo-radically to help other families in trouble or to make community life bet-ter. We are too consumed with our own family's well-being, which for some of us seems very, very difficult to secure.

Our own sins and our need for forgiveness should make all Christian families slow to judge others and quick to offer support, even while we persistently and courageously speak up for the family relationships and social conditions that we believe will enhance family life for all. The Chris-tian family is not the perfect family but one in which fidelity, compassion, forgiveness, and concern for others, even strangers, are known. In striving to embody these virtues, however imperfect its success, a family lives in the presence of God and begins to transform its surroundings. A Christian family is such a family.

Notes

Preface

1. The following recently published books make arguments in some ways similar to mine: Barend A. de Vries, *Champions of the Poor: The Economic Consequences of Judeo-Christian Values* (Washington, D.C.: Georgetown University Press, 1998); Michael G. Lawler, *Family: American and Christian* (Chicago: Loyola University Press, 1998); and Stephen G. Post, *More Lasting Unions: Christianity, the Family, and Society* (Grand Rapids, Mich.: William B. Eerdmans, 2000).

2. I use several terms to capture these situations: *family, the family,* and *families.* Critics of the industrial-age nuclear family rightly point out that it is neither the only nor the necessarily normative "family," and so eschew use of the phrase *the family,* as though only one form could be the proper subject of discussion. I occasionally use the term *the family* either to refer to debates that do take the "nuclear family" as normative or to indicate that family does exist as a cross-cultural institution that is recognizably the same (a form of social organization based on intergenerational kinship and marriage, augmented by "fictive" ties like adoption). I also use *family* to suggest the general but pliable nature of the human experience of family membership and *families* to indicate the variety of specific families that may exist in any given society.

3. Lisa Sowle Cahill, *Between the Sexes: Toward a Christian Ethic of Sexuality* (Philadelphia: Fortress Press, 1985). Elizabeth M. Bounds, in *Coming Together/ Coming Apart: Religion, Community, and Modernity* (New York and London: Routledge, 1997), states that my work "makes no attempt to consider issues of power, conflict or difference" (82). I am not sure I completely accept that characterization, but I do take well the point that the goal of gender equality within cooperative social relationships requires a radical critique of racist and classist institutions.

4. Lisa Sowle Cahill, *Sex, Gender, and Christian Ethics* (New York: Cambridge University Press, 1996).

5. My book *Sex, Gender, and Christian Ethics* was one of these. In addition, the following have been published as a series by Westminster John Knox Press: Max L. Stackhouse, *Covenant and Commitments: Faith, Family, and Economic Life* (1997); Phyllis D. Airhart and Margaret Lamberts Bendroth, eds., *Faith Traditions and the Family* (1996); Leo G. Purdue, Joseph Blenkinsop, John J. Collins, and Carol Meyers, *Families in Ancient Israel* (1997); Carolyn Osiek and David L. Balch, *Families in the New Testament World: Households and House Churches* (1997); Herbert Anderson, Don S. Browning, Ian S. Evison, and Mary Stewart van Leeuwen, eds., *The Family Handbook* (1998); Ted Peters, *For the Love of Children* (1996); Don S. Browning, Bonnie J. Miller-McLemore, Pamela Couture, K. Brynolf Lyon, and Robert M. Franklin, *From Culture Wars to Common Ground: Religion and the American*

Family Debate (1997); John Witte Jr., *From Sacrament to Contract: Marriage, Religion, and Law in the Western Tradition* (1997); Anne Carr and Mary Stewart van Leeuwen, eds., *Religion, Feminism and the Family* (1996); and K. Brynolf Lyon and Archie Smith Jr., eds., *Tending the Flock: Congregations and Family Ministry* (1998). In 1997 the Lilly Endowment gave the project an additional grant to support a second phase of research. This will include a series of books to be edited by Don S. Browning and John Wall. The first in the series is Stephen G. Post's *More Lasting Unions* (see note 1). Innovative chapters in Post's book address adoption as a Christian practice and family caregiving for the elderly.

Chapter 1: Families, Christian Ethics, and Civil Society

1. For an overview of the project, see Don S. Browning, Bonnie J. Miller-McLemore, Pamela D. Couture, K. Brynolf Lyon, and Robert M. Franklin, *From Culture Wars to Common Ground: Religion and the American Family Debate* (Louisville, Ky.: Westminster John Knox Press, 1997).

2. Barbara Dafoe Whitehead, "A New Familism?" *Family Affairs* 5/1–2 (summer 1992) 1. For a longer exposition of similar concerns, see the Council on Families in America, "Marriage in America: A Report to the Nation," in *Promises to Keep: Decline and Renewal of Marriage in America*, ed. David Popenoe, Jean Bethke Elshtain, and David Blankenhorn (Lanham, Md.: Rowman and Littlefield, 1996) 293–318.

3. See, for instance, Don S. Browning, "Biology, Ethics, and Narrative in Christian Family Theory," in Popenoe et al., eds., *Promises*, 119–56. If there is a "male problematic," I find it implausible, human nature being what it is, that there is not some sort of equally forceful "female problematic," and hence cannot accept that female behavior should be expected to accommodate male fallibility in an asymmetrical way. Moreover, I am enough of an optimist—or maybe perfectionist?—to think that social policy and especially Christian ethics should center our attention on humanity's nobler potentials and aspirations, not our lowest common denominators, even if we rarely manage to attain them.

4. Browning et al., *From Culture Wars*, 1–2.

5. For emphasis on feminist dimensions of the project, see Anne Carr and Mary Stewart van Leeuwen, eds., *Religion, Feminism and the Family* (Louisville, Ky.: Westminster/John Knox Press, 1996).

6. See Mary Ann Glendon, *Abortion and Divorce in Western Law: American Failures, European Challenges* (Cambridge, Mass.: Harvard University Press, 1987).

7. William Julius Wilson, *When Work Disappears: The World of the New Urban Poor* (New York: Random House, 1997).

8. Barbara Dafoe Whitehead, "Dan Quayle Was Right," *The Atlantic Monthly* (April 1993) 47–84.

9. Browning et al., *From Culture Wars*, 327–28. See also chapter 6, n. 4.

10. I learned of this initiative and its purpose in becoming an invited participant in a 1992 colloquium, "The Christian Family: A Domestic Church," sponsored by the Committee on Marriage and Family of the National Conference of Catholic Bishops.

11. See Stanley Hauerwas, *A Community of Character: Toward a Constructive Christian Social Ethic* (Notre Dame, Ind.: University of Notre Dame Press, 1981) 155–74.

12. This is the Browning et al. proposal. A critical familism quite properly employs criteria of full gender equality, and economic and social analysis of social supports for families. Further, it requires that families themselves be committed to the common good (*From Culture Wars*, 2). I heartily endorse all these qualifications. However, I also want to maintain a healthy skepticism about whether any ideology of "familism" is compatible with the compassionate inclusiveness of a "new family in Christ."

13. Wilson, *When Work Disappears*, 167. According to the popular stereotype, welfare mothers are young and black. Although some make the counterargument that in reality African Americans make up a minority of welfare recipients (39.2 percent in 1995, compared to 39.9 percent non-Hispanic white), this is still a disproportionate number in a black population that is only 12.4 percent of the total national population.

14. Ibid., 87–88.

15. Ibid., 164.

16. Reinhold Niebuhr, *Human Destiny*, vol. 2 of *The Nature and Destiny of Man* (New York: Charles Scribner's Sons, 1964) 212.

17. Carnegie Task Force on Meeting the Needs of Young Children, *Starting Points: Meeting the Needs of Our Youngest Children: The Report of the Carnegie Task Force on Meeting the Needs of Young Children* (New York: Carnegie Corporation of New York, 1994). The contents of the report and a table comparing statistics on child welfare from 1960 to 1990 are included in Susan Chira, "Study Confirms Worst Fears on U.S. Children," *New York Times* (12 April 1994) A1, 13.

18. Mary Ann Glendon, "Introduction," in *Seedbeds of Virtue: Sources of Competence, Character, and Citizenship in American Society*, ed. Mary Ann Glendon and David Blankenhorn (Lanham, Md.: Madison Books, 1995) 11.

19. See Nancy L. Rosenblum, *Membership and Morals: The Personal Uses of Pluralism* (Princeton, N.J.: Princeton University Press, 1998).

20. Robert D. Putnam, "Bowling Alone: America's Declining Social Capital," *Journal of Democracy* 6/1 (January 1995) 65–78.

21. Alexis de Tocqueville, "On the Use Which the Americans Make of Associations in Civil Life," in *Democracy in America*, vol. 2, ed. J. P. Mayer, trans. George Lawrence (New York: Doubleday, 1969 [originally published 1848]) 513, 515.

22. Putnam, "Bowling Alone," 72–73.

23. David Blankenhorn, "Conclusion," in Glendon and Blankenhorn, eds., *Seedbeds*, 280.

24. Ibid. See also William A. Galston, "The Reinstitutionalization of Marriage: Political Theory and Public Policy," in Glendon and Blankenhorn, eds., *Seedbeds*, 271–90.

25. William M. Sullivan, "Reinstitutionalizing Virtue in Civil Society," in Glendon and Blankenhorn, eds., *Seedbeds*, 185–201.

26. Alan Wolfe, *Whose Keeper? Social Science and Moral Obligation* (Berkeley: University of California Press, 1989) 77.

27. Ibid., 20

28. Ibid., 233.

29. Ibid., 52.

30. Alan Wolfe, *One Nation After All: What Middle-Class Americans Really Think about God, Country, Family, Racism, Welfare, Immigration, Homosexuality, Work, the Right, the Left, and Each Other* (New York: Viking, 1998).

31. A case that Americans are not so willing is forcefully made by Nicholas Lemann, "The New American Consensus: Government of, by and for the Comfortable," *New York Times Magazine* (1 November 1998) 37–38, 40–43.

32. See Paul Ricoeur, *Oneself as Another*, trans. Kathleen Blamey (Chicago: University of Chicago Press, 1992); Diana Fritz Cates, *Choosing to Feel: Virtue, Friendship, and Compassion for Friends* (Notre Dame, Ind.: University of Notre Dame Press, 1997); and Wendy Farley, *Eros for the Other: Retaining Truth in a Pluralistic World* (University Park: Pennsylvania State University Press, 1996). Don Browning argues similarly that Alan Wolfe needs to consider "the nature of human nature." Browning refers primarily to human biology as indicating that children are best raised by their two biological parents (Don S. Browning, "Altruism, Civic Virtue, and Religion," in Glendon and Blankenhorn, eds., *Seedbeds*, 110).

33. Alan Wolfe, "Is Civil Society Obsolete? Revisiting Predictions of the Decline of Civil Society in *Whose Keeper?*" *The Brookings Review* 15/4 (fall 1997) 11. See also Jean Bethke Elshtain, "Not a Cure-All," *The Brookings Review* 15/4 (fall 1997) 14.

34. William A. Galston and Peter Levine, "America's Civic Condition: A Glance at the Evidence," *The Brookings Review* 15/4 (Fall 1997) 24.

35. Ibid., 25. For the research, see Sidney Verba, Kay Lehman Schlozman, and Henry E. Brady, *Voice and Equality: Civic Voluntarism in American Politics* (Cambridge, Mass.: Harvard University Press, 1995).

36. John J. DiIulio Jr., "In America's Cities: The Church and the 'Civil Society Sector,'" *The Brookings Review* 15/4 (fall 1997) 27–35.

37. Theda Skocpol, ""Building Community, Top-Down or Bottom Up? America's Voluntary Groups Thrive in a National Network," *The Brookings Review* 15/4 (fall 1997) 19.

38. This oral history, titled "C. P. Ellis," appears in *Rereading America: Cultural Contexts for Critical Thinking and Writing*, ed. Gary Colombo, Robert Cullen, Bonnie Lisle (2d ed.; Boston: Bedford Books, 1992) 336–47. It originally appeared in Studs Terkel, *American Dreams* (New York: Random House, 1980).

39. "C. P. Ellis," 337.

40. Ibid., 338.

41. Ibid., 340.

42. Ibid., 346.

43. Monique P. Yazigi, "He Keeps the Blood True Blue," *New York Times* (1 February 1998) sec. 9, p.1, 7.

44. Wolfe, *Whose Keeper?* 12.

45. Reinhold Niebuhr, *Moral Man and Immoral Society* (New York: Charles Scribner's Sons, 1932).

46. Wolfe observes that, as a result of the modern globalization of social organization, "the scope of moral obligation . . . seems to be without limits" (*Whose Keeper?* 3).

47. As William Sullivan explains, "institutions are a name for the basic forms of life. . . . Good institutions are the crucial matrix of any effective virtues, while poor or badly functioning institutions are the source of prevalent vice. In its core sense an institution is a sanctioned set of social practices which actualize certain human capacities in a reasonably stable way" ("Reinstitutionalizing Virtue," in Glendon and Blankenhorn, eds., *Seedbeds*, 192).

48. Taken from the title of a book by James M. Gustafson, *Treasure in Earthen Vessels: The Church as a Human Community* (New York: Harper and Brothers, 1961). Gustafson, in turn, took the originally biblical phrase "earthen vessels" from a sermon by Julian Hartt.

Chapter 2: Family Bonds and Christian Community

1. For this project, see *Interpretation* 52/2 (April 1998), an issue on the family; see especially the essay by Sally B. Purvis, "A Question of Families: The Bible and Contemporary Challenges Facing the Family," 145–60.

2. K. C. Hanson and Douglas E. Oakman, *Palestine in the Time of Jesus: Social Structures and Social Conflicts* (Minneapolis: Fortress Press, 1998) 10.

3. Carolyn Osiek, "The Family in Early Christianity: 'Family Values' Revisited," *Catholic Biblical Quarterly* 58/1 (January 1996) 9–10.

4. Carolyn Osiek and David L. Balch, *Families in the New Testament World: Households and House Churches* (Louisville, Ky.: Westminster John Knox Press, 1997) 216.

5. Hanson and Oakman, *Palestine,* 22–23.

6. Bruce J. Malina and Richard L. Rohrbaugh, *Social-Science Commentary on the Synoptic Gospels* (Minneapolis: Fortress Press, 1992) 310. See also Halvor Moxnes, "Honor and Shame," *Biblical Theology Bulletin* 23 (April 1993) 167–76. Among the pivotal works in the study of honor and shame, as cited by Moxnes, are J. Pitt-Rivers, *The People of the Sierra* (Chicago: University of Chicago Press, 1961); J. G. Peristany, ed., *Honor and Shame: The Values of Mediterranean Society* (London: Weidenfeld and Nicholson, 1966); and J. G. Peristany and J. Pitt-Rivers, eds., *Honor and Grace in Anthropology* (Cambridge: Cambridge University Press, 1992). The pioneering work on honor and shame in early Christianity is Bruce J. Malina, *The New Testament World: Insights from Cultural Anthropology* (Atlanta: John Knox Press, 1981).

7. Hanson and Oakman, *Palestine,* 198.

8. Moxnes, "Honor and Shame," 168.

9. Malina and Rohrbaugh, *Social-Science Commentary,* 310–11; see also 76–77, 213–14.

10. Osiek, "Family in Early Christianity," 10. On the other side, husbands and wives increasingly willed property to one another, in disregard of the legal strictures.

11. Osiek and Balch, *Families,* 216.

12. Carolyn Osiek, "Women in House Churches," in *Common Life in the Early Church: Essays Honoring Graydon F. Snyder,* ed. Julian V. Hills and Richard B. Gardner (Harrisburg, Pa.: Trinity Press International, 1998). Read in manuscript; citation is on page 8.

13. Elaine Fantham, H. P. Foley, N. B. Kampen, and S. B. Pomeroy, *Women in the Classical World: Image and Text* (New York: Oxford University Press, 1994) 382.

14. Ross Shepard Kraemer, *Her Share of the Blessings: Women's Religions among Pagans, Jews, and Christians in the Greco-Roman World* (New York: Oxford University Press, 1992) 79.

15. Ibid., 77.

16. Fantham, *Women in the Classical World,* 383.

17. Kraemer, *Her Share,* 114, citing Philo, *On the Contemplative Life,* 68–69.

18. Ibid., 12.

19. Stephen C. Barton, *Discipleship and Family Ties in Mark and Matthew* (Cambridge: Cambridge University Press, 1994) 49, citing *Discourses* 3.22.69–72, Loeb Classical Library translation.

20. Ibid., 50, citing *Discourses* 3.22.81–82.

21. Ibid., 53.

22. Osiek, "Women in House Churches," 217.

23. See Joseph Blenkinsopp, "The Family in First Temple Israel," in Leo G. Perdue, Joseph Blenkinsopp, John J. Collins, and Carol Meyers, *Families in Ancient Israel* (Louisville, Ky.: Westminster John Knox Press, 1997) 50.

24. C. J. H. Wright, "Family," in *Anchor Bible Dictionary,* vol. 2, ed. David N. Freedman (New York: Doubleday, 1992) 761–69.

25. Richard A. Horsley, *Galilee: History, Politics, People* (Valley Forge, Pa.: Trinity Press International, 1995) 196–98.

26. Leo G. Perdue, "The Israelite and Early Jewish Family: Summary and Conclusions," in Perdue et al., *Families in Ancient Israel,* 167.

27. Moxnes, "Honor and Shame," 171.

28. Hanson and Oakman, *Palestine,* 44–46.

29. Carol Myers, "The Family in Early Israel," in Perdue et al., *Families in Ancient Israel,* 34–35.

30. Horsley, *Galilee,* 200–201.

31. Myers, "Family in Early Israel," 38.

32. Sarah J. Tanzer, "Ephesians," in *A Feminist Commentary,* vol. 2 of *Searching the Scriptures,* ed. Elisabeth Schüssler Fiorenza (New York: Crossroad, 1994) 330.

33. Horsley, *Galilee,* 201; see also 215, 220–21. See also Hanson and Oakman, *Palestine,* 86–90, on "social banditry" as a last resort of dispossessed peasants.

34. Richard A. Horsley, *Jesus and the Spiral of Violence: Popular Jewish Resistance in Roman Palestine* (San Francisco: Harper and Row, 1987) 152–53.

35. Barton, *Discipleship,* 37, citing Philo, *Vit.* 427.

36. J. W. Rogerson, "The Family and Structures of Grace in the Old Testament," in *The Family in Theological Perspective,* ed. Stephen C. Barton (Edinburgh: T. and T. Clark, 1996) 36.

37. Ibid., 37–38.

38. Perdue, "Israelite and Early Jewish Family," 167, 172.

39. Barton, *Discipleship,* 24, citing Philo, *Spec. Leg.* I.316–17, Loeb Classical Library translation.

40. Ibid., 38, citing *Bell.* II.120–21, Loeb Classical Library edition and translation.

41. Osiek, "Family in Early Christianity," 2.

42. Ibid., 4.

43. See Jim Francis, "Children and Childhood in the New Testament," in Stephen C. Barton, ed., *The Family,* 65–85.

44. See Elisabeth Schüssler Fiorenza, *Bread Not Stone: The Challenge of Feminist Biblical Interpretation* (Boston: Beacon Press, 1984) 74–77.

45. Elisabeth Schüssler Fiorenza, *In Memory of Her: A Feminist Theological Reconstruction of Christian Origins* (New York: Crossroad, 1983) 149–50.

46. Barton, *Discipleship,* 19. Although this summary statement is made specifically of Mark, it captures the general thesis of the book, with the qualification that Barton sees the conflict between Jesus and his kin as more pronounced in Mark than in Matthew or Luke.

47. Ibid., 123.

48. Matt. 5:31-32; 19:3-12; Mark 10:2-12; Luke 16:18; 1 Cor. 7:10-16. For a recent discussion, see Raymond F. Collins, *Divorce in the New Testament* (Collegeville, Minn.: Liturgical Press, 1992). In the period in which the New Testament was actually being written, for instance in the Pauline churches, some may have been initiating or asking about divorce for ascetic reasons.

49. Osiek, "Family in Early Christianity," 4–5.

50. Barton, *Discipleship,* 122.

51. Osiek and Balch, *Families,* 215.

52. Schüssler Fiorenza, *In Memory of Her,* 146.

53. Herman Hendrickx, C.I.C.M., "The 'House Church' in Paul's Letters," *Theology Annual* 12 (1990–1991) 154.

54. Eric M. Myers, "Synagogue," 255, and Rachel Hachlili, "Diaspora Synagogues," 262, in *Anchor Bible Dictionary,* vol. 6, ed. David N. Freedman (New York: Doubleday, 1992).

55. Wright, "Family," 768.

56. Hendrickx, "The 'House Church,'" 158–59.

57. Osiek and Balch, *Families,* 100. See also Wayne A. Meeks, *First Urban Christians: The Social World of the Apostle Paul* (New Haven, Conn.: Yale University Press, 1983) 51–73. A contrary opinion is offered by sociologist Rodney Stark, *The Rise of Christianity: A Sociologist Reconsiders History* (Princeton, N.J.: Princeton University Press, 1996). In chapter 2, "The Class Basis of Early Christianity," Stark's key argument is that new sects today (like the Christian Scientists) draw mostly from educated upper classes who are disenchanted with traditional beliefs. He then spends the bulk of the next chapter arguing that Christianity was largely a movement among diasporan Jews and that "Judaizing" tendencies persisted until well into the fifth century (65). This would suggest that it was more like a revival movement than the creation of a new religion or sect. Moreover, inferences

to the nature of early Christianity from the behavior of sects today have to be tested against available historical evidence of actual Christian membership. Osiek and Balch offer significant evidence that most Christians were from the middle strata of society (*Families*, 91–102).

58. Although Gerd Theissen (*The Social Setting of Pauline Christianity* [Philadelphia: Fortress Press, 1979]) has argued that Paul's "love patriarchalism" superimposes an internal attitude of equality on a social reality of vast inequality, it seems evident that imagery of equality in the body of Christ would begin to transform actions as well as dispositions. Evidence includes the actual female leadership in Paul's churches and his expectation of economic support and sharing among well-off and poor persons and churches.

59. Elizabeth Castelli, "Romans," in Schüssler Fiorenza, *A Feminist Commentary*, 279.

60. Abraham J. Malherbe, "God's New Family in Thessalonica," in *The Social World of the First Christians: Essays in Honor of Wayne A. Meeks*, ed. L. Michael White and O. Larry Yarbrough (Minneapolis: Fortress Press, 1995) 122, 124. See also O. Larry Yarbrough, "Parents and Children in the Letters of Paul," in the same volume, esp. 132.

61. Hendrickx, "The 'House Church,'" 159.

62. Osiek and Balch, *Families*, 54.

63. Schüssler Fiorenza, *Bread Not Stone*, 91.

64. Ibid., 2, citing *History* V.5 (in Hadas, *Tacitus*).

65. See also Osiek, "Family in Early Christianity," 16.

66. Jerome H. Neyrey, "Loss of Wealth, Loss of Family and Loss of Honour: The Cultural Context of the Original Makarisms in Q," in *Modelling Early Christianity: Social-Scientific Studies of the New Testament in Its Context*, ed. Philip F. Esler (New York: Routledge, 1995) 139–58.

67. Stark, *Rise of Christianity*, 82. The citation is from *Festival Letters*, quoted by Eusebius, *Ecclesiastical History* 7.22 (1965 ed.).

68. Ibid., 83.

69. Ibid., 84. As sources, Stark cites Paul Johnson, *A History of Christianity* (New York: Atheneum, 1976) 75, and David Ayerst and A. S. T. Fisher, *Records of Christianity*, vol. 1 (Oxford: Basil Blackwell, 1971) 179–81.

70. See David L. Balch, *Let Wives Be Submissive: The Domestic Code in 1 Peter* (Society of Biblical Literature Monograph Series; Chico, Calif.: Scholars Press, 1981); David L. Balch, "Household Codes," in *Anchor Bible Dictionary*, vol. 3, ed. Gary A. Herion and David N. Freedman (New York: Doubleday, 1992) 318–20; Schüssler Fiorenza, *In Memory of Her*; Schüssler Fiorenza, *Bread Not Stone*, 70–83; Clarice J. Martin, "The *Haustafeln* (Household Codes) in African American Biblical Interpretation: 'Free Slaves' and 'Subordinate Women,'" in *Stony the Road We Trod: African American Biblical Interpretation*, ed. Cain Hope Felder (Minneapolis: Fortress Press, 1991) 206–31; Mary Rose D'Angelo, "Colossians," in Schüssler Fiorenza, *A Feminist Commentary*, 313–24; and James D. G. Dunn, "The Household Rules in the New Testament," in Barton, *Family in Theological Perspective*, 43–63.

71. *Politics* 1.1253b.1–14.

72. Balch, *Let Wives,* 61, and "Household Codes," 318.

73. See Balch, *Let Wives,* 65–121; Schüssler Fiorenza, *In Memory,* 290–91.

74. Balch, *Let Wives,* 118; Dunn, "Household Rules," 53.

75. Barton, *Discipleship,* 6.

76. D'Angelo, "Colossians," 321–23.

77. Balch, "Household Codes," 319, and *Let Wives,* 121.

78. Osiek, "Women in House Churches," 7, 10 in manuscript.

79. Dunn, "Household Rules," 61.

80. Schüssler Fiorenza, *In Memory,* 291.

81. Osiek and Balch, *Families,* 102.

82. Ibid., 220.

83. Ibid., 46.

84. Halvor Moxnes, "The Social Context of Luke's Community," *Interpretation* 48 (1994) 382–83.

85. Robert L. Wilken, *The Christians as the Romans Saw Them* (New Haven, Conn.: Yale University Press, 1984) 36.

86. Stanley K. Stowers, "Greeks Who Sacrifice and Those Who Do Not: Toward an Anthropology of Greek Religion," in White and Yarbrough, eds., *Social World,* 330. Stowers refers to the work of Nancy Jay, *Throughout Your Generations Forever: Sacrifice, Religion, and Paternity* (Chicago: University of Chicago Press, 1992).

87. Ibid., 331.

88. Petros Vassiliadis, "Equality and Justice in Classical Antiquity and in Paul: The Social Implications of the Pauline Collection," *St. Vladimir's Theological Quarterly* 36/1&2 (1992) 59.

89. Moxnes, "Social Context," 387.

90. Wilken, *The Christians,* 36.

91. Halvor Moxnes, "Social Relations and Economic Interaction in Luke's Gospel: A Research Report," in *Luke–Acts: Scandinavian Perspectives,* ed. Petri Luomanen (Helsinki: Finnish Exegetical Society, 1991) 72.

92. Osiek, "Family in Early Christianity," 8.

93. Stark, *Rise of Christianity,* 212.

Chapter 3: Family as Church

1. See Carol Harrison, "The Silent Majority: The Family in Patristic Thought," in Stephen C. Barton, ed., *The Family in Theological Perspective* (Edinburgh: T. and T. Clark, 1996) 87–105, for an overview. David G. Hunter, ed., *Marriage in the Early Church* (Minneapolis: Fortress Press, 1992), offers selections from major writers, as well as an introduction to patristic thought on the subject in general.

2. John Chrysostom, *Homily 20 on Ephesians,* in Hunter, ed., *Marriage,* 87.

3. Augustine, *On the Goods of Marriage,* in Hunter, ed., *Marriage,* 102ff.

4. Peter Brown, *The Body and Society: Men, Women and Sexual Renunciation in Early Christianity* (New York: Columbia University Press, 1988) 399.

5. See also *On Continence,* an anti-Manichean tract in which Augustine defends the created goodness of the body and of the two sexes, as well as the unity of spirit and body, husband and wife, and Christ and church on the basis of the Pauline writings. The second in each pair is the inferior member.

6. See Elizabeth A. Clark, *Ascetic Piety and Women's Faith: Essays on Late Ancient Christianity* (Lewison, N.Y.: Edwin Mellen Press, 1986) 230, 246.

7. John Chrysostom, *On the Priesthood* 6.12, as cited by J. N. D. Kelly, *Golden Mouth: The Story of John Chrysostom—Ascetic, Bishop, Preacher* (London: Duckworth, 1995) 29.

8. John Chrysostom, *On Virginity* 27.1, as cited by Kelly, *Golden Mouth*, 45.

9. Kelly, *Golden Mouth*, 45–46.

10. John Chrysostom, *To a Young Widow* and *Single Marriage*, also discussed by Kelly, *Golden Mouth*, 46–48.

11. "Raise up an athlete for Christ! I do not mean by this, hold him back from wedlock and send him to desert regions and prepare him to assume the monastic life. It is not this that I mean. I wish for this and used to pray that all might embrace it; but as it seems to be too heavy a burden, I do not insist upon it. Raise up an athlete for Christ and teach him though he is living in the world to be reverent from his earliest youth" (John Chrysostom, *Address on Vainglory and the Right Way for Parents to Bring Up Their Children*, 19, in *Christianity and Pagan Culture in the Later Roman Empire*, ed. M. L. W. Laistner [Ithaca, N.Y.: Cornell University Press, 1951] 95).

12. Brown, *Body and Society*, 309, 313–15; David G. Hunter, "Introduction," in Hunter, ed., *Marriage*, 19.

13. Carol Harrison's phrase; see n. 1 above.

14. Kelly, *Golden Mouth*, 98, citing Chrysostom, *Homily on Matthew*, 79.1 (on the Parable of Judgment in Matt. 25).

15. Chrysostom, *Vainglory*, 40, in Laistner, ed., *Christianity and Pagan Culture*, 104–5.

16. John Chrysostom, *Homily 19 on 1 Corinthians 7*, in *St. John Chrysostom: Marriage and Family Life*, ed. and trans. C. P. Roth and D. Anderson (Crestwood, N.Y.: St. Vladimir's Seminary Press, 1986) 41.

17. Brown, *Body and Society*, 3–9, 311.

18. Kelly, *Golden Mouth*, 98–99; citing John Chrysostom, *Homily on the Psalms*, 110.3, and *On Almsgiving*, 6.

19. Brown, *Body and Society*, 316.

20. Unlike Augustine, John is conscious that adolescent girls and women may not be prone to lust in the same way or degree as their male counterparts and refrains from projecting the urgency of male sexual drives on women, much less blaming women for male excesses. "Young men are troubled by desire, women by love of finery and excitement" (Chrysostom, *Vainglory*, 90, in Laistner, ed., *Christianity and Pagan Culture*, 122). But he also depicts Potiphar's wife as carried away by her licentious, dishonorable impulses (Chrysostom, *Homily 19*, 38).

21. Chrysostom, *Vainglory*, 76, in Laistner, *Christianity and Pagan Culture*, 117.

22. Brown, *Body and Society*, 316, citing *Homily on Matthew*, 6:8. Showing, however, that John's insight is not unparalleled, Brown cites a similar text from Jerome's *Letters* 77.6.

23. Kelly, *Golden Mouth*, 97, citing *Homily on Matthew*, 37:6.

24. Chrysostom, *Vainglory*, 70, in Laistner, ed., *Christianity and Pagan Culture*, 115.

25. Ibid., 81–82, in Laistner, ed., *Christianity and Pagan Culture,* 119–20.

26. Brown, *Body and Society,* 313.

27. Chrysostom, *Vainglory,* 25, in Laistner, *Christianity and Pagan Culture,* 97.

28. Ibid., 14–15, in Laistner, *Christianity and Pagan Culture,* 93.

29. Chrysostom, *How to Choose a Wife,* in Roth and Anderson, eds., *St. John Chrysostom,* 96 and 100, respectively.

30. See, for example, Chrysostom, *Homily 20,* 6–7, in Hunter, ed., *Marriage,* 88–91.

31. Ibid., 7, in Hunter, ed., *Marriage,* 90–91.

32. Chrysostom, *How to Choose a Wife,* in Roth and Anderson, eds., *St. John Chrysostom,* 97.

33. Ibid., 97.

34. Ibid., 97–98.

35. See Brown, *Body and Society,* 399, 402.

36. Chrysostom, *Homily 12 on Colossians 4:18,* in Roth and Anderson, eds., *St. John Chrysostom,* 76. He makes the same point in *Homily 20,* 4, in Hunter, ed., *Marriage,* 83.

37. Chrysostom, *Homily 20,* 1, in Hunter, ed., *Marriage,* 78.

38. Ibid., 6, in Hunter, ed., *Marriage,* 87.

39. It also must be noted that neither John's fearlessness in denouncing extravagance and urging austerity nor his idealizations of the mutual love of spouses are matched by his attitude toward that other staple relationship of the classical household: enslavement (Kelly, *Golden Mouth,* 99–100). He sees slavery as a natural condition and regards slave behavior as inherently less likely to be virtuous. Yet he also advises that young men be taught not to expect slaves to wait on them hand and foot nor to treat slaves intemperately. Quoting Job, he counsels treating slaves "like brothers" and asks, "'Did not he that made me in the womb make them? Were we not fashioned in the same womb?'" (*Vainglory,* 72, in Laistner, ed., *Christianity and Pagan Culture,* 116).

40. Clark, *Ascetic Piety,* 31; and Elizabeth A. Clark, *Jerome, Chrysostom and Friends: Essays and Translations* (New York: Edwin Mellen Press, 1979) 31.

41. On Olympias, see Clark, *Ascetic Piety,* 210–12, and her *Jerome, Chrysostom,* which includes an introduction to and translations of the anonymous *Life of Olympias* and Sergia's *Narration Concerning St. Olympias,* 107–57. See also Kelly, *Golden Mouth,* 112–13.

42. Clark, *Ascetic Piety,* 211.

43. Clark, *Jerome, Chrysostom,* 112.

44. Clark, *Ascetic Piety,* 212.

45. Clark, *Jerome, Chrysostom,* 115.

46. Clark, *Ascetic Piety,* 31, 237, 245–46.

47. Georges Duby, *Love and Marriage in the Middle Ages,* trans. Jane Dunnett (Chicago: University of Chicago Press, 1994) 107–11.

48. See Ibid., 110–11; James A. Brundage, *Law, Sex, and Christian Society in Medieval Europe* (Chicago: University of Chicago Press, 1987) 134–35; Jean-Louis Flandrin, *Families in Former Times: Kinship, Household and Sexuality* (Cambridge:

Cambridge University Press, 1976) 58–59; and Charles J. Reid Jr., "The History of the Family," in L. S. Cahill and D. Mieth, eds., *The Family* (Maryknoll, N.Y.: Orbis Books, 1994) 12–14.

49. See Rosemary O'Day, *The Family and Family Relationships, 1500–1900: England, France and the United States of America* (New York: St. Martin's Press, 1994) 39–43.

50. Steven Ozment, *When Fathers Ruled: Family Life in Reformation Europe* (Cambridge, Mass.: Harvard University Press, 1983) 1–2.

51. Martin Luther, "The Estate of Marriage," *Luther's Works* (Philadelphia: Fortress Press, 1962) 45:49. *Luther's Works* will hereafter be cited as LW. The general editors are Jaroslav Pelikan for volumes 1–30 (St. Louis, Mo.: Concordia House, 1955–1986) and Helmut T. Lehmann for volumes 31–55 (Philadelphia: Fortress Press, 1957–1986). See also the "Lectures on Genesis": after the fall, "we are begotten and also born in sin. And yet . . . in so wretched a state, the Lord fulfills His blessing, and people are begotten, though in sin and with sin" (LW 1:116). Or: "We are in the state of sin and of death; therefore we also undergo this punishment, that we cannot make use of woman without the horrible passion of lust and, so to speak, without epilepsy" (119). The *Lectures on Genesis* date from the last years of Luther's life. The often-cited reference to marriage as a "hospital for incurables" comes from a sermon of 1519, while Luther still considered marriage a sacrament ("A Sermon on the Estate of Marriage (1519)," LW 44:9).

52. Martin Luther, "The Estate of Marriage (1522)," LW 45:18–19, 21.

53. Ibid., 18; Martin Luther, "On Marriage Matters (1530)," LW 46:265.

54. Luther, "Lectures on Genesis," LW 1:115, 202.

55. "Dr. Luther said one day to his wife: You make me do what you will; you have full sovereignty here, and I award you, with all my heart, the command in all household matters, reserving my rights in other points," in Martin Luther, *Table Talk*, trans. W. Hazlitt (London: HarperCollins, 1995) 335.

56. Luther, "On Marriage Matters," 304.

57. Luther, "Estate of Marriage," 30–35. See also "Commentary on 1 Corinthians 7," LW 28:32.

58. Ibid., 35 and 20, respectively.

59. See Martin Luther, "Temporal Authority: To What Extent It Should be Obeyed," LW 45:90–93.

60. Luther, "Lectures on Genesis," LW 1:104, 115.

61. Ibid., 117.

62. Ibid., 115, 202.

63. Ibid., 138, 202.

64. Ibid., 132–34.

65. Ibid., 137.

66. LW 49:117, as cited in Eric W. Gritsch, *Martin—God's Court Jester: Luther in Retrospect* (Philadelphia: Fortress Press, 1983) 159.

67. See, for examples, the "Lectures on Genesis" (98–99, 200), in which Luther contrasts women's state now with that of Eve. Pregnancy is "beset with severe and sundry ailments. From the beginning of that time a woman suffers very painful

headaches, dizziness, nausea, an amazing loathing of food and drink, frequent and difficult vomiting, toothache, and a stomach disorder which produces a craving, called pica, for such foods from which nature normally shrinks. Moreover, when the fetus has matured and birth is imminent, there follows the most awful distress, because only with utmost peril and almost at the cost of her life does she give birth to her offspring" (200).

68. LW 50:238, as cited in Ozment, *When Fathers Ruled,* 168.

69. Luther, "The Estate of Marriage," LW 45:45.

70. Ibid., 43.

71. Martin Luther, "Sermon at the Marriage of Sigismund von Lindenau," LW 51:358.

72. Ibid., 359.

73. Ibid., 360.

74. Ibid., 365.

75. Martin Luther, "An Exhortation to the Knights of the Teutonic Order that They Lay Aside False Chastity and Assume the True Chastity of Wedlock," LW 45:155.

76. Luther, "Sermon on the Estate of Marriage," LW 44:12.

77. Ibid., 12. See also Luther, "The Estate of Marriage," LW 45:46.

78. Martin Luther, "To Hans Luther," LW 48:332.

79. Ibid., 335.

80. Luther, "On Marriage Matters," LW 46:268, 306. See also Martin Luther, "That Parents Should Neither Compel Nor Hinder the Marriage of Their Children, and That Children Should Not Become Engaged without Their Parents' Consent," LW 45:385–93. Ozment, *When Fathers Ruled,* 37ff., discusses the cultural context.

81. Luther, "Sermon on the Estate of Marriage," LW 44:13.

82. Luther, "The Estate of Marriage," LW 45:46.

83. Martin Luther, "The Order of Marriage for Common Pastors," LW 53:114.

84. Ibid., 114–15; "Lectures on Genesis," LW 1:201; "The Estate of Marriage," LW 45:40.

85. "Hence, as our heavenly Father has in Christ freely come to our aid, we also ought freely to help our neighbor through our body and its works, and each one should become as it were a Christ to the other that we may be Christs to one another and Christ may be the same in all, that is, that we may be truly Christians" (Martin Luther, *Christian Liberty,* ed. H. J. Grimm [Philadelphia: Fortress Press, 1957] 30–31). Note the correspondence of St. Paul's reference to the husband's body, Luther's connection of love to bodily works, and the bodily texture of his empathy for women's situation.

86. See n. 67 above.

87. Luther, "The Estate of Marriage," LW 45:40; cf. 39.

88. Luther, "The Large Catechism: Exposition of the Ten Commandments," in W. Beach and H. R. Niebuhr, eds., *Christian Ethics: Sources of the Living Tradition* (New York: Ronald Press, 1973) 250. See also "The Estate of Marriage," LW 45:46.

89. Luther, *Table Talk,* 333.

90. Luther, "Parents Should Neither Compel," LW 45:392.

91. John Calvin, *Commentaries on the First Book of Moses, Called Genesis, Volume First*, trans. John King (Grand Rapids, Mich.: Baker Book House, 1981) 172. This is Calvin's commentary on Genesis 3:13.

92. Robert T. Handy, *A Christian America: Protestant Hopes and Historical Realities* (2d ed., rev. and enl.; New York: Oxford University Press, 1984) 7.

93. See M. Eugene Osterhaven, "Calvin on the Covenant," in *Readings in Calvin's Theology*, ed. Donald K. McKim (Grand Rapids, Mich.: Baker Book House, 1984) 89–106.

94. John Calvin, *Institutes of the Christian Religion*, 2.8.20.

95. G. S. M. Walker, "Calvin and the Church," in McKim, ed., *Readings in Calvin's Theology*, 212.

96. John Calvin, *Commentary on 1 Corinthians* 16:19, as quoted in Walker, "Calvin and the Church," 220.

97. Edmund S. Morgan, *The Puritan Family: Religion and Domestic Relations in Seventeenth-Century New England* (new ed., rev. and enl.; Westport, Conn.: Greenwood Press, 1980) 7.

98. Ibid., 9.

99. Thomas Taylor, *Works* (1653) 190–92; as cited in Christopher Hill, *Society and Puritanism in Pre-Revolutionary England* (London: Secker and Warburg, 1964) 393.

100. They are all cited by Anthony Fletcher in *Gender, Sex and Subordination in England 1500–1800* (New Haven, Conn.: Yale University Press, 1995) 204–5.

101. All cited in Morgan, *Puritan Family*, 143–44.

102. Janet Fishburn, *Confronting the Idolatry of Family: A New Vision for the Household of God* (Nashville: Abingdon Press, 1991) 35.

103. Fletcher, *Gender, Sex*, 101.

104. Fletcher, *Gender, Sex*, 103–4.

105. Hill, *Society and Puritanism*, 385.

106. William Perkins, as cited by Hill, *Society and Puritanism*, 398–99.

107. Morgan, *Puritan Family*, 91–94.

108. Anthony Fletcher, "The Family, Marriage, and the Upbringing of Children in Protestant England," in Barton, ed., *Family in Theological Perspective* (Edinburgh: T. and T. Clark, 1996) 118.

109. "The Family," as cited by Fletcher, *Gender, Sex*, 120.

110. Anthony Fletcher, "Prescription and Practice: Protestantism and the Upbringing of Children, 1560–1700," in Diana Wood, ed., *The Church and Childhood* (Oxford: Blackwell, 1994) 334.

111. Morgan, *Puritan Family*, 77; Fletcher, *Gender, Sex*, 211–12.

112. Fletcher, *Gender, Sex*, 302.

113. Morgan, *Puritan Family*, 84.

114. Richard Baxter, *A Christian Directory: Or, a Summ of Practical Theologie, and Cases of Conscience* (1673) cited in Joyce L. Irwin, *Womanhood in Radical Protestantism 1525–1675* (New York: Edwin Mellen Press, 1979) 112.

115. William Gouge, *Of Domestical Duties*, Eight Treatises (1622) cited in Irwin, *Womanhood*, 87, 89, 100, 103. On marital violence, see Fletcher, *Gender, Sex*, 192–203.

116. Fletcher, *Gender, Sex,* 186.

117. Ibid., 348.

118. Merry E. Weisner, "The Early Modern Period: Religion, the Family, and Women's Public Roles," in Anne Carr and Mary Stewart van Leeuwen, eds., *Religion, Feminism and the Family* (Louisville, Ky.: Westminster/John Knox Press, 1996) 160.

119. Fletcher, *Gender, Sex,* 159.

120. Ibid., 179. Fletcher cites A. D. Wall, "Elizabethan Precept and Feminine Practice: The Thynne Family of Longleat," *History* 75 (1990) 32–35.

121. Ibid., 124.

122. Ibid., 243–46.

123. Fletcher, *Gender, Sex,* 139–44.

124. Hill, *Society and Puritanism,* 219.

125. Ibid., 235.

126. Fletcher, *Gender, Sex,* 267.

127. The first edition was published in 1944, with a revised edition appearing in 1966.

128. Morgan, *Puritan Family,* 173, 174.

Chapter 4: Domestic Church

1. John Paul II, *On the Family* (Apostolic Exhortation, *Familiaris Consortio*) (Washington, D.C.: United States Catholic Conference, 1981). Reference to this and other official Catholic documents will be made by section or paragraph number, not page. This customary means of citation enables reference across languages and editions. *On the Family* (no. 49) defines the family as a domestic church or church in miniature.

2. Family prayer and spirituality will not be addressed at length in the present work, though they are important in a Christian family perspective. A more extended treatment may be found in Florence Caffrey Bourg, *Christian Families as Domestic Churches: Insights from the Theologies of Sacramentality, Virtue, and the Consistent Ethic of Life* (Ph.D. diss., Boston College, 1998). Bourg is assistant professor of theology at the College of Mount St. Joseph in Cincinnati, Ohio.

3. *On the Family,* no. 41.

4. Ibid., no. 42.

5. Ibid., no. 22.

6. John Paul II discusses Ephesians 5 many times in his writings, using it as a model of marital love, without ever endorsing female submission or male "headship." Perhaps the most explicit treatment of this topic occurs in *On the Dignity and Vocation of Women* (*Mulieris Dignitatem,* 1988), *Origins* 18/17 (6 October 1988) 261–83. The pope interprets Eph. 5:22-23 to mean "mutual subjection out of reverence for Christ" (cf. Eph. 5:21). He specifically limits the analogy of spousal subjection to the relation between Christ and church, since, whereas in the latter, "the subjection is only on the part of the church; in the relationship between husband and wife the 'subjection' is not one-sided but mutual" (no. 24).

7. Walter Rauschenbusch, *Dare We Be Christians?* (Cleveland, Ohio: Pilgrim Press, 1993) 21–22. This work was published originally in 1914.

8. National Conference of Catholic Bishops' Committee on Marriage and Family, "Always Our Children: A Pastoral Message to Parents of Homosexual Children and Suggestions for Pastoral Ministers," *Origins* 27/17 (9 October 1997) 285, 287–91.

9. Leo XIII, *On the Condition of Labor (Rerum Novarum)*, no. 35, in William J. Gibbons, *Seven Great Encyclicals* (Paramus, N.J.: Paulist Press, 1966).

10. Ibid., no. 44.

11. See Christine Firer Hinze, "Bridge Discourse on Wage Justice: Roman Catholic and Feminist Perspectives on the Family Living Wage," in *Feminist Ethics and the Catholic Moral Tradition,* ed. Charles E. Curran, Margaret Farley, Richard A. McCormick (Mahwah, N.J.: Paulist Press, 1996) 511–40. This essay first appeared in *The Annual of the Society of Christian Ethics* 1991.

12. Leo XIII, *On the Condition of Labor,* no. 20.

13. John Paul II, *On Human Work (Laborem Exercens)*, no. 19 (Washington, D.C.: United States Catholic Conference, 1981). See Hinze, "Bridge Discourse," in Curran et al., *Feminist Ethics,* 521.

14. Hinze, "Bridge Discourse," 31–32.

15. Leo XIII, *On Christian Citizenship (Sapientiae Cristianae,* 1890), no. 42, in Etienne Gilson, ed., *The Church Speaks to the Modern World: The Social Teachings of Leo XIII* (New York: Doubleday, 1954).

16. Leo XIII, *On Christian Marriage (Arcanum Divinae Sapientiae)*, no. 11, in Gilson, ed., *Social Teachings of Leo XIII.*

17. Ibid., nos. 12 and 15.

18. Pius XI, *On Christian Marriage (Casti Connubii,* 1930), no. 26, in Terence P. McLaughlin, ed., *The Church and the Reconstruction of the Modern World: The Social Encyclicals of Pius XI* (New York: Doubleday, 1957).

19. Ibid., no. 24. Although like earlier popes and theologians, both Catholic and Protestant, Pius XI still maintains that procreation is the primary purpose of sex and marriage, he makes increasingly central the mutual and equal love of spouses. The marital love that is intrinsic to "the blending of life as a whole" "can in a very real sense . . . be said to be the chief reason and purpose of matrimony."

20. Ibid., no. 74.

21. See David Hollenbach, *The Right to Procreate and Its Social Limitations: A Systematic Study of Value Conflict in Roman Catholic Ethics* (Ph. D. diss., Yale University, 1975) 326–27.

22. Pius XI, *On Christian Marriage,* nos. 120–22.

23. Paul VI, *On the Development of Peoples (Populorum Progressio,* 1967), nos. 23, 26, 44, 48 (New York and Mahwah, N.J.: Paulist Press, 1967).

24. Ibid., no. 80.

25. John Paul II, *On Social Concerns (Sollicitudo Rei Socialis,* 1988), no. 42, *Origins* 17/38 (3 March 1988).

26. Ibid., no. 46; see also no. 39.

27. John Paul II, *The Hundredth Year (Centesimus Annus)*, nos. 15, 39, *Origins* 21 (1991).

28. Ibid., no. 43.

29. John Paul II, *On the Family,* no. 6.

30. Ibid., no. 17.

31. Ibid., nos. 42, 46.

32. Ibid., no. 47.

33. Ibid., no. 7.

34. Ibid., no. 21. The reference given for the phrases "domestic church" and "school of deeper humanity" are two documents of the Second Vatican Council, *Lumen Gentium*, no. 11, and *Gaudium et Spes* 52, respectively. The phrase "'church in miniature' (*ecclesia domestica*)" occurs within a discussion of evangelization and in building up the kingdom of God in history (no. 49).

35. Ibid., no. 44.

36. Ibid., no. 45.

37. Ibid., no. 23.

38. See virtually all of the essays in Curran et al., eds., *Feminist Ethics and the Catholic Moral Tradition*, especially those by Barbara Andolsen, Christine Gudorf, and Anne Patrick. See also Margaret A. Farley, "The Church and the Family: An Ethical Task," *Horizons* 10/1 (1983) 50–71.

39. John Paul II, *On the Family*, no.25.

40. The "charter document" for these views is John Paul II, *On the Dignity and Vocation of Women* (*Mulieris Dignitatem*, 1988), *Origins* 18/17 (6 October 1988) 261–83. See especially nos. 28, 30, 31.

41. Farley, "Church and the Family," 67.

42. John Paul II, *Letter to Women*, no. 2, *Origins* 25/9 (27 July 1995).

43. Ibid., no. 3.

44. Ibid., no. 6.

45. Ibid., no. 4.

46. Ibid., no.5.

47. Ibid., no. 12.

48. Ibid., no. 11.

49. *Letter to Families*, no. 15.

50. Ibid., no. 16. Italics added.

51. Ibid., no. 21ff.

52. Ibid., nos. 8, 10, 16.

53. *Charter on the Rights of the Family* (22 October 1983). Obtained on the Internet from Catholic Resources on the Internet: http://www.cs.cmu.edu/People/spok/catholic.

54. Ernie Cortes, "Reflections on the Catholic Tradition of Family Rights," in *One Hundred Years of Catholic Social Thought: Celebration and Challenge*, ed. John A. Coleman (Maryknoll, N.Y.: Orbis, 1991) 158.

55. Ibid., 157.

56. Dorothy M. Brown and Elizabeth McKeown, *The Poor Belong to Us: Catholic Charities and American Welfare* (Cambridge, Mass.: Harvard University Press, 1997).

57. Ibid., 3.

58. Ibid., 194–95.

59. Ibid., 171. Many of these same concerns are echoed by James and Kathleen McGinnis, "Family as Domestic Church," in Coleman, ed., *One Hundred Years*, 120–34. They speak from the experience of parents who seek concrete ways to

educate families for the values Catholic social tradition espouses in principle. In particular, they address briefly materialism, individualism, racism, sexism, and violence or militarism.

60. Brown and McKeown, *The Poor,* 193–94.

61. These are all published by the United States Catholic Conference, Washington, D.C.; they are also available in the journal *Origins.*

62. The conference was organized by the staff of the University of Dayton Center for the study of Family Development. The papers delivered are collected in Patricia Voydanoff, ed., *Families and Communities in Partnership* (Lanham, Md.: University Press of America, 1996). Similar ventures and publications have emerged from the Boston College Center for Child, Family, and Community Partnerships. Center Director Richard M. Lerner has recently published *University-Community Collaborations for the Twenty-First Century: Outreach Scholarship for Youth and Families* (New York: Garland Publications, 1998), edited with Lou Anna K. Simon. See also Richard M. Lerner, *America's Youth in Crisis: Challenges and Options for Programs and Policies* (Thousand Oaks, Calif.: Sage Publications, 1995).

63. Robert N. Bellah, "Families in the Context of Community," in Voydanoff, ed., *Families and Communities,* 15.

64. James Healy, "Balance, the Presence of Men, and Collaboration in Caring for Families," in Voydanoff, ed., *Families and Communities,* 130.

65. To take examples just from the limited area of Hispanic presence in Catholic theology, note the new *Journal of Latino-Hispanic Theological Studies,* founded and edited by Orlando Espín at the University of San Diego, and the thriving professional society, Association of Catholic Hispanic Theologians in the U.S.

66. Gary Bryner, *The Great American Welfare Reform Debate: Politics and Public Morality* (New York: W. W. Norton, 1998) xiii.

67. Charles Murray, *Losing Ground: American Social Policy 1950–1980* (New York: Basic Books, 1984).

68. Bryner, *Welfare Reform Debate,* xxiii.

69. For "welfare devolution," ibid., xiv; ibid., 173, for the Moynihan quote, which Bryner cites from 140 *Cong. Rec.,* S. 9322-23 (1 August 1996).

70. Ibid., xv.

71. Consult *Welfare to What? Early Findings on Family Hardship and Well-Being* (December 1998), released jointly by the Children's Defense Fund (CDF) and the National Coalition for the Homeless. The report is available from the CDF, 25 E St., Washington, DC 20001; or on the CDF Web site: http://www.childrensdefense.org. See also Pamela Loprest, "Families Who Left Welfare: Who Are They and How Are They Doing?" *Assessing the New Federalism* (discussion paper no. 99-02; Washington, D.C.: Urban Institute, 1999), available at www.urban.org., and Cecilio Morales, "Has Welfare Reform Helped the Poor?" *America* 181/5 (28 August 1999) 16–18.

72. Jason DeParle, "Leftover Money for Welfare Baffles, or Inspires, States," *New York Times* (29 August 1999) A1, 20.

73. Peter Edelman, "Clinton's Cosmetic Poverty Tour," *New York Times* (8 July 1999) obtained on the Internet (http://www.nytimes.com).

74. Bryner, *Welfare Reform Debate,* 315.

75. Ibid., 337.

76. Thomas Massaro, *Catholic Social Teaching and United States Welfare Reform* (Collegeville, Minn.: Liturgical Press, 1998)152–67.

77. United States Catholic Conference (USCC) Administrative Board, "Moral Principles and Policy Priorities on Welfare Reform," *Origins* 24/41 (1995) 673, 675–78.

78. Ibid., 677.

79. Ibid., 676.

80. National Conference of Catholic Bishops, *Economic Justice for All: Pastoral Letter on Catholic Social Teaching and the U.S. Economy* (Washington, D.C.: United States Catholic Conference, 1986).

81. Harvey Cox, "The Market as God," *The Atlantic Monthly* (March 1999) 18.

82. Ibid., 23.

83. John B. Cobb Jr., "Liberation Theology and the Global Economy," in Joerg Rieger, ed., *Liberating the Future: God, Mammon, and Theology* (Minneapolis: Fortress Press, 1998) 32.

84. Joerg Rieger, "Introduction: Watch the Money," in Rieger, ed., *Liberating the Future,* 3.

85. Ibid., 6.

86. Mary E. Hobgood, *Catholic Social Teaching and Economic Theory* (Philadelphia, Pa.: Temple University Press, 1991), and "Poor Women, Work, and the U.S. Catholic Bishops: Discerning Myth from Reality in Welfare Reform," *Journal of Religious Ethics* 25/2 (1997) 307–33. The same journal issue includes helpful responses to Hobgood from Daniel Rush Finn, Harlan Beckley, and Carol S. Robb, as well as Hobgood's reply.

87. Hobgood, "Poor Women, Work," 315. Gary Bryner supports the hypothesis that forcing welfare recipients into work could depress wages and increase competition for otherwise undesirable jobs (Bryner, *Welfare Reform Debate,* xxi).

88. Hobgood, "Poor Women, Work," 319.

89. Ibid., 320.

90. Ibid., 328.

91. Cobb, "Liberation Theology," in Rieger, ed., *Liberating the Future,* 38.

92. Massaro, *Catholic Social Teaching,* 234.

93. Ibid., 236.

94. Daniel R. Finn, "John Paul II and the Moral Ecology of Markets," *Theological Studies* 59/4 (1998) 662–79.

95. Ibid., 670–71.

96. USCC Administrative Board, "Moral Principles," 677.

97. Mary Jo Bane, "Poverty, Welfare and the Role of the Churches," *America* 181/18 (4 December 1999) 8–11.

98. Ibid., 9.

99. Ibid., 10.

100. Ibid., 11.

Chapter 5: Lessons from African American Families

1. Toinette M. Eugene, "African American Family Life: An Agenda for Ministry within the Catholic Church," *New Theology Review* 5/2 (1992) 33–47, and "'Lift-

ing as We Climb': Womanist Theorizing about Religion and the Family," in Anne Carr and Mary Stewart van Leeuwen, eds., *Religion, Feminism and the Family* (Louisville, Ky.: Westminster/John Knox Press, 1996) 330–43. See also J. Deotis Roberts, *Roots of a Black Future: Family and Church* (Philadelphia: Westminster Press, 1980); and Thea Bowman, ed., *Families: Black and Catholic, Catholic and Black* (Washington, D.C.: United States Catholic Conference, 1985).

2. Eugene, "Lifting as We Climb," in Carr and van Leeuwen, eds., *Religion, Feminism*, 330; citing from Roberts, *Roots*, 108.

3. Eugene, "Lifting as We Climb," 335.

4. Thea Bowman, "Introduction," in Bowman, ed., *Families*, 11.

5. Sara McLanahan and Gary Sandefur, *Growing Up with a Single Parent: What Hurts, What Helps* (Cambridge, Mass.: Harvard University Press, 1994) 38.

6. Stephanie Coontz, *The Way We Really Are: Coming to Terms with America's Changing Families* (New York: HarperCollins, 1997) 101.

7. Donna L. Franklin, *Ensuring Inequality: The Structural Transformation of the African-American Family* (New York: Oxford University Press, 1997) 30.

8. Ibid., 31.

9. Ibid., 43.

10. Ibid., 65–66.

11. One sociologist has identified a twelve-part typology, based on the three major structures of nuclear families, extended families, and augmented families (where people without blood or marital ties are appropriated into the family structure and treated as kin). These three can be broken into further categories, depending on the gender and marital status of family heads and the presence or absence of children. See Andrew Billingsley, *Climbing Jacob's Ladder: The Enduring Legacy of African-American Families* (New York: Simon and Schuster, 1992) 27–64. Billingsley also states that African kinship systems emphasize consanguinity over conjugality in defining family, though both ties are important. Thus the African American extended family tends to prioritize intergenerational biological links, although relations by marriage and "appropriated" kin are widely incorporated into extended family networks (28).

12. E. Franklin Frazier's *The Negro Family in the United States* (Chicago: University of Chicago Press, 1939) argued that slavery had spawned instability in the black family because slave owners forbade slave marriage, disrupted families, and thereby undermined the formation of permanent family ties. Many subsequent authors, especially African Americans, dispute this analysis and highlight the strengths of black families in surviving and recuperating from slavery. See Herbert Gutman, *The Black Family in Slavery and Freedom, 1750–1925* (New York: Pantheon Books, 1976); Wallace Charles Smith, *The Church in the Life of the Black Family* (Valley Forge, Pa.: Judson Press, 1985); and Billingsley, *Jacob's Ladder*. For a general discussion, see Don S. Browning, Bonnie J. Miller-McLemore, Pamela D. Couture, K. Brynolf Lyon, and Robert M. Franklin, *From Culture Wars to Common Ground: Religion and the American Family Debate* (Louisville, Ky.: Westminster John Knox Press, 1997). 222–31. I assume that this section shows the hand of African American co-author Robert M. Franklin.

13. Eugene, "African American Family Life," 39.

14. Browning et al., *From Culture Wars*, 229.

15. Billingsley, *Jacob's Ladder*, 334.

16. Browning et al., *From Culture Wars*, 223.

17. Ibid., 134–35.

18. Sylvia Ann Hewlett and Cornel West, *The War against Parents: What We Can Do for America's Beleaguered Moms and Dads* (New York: Houghton Mifflin, 1998) 77. For a corroborating indictment of the effect of market values on the institutions of black civil society, see Cornel West, *Race Matters* (reprint; New York: Vintage Books, 1994).

19. William Julius Wilson, *When Work Disappears: The World of the New Urban Poor* (New York: Random House, 1996) 20.

20. Ibid., xiii–xiv.

21. John J. DiIulio Jr., "The Church and the 'Civil Society Sector,'" *The Brookings Review* 15/4 (fall 1997) 28.

22. Wilson, *When Work Disappears*, 56.

23. Ibid., 58.

24. E. J. Dionne, "Jobs Work: The Best Social Policy," *Commonweal* 126/12 (18 June 1999) 6, which cites a 1999 study on fourteen metropolitan areas where the percentage of young black men working rose from 52 percent in 1992 to 64 percent in 1999.

25. June Gary Hopps, Elaine Pinderhughes, and Richard Shankar, *The Power to Care: Clinical Practice Effectiveness with Overwhelmed Clients* (New York: Free Press, 1995) 148.

26. Wilson, *Work*, 87.

27. Ibid., 91.

28. Ibid., 105.

29. Ibid., 107.

30. D. Franklin, *Inequality*, 130–32.

31. Ibid., 204.

32. Mary Jo Bane and David T. Ellwood, *Welfare Realities: From Rhetoric to Reform* (Cambridge, Mass.: Harvard University Press, 1994) 55. Welfare reformers are divided over the preferable model for realizing this goal. The "labor force attachment" model views the welfare system as essentially a job search and placement service through which recipients move as quickly as possible before entering some type of employment, however unskilled or low paid. The "human capital development" model seeks to provide or improve the preparation of recipients to enter the workforce by providing basic education or vocational and on-the-job training. The latter model clearly promises more long-term satisfaction for recipients but is just as clearly more expensive. It is in fact cheaper to hand the unemployed a welfare check than to equip them to be competitive in the labor market, much less to expand that market to accommodate all potential job seekers with work (Gary Bryner, *The Great American Welfare Reform Debate: Politics and Public Morality* [New York: W. W. Norton, 1998] 218).

33. William Julius Wilson, "Foreword," in Hopps et al., *Power to Care*, viii.

34. I see Richard Herrnstein and Charles Murray's *The Bell Curve: Intelligence and Class Structure in American Life* (New York: Free Press, 1994) as a rationalization of just this sort.

35. Ibid., 158–59, 164.

36. Billingsley, *Jacob's Ladder*, 393.

37. D. Franklin, *Inequality*, 228–32.

38. Ibid., 236.

39. Black Bishops of the United States, *What We Have Seen and Heard* (Cincinnati, Ohio: St. Anthony Messenger, 1984), excerpts reprinted in Bowman, *Black and Catholic*, 137–40.

40. Ibid., in Bowman, ed., *Black and Catholic*, 137.

41. Ibid.

42. Ibid., 138.

43. Billingsley, *Jacob's Ladder*, 349.

44. Ibid., 377.

45. Thea Bowman, "Sexuality and the Black Catholic Family: An Interview with Dr. Edwin J. Nichols," in Bowman, ed., *Black and Catholic*, 45.

46. Browning et al., *From Culture Wars*, 230; Eugene, "Lifting as We Climb," 332–34.

47. See chapter 5, n. 12 above.

48. Browning et al., *From Culture Wars*, 226–27. These authors define a Protestant concept of "domestic church" as mediating a direct experience of God through the intimacy of family life (not through the institutional church or the sacraments) and in a dialogue between God's covenant with the family and God's covenant with the church (308).

49. Toinette M. Eugene, "The Black Family That Is Church," in Bowman, ed., *Black and Catholic*, 58.

50. Ibid.

51. Eugene, "African American Family Life," 41.

52. Hewlett and West, *War against Parents*, 184.

53. Ibid., 186.

54. Ibid., 189.

55. Eugene, "Lifting as We Climb," 332, 336. For the landmark exposition of womanist theology, see Katie G. Cannon, *Black Womanist Ethics* (Atlanta: Scholars Press, 1988).

56. Eugene, "Lifting as We Climb," 341.

57. Black Bishops of the United States, *What We Have Seen and Heard*, 138–39. A statement on "father absence in black America" cosponsored by the Morehouse Research Institute and the Institute for American Values likewise affirms a preference for marriage and gender equality in marriage while acknowledging a seemingly major fault line within the group about whether nonmarriage and father absence are due primarily to economic causes or to cultural attitudes and about appropriate policy responses to father absence (*Turning the Corner on Father Absence in Black America*, A Statement from the Morehouse Conference on African American Fathers (Atlanta: Morehouse Research Institute, 1999).

58. DiIulio, "Church and 'Civil Society Sector,'" 27.

59. Billingsley, *Jacob's Ladder*, 393.

60. Stephan Thernstrom and Abigail Thernstrom, *America in Black and White: One Nation, Indivisible* (New York: Simon and Schuster, 1997).

61. The term comes from Marvin L. Krier Mich, "Ecclesial and Racial Revolutions: *Gaudium et Spes, Justice in the World,* and Racism," in *Catholic Social Teaching and Movements* (Mystic, Conn.: Twenty-Third Publications, 1998). Mich documents the history of racism in the Roman Catholic Church and presents the work of contemporary black Catholic theologians. For a more general analysis of the continuing existence of racism in America, see Orlando Patterson, *The Ordeal of Integration: Progress and Resentment in America's "Racial" Crisis* (Washington, D.C.: Civitas/Counterpoint, 1997).

62. Wilson, *When Work Disappears,* 229.

63. D. Franklin, *Inequality,* 234.

64. In *The Way We Really Are,* Coontz documents the effects of economic trends and changing gender roles on families. She argues that the recovery of a mythic 1950s nuclear family is a misguided ideal, especially since the myth's appeal is due largely to nostalgia for the economic boom of the post–World War II years, rather than to a bygone family structure. According to Coontz, working mothers, single parents, blended families, and gay parents are here to stay. We must look for institutional forms of family support that encourage family stability and child welfare without ignoring or punishing these new realities.

Chapter 6: A Christian Family Vision

1. Diana Fritz Cates, *Choosing to Feel: Virtue, Friendship and Compassion for Friends* (Notre Dame, Ind.: University of Notre Dame Press, 1997).

2. On this point, see Barbara Deveny Redmond, *The Domestic Church: Primary Agent of Moral Development,* (Ph.D. diss., Boston College; Ann Arbor, Mich.: UMI, 1998).

3. Stephen G. Post, *More Lasting Unions: Christianity, the Family, and Society* (Grand Rapids, Mich.: William B. Eerdmans, 2000) 178–79.

4. Don S. Browning, Bonnie J. Miller-McLemore, Pamela Couture, K. Brynolf Lyon, and Robert M. Franklin, *From Culture Wars to Common Ground: Religion and the American Family Debate* (Louisville, Ky.: Westminster John Knox Press, 1997) 308–9.

5. Ibid., 309–34. They suggest, for example, that social scientific evidence indicates that both spouses or coparents will be more satisfied and fulfilled if they have opportunities to engage in domestic work and in some form of paid employment outside the home. They also conclude that a sixty-hour *family* work week should be the norm and should be supported by appropriate employment flexibility and child care. Moreover, single parents, including those receiving public assistance, should only be expected to devote thirty hours to outside work and should receive the necessary funding to make this possible, in cases in which the co-parent is not contributing to family support.

Index

adoption, family structure and, xi–xiv

African American churches
  domestic church metaphor in, 121–26
  support for families from, 2

African American community
  Catholic social teaching and, 126–29
  Catholic theology and, 84, 86
  community-based solutions in, 119–21
  history of family in, 112–14
  marriage rates linked to educational levels in, 5
  overrepresentation of, in welfare profiles, 5, 140n.13

African American family ethics
  characteristics of, 102–103, x–xiv
  domestic church metaphor and, 111–29
  socioeconomic factors in, 114–19

Aid to Families with Dependent Children (AFDC), 99–103, 118–19

Alexander III (Pope), 61

altruism
  in civil society, 9–12, 15–16
  in early Christian community, 38

animal sacrifice, in early Christianity, 43–44

Aristotle, 39

association membership, civil society and, 7–8, 11–14

Augustine (bishop of Hippo), 52–54
  Luther and, 60, 62
  on marriage, 57
  moral priorities of, 54

Balch, David, 33, 39, 42, 145n.47

Bane, Mary Jo, 109, 118–19

barriers to employment, welfare reform and, 103–10

Barton, Stephen, 26–27, 31–32, 144n.46

Baxter, Richard, 75–76

Beatitudes
  honor and shame depicted in, 28–29, 38

Bellah, Robert, 98

Bernardin, Cardinal Joseph, 3

Bethune, Mary McLeod, 125

Billingsley, Andrew, 111, 114, 119–23, 127, 157n.11

Blankenhorn, David, 8

Bowman, Thea, 112, 157nn.1,4, 159n.45

Braithwaite, Richard, 72

Bretton Woods institution, 105

brother-ethic, concept of, in early Jewish communities, 27–28

Brown, Dorothy, 97–98

Brown, Peter, 55–56

Browning, Don, 2–3, 132
  critique of Alan Wolfe by, 141n.32

Bryner, Gary, 100–101, 103, 156n.87

Calvin, John, 68–79, 81
  Catholic theology and, 84

capitalism. *See also* global capitalism; market systems
  Catholic social teachings and, 86–89, 106–10

Carnegie Corporation Report on family, 7

Cates, Diana Fritz, 131

Catholic Church
  African American family norms and, 111–29, 122–23, 125–29
  domestic church metaphor in, 3–7, 83–110
  ethnic diversity in, 84
  grassroots response to messages of, 95–99
  recent themes in, 85–86
  social institutions and collaboration with, 98–99
  social teachings and family ethic, 86–89, 103–10, 126–29
  welfare reform and response to, 99–103

Catholic Theological Society of America (CTSA), 3